EXPLORING CHRISTIANITY
an introduction

Robert C. Monk
Joseph D. Stamey

PRENTICE-HALL, INC.
Englewood Cliffs, New Jersey 07632

Library of Congress Cataloging in Publication Data

Monk, Robert C.
  Exploring Christianity.

  Bibliography: p.
  Includes index.
  1. Christianity.   I. Stamey, Joseph D.   II. Title.
BR121.2.M583   1984   200   83-17646
ISBN 0-13-296385-X

Editorial/production supervision: Cyndy Lyle Rymer
Cover design: Diane Saxe
Manufacturing buyer: Harry P. Baisley

Scripture passages throughout the text have been reprinted
with permission from the *Revised Standard Version of the Bible,*
copyrighted © 1946, 1952, 1971, 1973.

Printed in the United States of America

10   9   8   7   6   5   4   3   2   1

ISBN 0-13-296385-X

Prentice-Hall International, Inc., *London*
Prentice-Hall of Australia Pty. Limited, *Sydney*
Editora Prentice-Hall do Brasil, Ltda., *Rio de Janeiro*
Prentice-Hall Canada Inc., *Toronto*
Prentice-Hall of India Private Limtied, *New Delhi*
Prentice-Hall of Japan, Inc., *Tokyo*
Prentice-Hall of Southeast Asia Pte. Ltd., *Singapore*
Whitehall Books Limited, *Wellington, New Zealand*

CONTENTS

PREFACE

Exploring Christianity has been designed as a comprehensive introductory text for use in studying Christianity, its history and development, and the variety and unity of its beliefs, traditions, practice, and organizational structures. It has grown from our experience, during the past fifteen years, in teaching a number of rather different college-level courses in religion. One of these is a recently initiated semester-long "Introduction to Christianity" course, the successor of a course called "Introduction to Religion." "Introduction to Religion" focused on several of the world's religions, usually allocating from three to five weeks to the study of Christianity. We believe that *Exploring Christianity* can be used for courses of either type. It was largely our sense of need for a text that can be used either as a main text for a semester-long study of Christian traditions or for a more concentrated shorter unit that influenced our attempt. We have also drawn on our experience in courses on "Religion and Society" and "Christianity and Human Problems," in each of which we felt the need for a brief, comprehensive introductory study of Christian groups and traditions.

There are a number of excellent works dealing with the history of Christianity. We have often found these useful, but too detailed or technical for the courses we were conducting. There are also a number of available introductory texts that treat Christianity. Most of these have strong points to recommend them. However, most of the ones we attempted to use seemed, like the works on church history, better suited for other kinds of course; they were either too detailed or too special-ized. We set ourselves the task of developing a text that can be used either as the principal text for an entire course dealing with Christian religious tradition or for a unit in a course dealing with comparative or world religions, religion and society, Western civilization, or religion and contemporary issues. We realize that our text will be vulnerable to the criticism we have made of others and to some unique to it; however, we have aimed at producing a book that can be used flexibly and that will provide an adequate and comprehensive, but not overly technical or specialized, introduction to the study of Christianity.

Exploring Christianity is not a history of Christianity, though we believe it will give the student adequate acquaintance with the major outlines of Chris-tianity's historical development. Chapters One through Four follow essentially a chronological, or historical, outline from the Jewish backgrounds of Christianity to its emergence as a truly world religion in the nineteenth and twentieth centuries. They do not attempt historical completeness, which would be impossible in a book of this size. Rather, they attempt, through selective thematic emphasis, to give an adequate introduction to the configuration and variety of forms and groups within Christianity. Major developments in the evolution and diversification of Christian bodies, movements and practices are sketched and traced; in fact, they are explored in terms of their overall significance and impact on Christian development. Other chapters (Five to Nine) deal with central issues and topics in other than historical orderings. Still, an understanding of the movements, persons, and ideas discussed in those chapters will be greatly enhanced by the historical framework of the earlier chapters.

Chapter One deals with Jewish religious history from its beginnings through the first and second centuries of the Roman Empire, especially as this history pro-vides background for understanding the emergence and development of Christian-ity. One of the distinctive features of the book is that in subsequent chapters the story of Jewish-Christian interaction is resumed, with some features highlighted. This reflects our belief that later Christian history, and the nature of Christianity as a world religion, becomes clearer in light of the continuing "uneasy kinship" between the two religious traditions.

Chapter Two deals primarily with the mission and message of Jesus. A brief introductory section introduces the student to the academic context in which discussions of historical knowledge about Jesus take place, the major trends in historical-critical studies of the gospels during the past hundred years. Such an introduction is indispensable if the student is to make sense of any presentation of "the message of Jesus," but a lengthy presentation of technical information that would be relevant in a New Testament text would be out of place here. We have aimed at avoiding both oversimplification and perplexing complications in trying to deal responsibly with issues that inevitably arise early on as the student approaches the beginnings of Christianity and its continuing development.

Chapter Three traces the emergence of Christianity from obscurity as a Jewish sect in the early Roman Empire to its commanding position as a spiritual,

cultural, social, and political force in medieval European and Byzantine civilizations. Chapter Four continues the story of Christianity's development from its
Western Renaissance and Reformation settings up to the present.

Chapter Five focuses on the variety and development of Christian organizational and liturgical practice. As in the earlier chapters, we characterize, by means
of comparison and contrast, the major strands of Christian tradition—Eastern
Orthodox, Western Catholic, Protestant, churchly, denominational, sectarian, and
cultic. Common and diverse elements in Christian practice, Christian popular
religion, mysticism, and devotional life, as well as various Christian "offshoots"
are considered.

Chapter Six discusses a cluster of topics that are indispensable for understanding the content of Christian belief and the development and role of Christian
institutions. First, the relationship of Christian approaches to "the knowledge of
God," as discussed in Greek philosophical schools, and the basis of Christian
approaches to knowledge of God in Judaism are examined. Five—or six, if Christian
mysticism in considered a separate approach—Christian approaches to the question
of revelation and reason are explored. Also, the relation of faith to scientific
method and theorizing, recent and classical discussions of the nature of religious
language, and questions concerning the sources and nature of authority in Christian
traditions are presented and examined.

Chapter Seven characterizes the major Chrisitian beliefs as they have been
confessionally and theologically expressed. The chapter follows the traditional
credal or confessional outline used in much of systematic theology. Here we
attempt to be as nontechnical as possible, but do not avoid names and terms (*e.g.*,
"Christology," "modalism") that figure prominently in theological discussion. We
must emphasize that this work is not intended to be a *history* or an *encyclopedia* of
Christian thought. To take one example: Although we characterize Trinitarian and
Christological controversies, we do not attempt to characterize or trace the development of all, or even many, of the variant positions relative to these issues, many of
which had great numbers of adherents. However, we hope we have avoided neglecting concepts and positions requisite to genuine understanding of the dynamic unity
and variety of Christian belief.

Chapter Eight presents a variety of creative figures and related movements
from Christian history—reformers and renewers. Certain of these are dealt with to
some extent in other parts of the book. Here, the emphasis is on variety and
diversity—richness—to be found in individual and group expression within Christian
history. Certain individuals and movements would have had to be treated in any
introductory discussion of Christianity—Paul; monastic reformers like Basil,
Benedict, Francis of Assisi, and Loyola; Luther and Calvin; and Teresa of Avila.
Other individuals are chosen to represent the wide variety of men and women of
diverse historical, cultural, and ethnic backgrounds who have contributed to the
variably shaped thrust of Christianity as it has sought to renew and extend itself
in its historical settings.

Chapter Nine describes some of the major contemporary issues faced by

Christian groups against the background of a characterization of contemporary society and its international setting. Here, too, we give interpretations of the major trends of Christian organizational and individual response to the contemporary issues and setting.

At the end of each chapter is a list of questions that systematically cover the materials discussed in the chapter. Possibly many instructors will find it useful to call these questions to the attention of students when making reading assignments. Some instructors may use them as written assignments or for class discussion or review sessions.

Each chapter also has a list of additional readings. These are not intended to be chapter bibliographies. They are given to provide guidance for readers who may wish to pursue topics discussed in the chapter and may be useful to instructors in assigning additional readings.

In using *Exploring Christianity*, one will find a certain overlapping of material. For instance, Martin Luther and the Protestant Reformation are dealt with (to some extent) in Chapters Four, Five, Six, Seven, and Eight. Albert Schweitzer is dealt with in Chapters Two and Eight. Other figures appear and reappear in various chapters. In a few cases, as in Luther's, our approach has resulted in a degree of repetition. What will ordinarily be found will—we hope—not be repetition but enrichment. Our fundamental approach is, for want of better terms to describe it, thematic and contextual. Each chapter is relatively self-contained, complete. However, the student's understanding of Luther's role in the Protestant Reformation (Chapters Four and Five) will be enriched by the discussion of Luther's personal religious experience (Chapter Eight), of his attitude toward the relation of revelation to reason (Chapter Six), and even of the discussion of how trends toward the development of national states in sixteenth-century Europe affected the forms of emerging religious organizations (Chapter Nine).

We do not intend to evaluate the various positions or views of the Christian groups described in this book. Even when a position is referred to as "heretical," this should be taken by the readers to mean the leadership or majority of members of groups we are describing considers the position to be divergent from orthodox positions. Similar considerations should be taken as applying to our characterization of various positions or beliefs as "orthodox" or otherwise.

We have attempted throughout *Exploring Christianity* to use language that will not be offensive to readers of various backgrounds and affiliations. Thus, we have not used the term "Old Testament" to characterize the Scriptures of Judaism, through we have used the term to characterize or describe a traditional *Christian* theological concept and use of the Jewish scriptures. This may seem almost to be a distinction without a difference, but we believe it is a distinction worth making. In the same spirit, we have used the descriptions B.C.E. (Before the Common Era) and C.E. (Common Era) to refer to the periods (roughly) before and after the birth of Jesus.

We have included a discussion of the Christian theological stance with respect to the appropriateness or inappropriateness of the use of sexual characteristics or sexually specific pronouns when speaking of God. However, when we describe and use traditional Christian expressions referring to God, we have usually let the masculine pronoun stand—otherwise, we would have falsified the tradition and imposed a "let's pretend" resolution to issues still very much alive.

We must express our appreciation to colleagues at our own college and at other colleges and universities who have helped with criticism and encouragement. Particularly, thanks should go to Professors William Barrick and Johnnie Kahl of the faculty of McMurry College and to students who have allowed us to try out some of the material embodied in *Exploring Christianity* in various forms in the courses described or mentioned above. We also thank the reviewers of our original proposal and of a preliminary version of our text, who, we hope, will be able to see that we have adopted the majority of their suggestions and have taken account of the others. It is not going too far to say that constructive suggestions of these reviewers caused us to reshape major sections of our book in ways that we believe have much improved it.

Our participation in a seminar on Catholic Christianity held at various universities and theological seminaries in the southwest during the past sixteen or more years has contributed probably much more than we realize to our ideas about many of the topics discussed herein. Also, a generous grant from the Sam P. Taylor Foundation to one of the authors contributed to the development of some of the ideas expressed in Chapter Nine. Finally, we express our gratitude to our diligent and able typist, Ms. Pat Shackelford.

chapter one
CHRISTIANITY:
ITS JEWISH CONTEXT

Most Christians and Jews are aware that Christianity emerged from first-century Judaism. However, many have only vague ideas about the relationship of these two religious traditions either in their beginnings or throughout their continuing history. A common mistake made among Christians is to assume that at the formation of a Christian community in Jerusalem immediately following the death of Jesus there was a complete separation of the two traditions and that thereafter there was little significant contact between them. In fact, the separation was much slower, and inter-action between Judaism and Christianity has been continuous—sometimes friendly, sometimes turbulent—since that time. Historically, an important part of Christian-ity's self-definition has been derived from its interpretation of its original and con-tinuing relation to Judaism. This chapter investigates the kinship of these two major religious traditions. Because both are living traditions that have changed and continue to change, it is not possible to understand the relationship of one to the other by focusing only on the historical beginnings of Christianity within Judaism. Their relationship today affects our understanding of each tradition, both in the past and in the present.

THE JEWISH SETTING OF CHRISTIANITY

Jesus and his immediate followers were Jews living in the Palestinian homeland that had been identified with their forefathers from at least 1200 B.C.E.[1] Known as Hebrews, a name derived from nomads called *Habiru* or *Apiru*, they were originally part of a large group of nomadic wanderers that inhabited the fringes of the more "civilized," or agricultural, territories of the Mesopotamian, Egyptian, Syrian, and Canaanite regions. The Hebrews emerged as an identifiable community around 1200 B.C.E.

During the next several centuries they developed beliefs and practices that separated them from the societies surrounding them. Central among these beliefs was the affirmation of *one* God who had chosen the Hebrews to be his special people. In a world where polytheism was common, the identification of one God with a specific people was not unusual. However, the claim that this God, Yahweh, was the *only* God, that He possessed transcendent power over all reality, and that He had chosen Israel to be *His* people to represent Him to all other nations was significantly different. The Hebrews further saw themselves as subject to Yahweh's demand for exemplary conduct, which emphasized a distinctive pattern of moral and ritual holiness. This code incoporated prescribed religious rites, dietary taboos, and moral commandments. By the time of Jesus, the code had been formulated in minute detail, with exacting standards defining every aspect of behavior. The Hebrews also believed that Yahweh actively participated in history to guide, discipline, and sustain them. Continuously relating Himself to human history, Yahweh became for the Hebrews a personal God with whom each individual could have a direct relationship and from whom they derived value and meaning for their lives.

The history of Yahweh's involvement in the life of the Hebrews and the ritual-ethical codes He gave them were incorporated in the Torah (the first five books of what Christians know as the Old Testament). To these materials were added the words of Hebrew prophets and other writings.[2] These sacred writings were a central source of religious belief and ethical practice. Confident that Yahweh is a God of history, the Hebrews believed that He had guided their destiny and would always do so. By the first century this belief had crystalized into the expectation that He would, through the sending of a Messiah (an anointed deliverer), bring the Hebrews and the world into a new day.

Those who followed Jesus and his teachings shared these central Jewish beliefs, and built upon them. Over the centuries, the Christian superstructure built on Jewish history, tradition, and scriptures came to differ significantly from Judaism, but the two religious traditions remain significantly intertwined, reflecting their common foundation and similar beliefs.

---

[1] C.E. in this text refers to the common era shared by Christians and Jews. B.C.E., Before the Common Era, refers to the time before the origin of Christianity.

[2] See Appendix I for a listing of Hebrew Scriptures.

JEWISH HERITAGE PRIOR
TO THE FIRST CENTURY C.E.

The beliefs and practices of the Hebrews developed from a long and complex history. Jews trace their origin to Abraham, although the Biblical account begins with stories about the creation of the world and human life. Abraham, a native of Mesopotamia, migrated into Canaan around 1800 B.C.E. There, according to the book of Genesis, he and his son, Isaac, and grandson Jacob, lived as nomadic sheep and cattle herders. The same tradition states that Jacob—whose name was changed to "Israel" after an encounter with God—went with his sons into Egypt during a period of famine to live with one of his younger sons, who had become a man of power. They stayed for centuries, but eventually were reduced to the status of slaves.

During this period a primary religious conviction emerged. Abraham had come into Cannan under the guidance and sustaining power of God. He left the gods of Mesopotamia to serve a God who had made him a promise—that Abraham would be father of a great people, and that through him (and his descendants) "the families of the earth shall bless themselves" (Genesis 12:1-3). So the "children" or "sons of Israel" came to believe in their particular and unique relationship to God.

Their status as slaves in Egypt became the setting for a renewed relationship between God and Abraham's descendants. Moses, called by God, led them out of their Egyptian bondage (ca. 1290 B.C.E.). After wandering in the Sinai for a generation, they entered Palestine, understanding it to be the Promised Land given to them by Yahweh. During this wilderness experience a decisive event occurred, ultimately perhaps more important than the escape from Egypt. The promise made by God to Abraham was renewed through a covenant (a contract) wherein God was to be the God of the descendants of Israel and they were to be His people. The covenant was God's promise to be their God forever and their promise to be His people. Their commitment meant following a specific religious and ethical code represented first by the Ten Commandments and also by a multitude of other moral and cultic regulations.

After a period during which the political organization of the descendants of Israel was a loosely structured confederacy of tribes, a nation, known as Israel, emerged under the leadership of David in 1000 B.C.E. Under David, Israel reached its height of political ascendancy, occupying a position of importance among the nations of the Eastern Mediterranean. After the reign of David's son, Solomon, the Israelite state split into two kingdoms: Judah and Israel. For several centuries these kingdoms enjoyed political freedom, although for much of that time they were threatened by and often subservient to the "superpowers" of the period, Egypt and the kingdoms that successively controlled the Mesopotamian valleys.

From its beginning, Israel's relationship to God had been celebrated and reinforced through stories recounting its history, distinctive cultic patterns of worship, and elaborate codes of moral instruction. At first passed from generation to generation in oral traditions, some of these acquired written forms early. Together, these oral and written traditions formed the basis of the Torah (the body of Israelite law and covenant), which from the time of David was shaped into an organized pattern. As the nation consolidated its social and political structure, the written Torah took on more significance, reflecting the changing social patterns, since trading and political activity depended on writing. Oral traditions continued, however, to supplement and interpret the written forms.

Distinctive religious concepts progressively developed among the Israelites. David and his successors were never deified, as many rulers were in ancient civilizations. God was understood to be ruler of Israel; the king of Israel was always God's servant but only a viceregent for God.

In the southern kingdom, Judah, worship slowly became centralized in a Temple in Jerusalem. This centralization of worship was one response to the constant temptation to conflate and intermix Israel's religion with the worship of the peoples among whom Israelites lived. Canaanite polytheistic worship of agricultural gods who promised fertility of the land was especially attractive to the Israelites as they settled from nomadic life to agriculture. These surrounding religions also claimed to provide political prowess and success to their adherents. Consequently, Israel's monotheistic faith was constantly challenged by the idolatry (worship of gods other than Yahweh) of its neighbors.

As the political fortunes of the Israelite kingdoms rose and fell there arose the voice of prophets (messengers of God), to remind Israel of the ancient covenant. According to the prophets, idolatry and the failure to adhere to the moral commandments were causing political chaos that cold be corrected only by returning to the worship of Yahweh. These prophets, interpreting political events within the framework of religious allegiance and moral discipline, inserted into Israelite beliefs a principle that was eventually to become more important than participation in ritual observances of the temple cult. Prophetic tradition claimed that the relationship went beyond observance of ritual and external moral commandment: What God demanded was an inner commitment to justice, mercy, loving kindness, and "humbly walking" with Him (Micah 6:8).

Israel was conquered by Assyria in 722 B.C.E. and Judah by Babylon in 587 B.C.E. The dissolution of the kingdoms brought political and religious crises. The descendants of Israel were not to be a national entity or enjoy political freedom again until the modern period, except for a brief respite under the Maccabees (165-63 B.C.E.). Nevertheless, the religious crisis was more significant. After 722 B.C.E. the Northern Kingdom effectively disappeared from history. With the Jerusalem Temple's destruction and the removal of many of the southern nation's elite, including the priests, to Babylon, the meaning of Israel's relationship to God had to be reinterpreted.

Jerusalem continued to have a very important symbolic significance as the City of God. However, one especially significant reformulation of belief was the recognition that worship could take place wherever believing descendants of Israel gathered. In exile, the community's attention focused on the ancient tradition of the covenant and the laws that were derived from it. The patterns of worship and the moral conduct demanded by ancient tradition did not require a physical temple, even though many of the exiles fervently hoped for a return to Palestine and the rebuilding of God's temple. Out of this new insight and the cultural realities of exile rose the *synagogue,* a setting for local worship outside Jerusalem and a place for the study of ancient tradition. Written forms of the tradition were by this time elaborated in the Torah.

A reinterpretation of Israel's destiny also became prominent during the exile. Prophetic voices, noting God's reliability and justice in His punishment of Israel's unfaithfulness, also emphasized the steadfastness and kindness of His love that followed them into exile. Together, these formed the basis of a renewed hope for the restoration of Israel. In this restoration Israel would fulfill its role as a "light to the nations" (Isaiah 49:6) revealing God's power and His love to all peoples. Israel would realize the completion of God's promise to Abraham.

The Persian emperor, Cyrus, after conquering the Babylonians, released the Judeans to return to Jerusalem in 538 B.C.E. The return was made by only a portion of the Judean exiles, but these persons were convinced that the prophecy of restoration was taking place. In this period the descendants of Israel came to be known as Jews, a name derived from Judah, the territory of Palestine in which they relocated. After delay and the overcoming of many obstacles, a "Second Temple" was built (ca. 520-515 B.C.E.). Because the Jews remained politically subservient to the Persians, religion became more than ever the binding force among the Jews. Ezra, a returning priest, brought about a renewal of interest in the Torah, now nearing its final written form as the first five books of the Hebrew Scripture. With the public reading of the Torah by Ezra (Nehemiah 8:2ff), the descendants of Israel renewed the ancient covenant, resolving again to live by its precepts.

The written Torah became a central focus of interest because it prescribed belief, worship patterns, and social as well as ethical behavior. Its laws extended to many details of daily life: Dietary taboos defined clean and unclean food, circumcision was required of all males to distinguish men of the covenant, marriage with non-Jews was forbidden, ethical instructions emphasized the sanctity of human life.

The transmission of the Torah became essential and produced a group of scribes responsible for its exact preservation and interpretation. The Torah of necessity had to be interpreted and reinterpreted in order to be applied to each new historical situation. Oral interpretative traditions continued to exist along with the written Torah, and were believed by many Jews to be equally as ancient and as binding as the written Torah. The necessity of preserving and interpreting these traditions created a need for trained, judicious scholars and teachers.

The relatively brief interlude of political independence for Palestinian Jews won by the Maccabees resulted from Jewish insistence on the worship of no God but Yahweh. Antiochus IV, a Greek-Syrian King, insisted that all his vassal states, including Israel, should worship Zeus, the chief of the Greek gods, of whom Antiochus claimed to be an earthly manifestation. This call to worship another god was accompanied in Judah by active desecration of Jewish sacred places and books.

A country priest, Mattathias, and his sons revolted and refused to worship any God but Yahweh. Known as the Maccabees, they led their countrymen to a period of political independence. The motive for the revolution was religious—a concern for the freedom to live as Jews without being compelled to worship non-Jewish gods or abandon the cultic and dietary practices that set them apart from other inhabitants of the Greek-Syrian empire.

In the postexilic period, Judaism also became geographically diverse. A portion of the Jews who were taken into captivity in Babylon chose to remain there, founding and maintaining a significant Jewish community. From there, they scattered throughout the Eastern Mediterrean world. By the time of Jesus, Jews of the dispersion, or Diaspora, as these non-Palestinian Jews came to be called by historians, outnumbered those in the homeland.

JEWISH RELIGIOUS PARTIES

While the Jewish community was bound together by its religious beliefs and practices, first-century Judaism was anything but a monolithic entity. The appeal to Rome for support by feuding factions of the Maccabean royal household brought Pompey in 63 B.C.E. to establish an uneasy Roman overlordship of Judah. Roman control allowed the continuation of a limited and subservient Jewish monarchy, unified until after the reign of Herod the Great, then divided geographically among Herod's sons in 4 B.C.E. Political control was thereafter variously effected, with Rome sometimes exercising direct rule over parts of Palestine and sometimes ruling through Herod's descendants.

The social and religious divisions that developed during postexilic Judaism had a far-reaching effect on Judaism and the development of Christianity. Josephus, a Jewish historian writing at the close of the first century C.E., lists four major groups influencial in the Jewish community. The priests related to the Temple in Jerusalem and the wealthy Jerusalem landowners constituted a group known as *Sadducees.* The Sadducees accepted only the written Torah as authentic spiritual authority, since it described Temple ritual and practice. To the extent they entertained Messianic beliefs at all, they held a conservative view of the "kingly" Messiah who would guarantee proper temple worship. It is possible that some of the early Sadducees identified the Messiah with Simon, the youngest of the Maccabean brothers who had ca. 140 B.C.E. taken upon himself the offices of both king and high priest. Because of their position as spiritual and economic leaders of the community, the Sadducees were in greater contact with Greek and Roman culture. They tended to accept social and cultural changes brought by contact with Rome, but continued to be conservative in worship.

The *Pharisees* were a successor group to the Hasidim (the loyal, or pious ones) who had emerged as early resisters to the Hellenization of Israel, brought about through contact with Greek culture after the exile. The Pharisees of the first century followed the Hasidim in their concern to interpret and apply the Torah to everyday life. For them Torah was not simply the written forms of the first books of the Bible, but included the commandments of the Oral Torah handed down from generation to generation by the great teachers of Israel. The Pharisees also recognized as authenic teachings the works of the prophets and a group of materials probably written after the exile known as the "writings." Knowledge and instruction in these works, and their application to everyday life, fell to the rabbi or teacher among the Pharisees. Normally laymen, the Pharisees could be from any segment of society, but were particularly drawn from craftsmen, artisans, and merchants. As a group they enjoyed religious prestige and influenced the understanding of the "law" among the general populace. They expected a Messiah who would institute a kingdom of righteous people—those who would assiduously follow the Torah, both written and oral.

The *Zealots* were, as the name has come to indicate, a radical group. They were dedicated to overthrowing Roman political control of the Jews by whatever means. Religiously, they probably were drawn from all segments of society, although they were most closely related to the Pharisees. Their Messianic expectations were for a king who would reestablish the Davidic kingdom.

Each of these groups is mentioned in the New Testament, and Jesus' teachings are often contrasted with these teachings and attitudes. The fourth party mentioned by Josephus was the *Essenes*. Until recently little was known about the group. Scrolls found hidden in Dead Sea caves in the twentieth century are thought by many scholars to give much information about the Essenes. The group formed an ascetic community that was generally withdrawn from Jewish society. They expected the reestablishment of "pure" Judaism only when the sinfulness of the community would be cleared away in a great holocaust allowing God's goodness to triumph over the evil of the world. This event would end the present world and establish a righteous and pure community. The new age instituted by this event would result from the coming of two Messiahs: The Messiah of Israel would lead the war against evil and the Messiah of Aaron would establish the New Jerusalem and its new Temple. For the Essenes, one of the signs of the corruption of the age was that even the Jerusalem Temple had been desecrated. In their understanding, it was presided over by the line of false and unrighteous priests stemming from the Maccabean period.

While these identifiable religious groups held roles of leadership in the society, most first-century Jews belonged to none of them. By their very nature the parties limited their membership to relatively small percentages of the population. The common people followed the Torah commandments as best they could and worshipped at the Temple and the local synagogues. Undoubtedly, they were influenced and swayed by the opinions and practices of the religious parties. Typically, they obeyed the Sadducees, perhaps admired the Pharisees, sympathized with the Zealots, and held the Essenes in awe. Judaism at the time of Jesus provided a rich tapestry of religious ideas and expectations within a framework of central commitment to Yahweh, His covenant, and His commandments.

A central theme of Jewish life in the first century was the expectation of one who could renew Israel's relationship to Yahweh through the purification of the community and the fulfilling of the ancient promises made to Abraham and his descendants. Such expectations were part of the fabric of Jewish religion from the time of the prophets. This element of Jewish faith intensified during the political and social changes wrought by their postexilic encounter with Greek and Roman culture. For most Jews, some form of Messianic belief probably figured as an important part of their religious background. For some, perhaps many, it was a fervent hope. The identification of Jesus as the Messiah was a natural development for Jews who accepted his teachings.

JESUS AND THE JEWISH COMMUNITY

Jesus entered the Jewish scene as a public figure when he began a teaching ministry using methods similar to those of other Jewish teachers. He gathered a group of disciples and taught them by commenting on and interpreting ancient Jewish beliefs and laws. However, he claimed an authentication that did not depend on previous teachers, thereby questioning traditional interpretations of the Torah. His teachings emphasized doing the "will of God" rather than rigorous adherence to the commonly accepted Pharisaic and Sadducean interpretations of the Torah commandments. Accompanying Jesus' teaching was a healing ministry seen by the ordinary people as a sign of unusual spiritual powers. His images of the Messianic age suggested a servant role for the Messiah, whose kingdom would be found where the faithful followed God's will by selflessly serving others. These Messianic ideas contrasted with those of the Jewish parties and were not attractive to those who expected immediate deliverance from the power of evil experienced in the rule by Rome. Also, unlike the renowned rabbis of the time, Jesus took his teachings to the ordinary people, rather than to the cultural and religious leaders. His teachings, and some of his actions, ultimately led to Jesus' death. Accused of blasphemy for appealing to the authority of God rather than that of tradition, and apparently for his attacks on the authority of the Pharisaic scribes and the Sadducean priesthood and Temple cult, he was crucified by the Romans for insurrection (on the basis of a supposed assertion that he was the king of the Jews).

At first disillusioned and scattered at Jesus' death, his followers quickly came to proclaim that they had witnessed the presence of a living, resurrected Jesus. They took his resurrection to be confirmation that Jesus' teachings and action were those of God himself. Jesus was the anointed of God and, therefore, the long-expected Messiah. As such, he had inaugurated in his life, death, and resurrection the kingdom so anxiously awaited by the Jews. This Messiah was not one who brought political independence or ritual and moral righteousness, but one who brought a new expression of Yahweh's love centered in selfless giving.

The followers of Jesus, soon known as Christians for their proclamation that Jesus was the Christ (the Greek translation of Messiah), at first challenged the

Jewish community at large to believe with them that Jesus was the Messiah—the anointed one of God. Early Christian writers went to great pains to show that Jesus fulfilled the ancient prophetic expectations (Matthew 1:22; 2:17; 12:17). However, this proclamation was accepted by only a small minority of Jews. Most continued to believe a Messiah would fulfill their dreams of restored political independence and religious purification.

Conflicts in the earliest Jewish Christian community.   Those who accepted Jesus as the Christ soon found their numbers increasing. Included in the expanding community were Hellenists (Acts 6:1). These were either Greek-speaking Jews of the dispersion who, in Jerusalem for the passover, were attracted to Christianity; Jews who had acquired Greek customs; or perhaps Greek and Roman proselytes to Judaism who now accepted Christianity. In any case, they constituted a large enough group in the Jewish Christian community to be recognized, and to complain about their treatment by "the Hebrews," or Jerusalem Jews. This distinction be- tween the Jews of Palestine and the Jews or proselytes who reflected a broader exposure to the Greco-Roman culture expanded as Christian evangelism moved outside of Palestine. Since most of the first Christians were Jewish (Hebrews or Hellenists), the proclamation was taken into the Jewish synagogues of the disper- sion (Acts 13:5, 17:1). Reception was mixed and often negative. The Christian message, nevertheless, found fertile soil among the "gentiles"—non-Jewish neighbors in the Greco-Roman society, many of whom had admired Jewish mono- theism and the Torah's moral code.

The Apostle Paul, a Hellenistic Jew who originally had bitterly opposed those who proclaimed Jesus to be the Messiah, after his conversion to Christianity took it as his special mission to preach to the gentiles (Galatians 1:17). Because of Paul's and others' missions, by the late first century the majority of the Christians were gentiles. This created a crisis in the church. If persons converted to Christianity were not Jews through birth or covenant, was it necessary for them to become practicing Jews, keeping the dietary and ritual laws of the Torah? Paul, appearing before a council of Christian elders in Jerusalem, argued that it was neither neces- ary nor wise. A decision was made that gentiles did not have to follow the Jewish law in all its detail (Galatians 2:1f; Acts 15:6-21). This decision, which perhaps only recognized accepted practice by that time, indicates the development of another early distinction among Christians. Two distinct groups existed side by side: Jewish Christians, who practiced the precepts of the Jewish law, and gentiles, who did not. The tensions created by this situation lessened with the passing years, for the Christian mission found abundant fruit among the gentiles and had limited success among the Jews. After the destruction of Jerusalem by the Romans in 70 C.E., there was no significant geographical center left for Jewish Christianity. Christianity, like Judaism, spread throughout the empire with no early central authority.

THE JEWISH WAR AGAINST THE ROMANS

The single most important event in Jewish history in the first century was the war fought to throw off the Roman yoke in 66-73 C.E. Zealot patriots dominated the political events of the latter part of the century and succeeded in fomenting a war which resulted in the destruction of Jerusalem and the Temple in 70 C.E. These Messianic patriots continued their influence until a final and catastrophic conflict (132-135 C.E.) under the leadership of Simon Ben Kosifa (Bar Kokhba). This conflict destroyed Jerusalem and effectively scattered the remaining Palestinian Jews. There was no significant Jewish political community in Palestine from that time until the events leading to establishment of modern Israel in 1948.

The political and religious consequences of the destruction of the Temple were revolutionary. The destruction eliminated the worship centered there and the role of those responsible for it—the priests. Their colleagues, the landowners, were also displaced, so that the influence of the traditional Sadducees was lost forever. The Zealots, having lost the war with Rome, were eliminated; their reason for existence was lost in the Jewish defeat. While the exact fate of the Essenes is unknown, their Dead Sea community was evidently destroyed during the war or its aftermath.

The Jewish group that survived the wars was the Pharisees. Their interests did not demand a Temple, for the Torah could be studied and applied anywhere. The concerns and methods of the Pharisees by this time already dominated the Dispersion synagogues. Their chief emphasis centered on preservation of the Torah, knowledge of its teachings and application of these to everyday life. Such emphases gave stability and content to the Judaism that survived. It was around this Pharisaical leadership that post-Jerusalem Israel coalesced. Jacob Neusner suggests that the priestly interests also were not totally lost after the fall of Jerusalem. The synagogue already served as a place of worship as well as teaching. The priestly concern for regularity, order, and continuity survived in post-Jerusalem Judaism in synagogue and family worship.[3] The Judaism that emerged in the next few centuries welded together these interests into what became Rabbinic Judaism: the classical pattern that has survived almost unchanged for eighteen centuries.

HEBREW SCRIPTURES

The patterns of pharisaical Judaism that developed before the destruction of the Temple allowed Judaism to survive repeated crises in the ensuing centuries. In the post-Jerusalem community, the pharisaical system of education and reformulation of the law assumed a central role in the preservation and systematization of the Hebrew law and its scriptures. Highly influential in the synagogues where most male

---

[3] Jacob Neusner, *The Way of the Torah* (North Scituate, Mass.: Duxbury Press, 1979), pp. 12-13.

Jews learned to read and write through the study of the Torah, the Pharisees had by the time of Jesus established *academies* for advanced study of oral and written Scriptures. In these academies disciples gathered around renowned teachers (rabbis). The most famous of these institutions were the schools of Hillel and Shammai. In these academies ancient patterns of interpretation were expanded. Central to the method was refinement of traditional answers given to questions raised by the constant adjustment of the understanding of the Torah to changing social and historical conditions. Clarification of issues, debate about appropriate answers, and amplification by the teacher led to new interpretations and the rise of classical rabbinical learning, an expansion of the oral tradition. Different academies developed unique patterns of interpretation, giving a dynamic quality to the total endeavor.

After the destruction of Jerusalem, the Jews were anxious to stabilize their precarious situation. One concern of the period was the establishment of a "regular list" or "canon" of the ancient scriptures. The Pharisees had from an early time accepted a broader group of scriptures than the priests. For the Pharisees, the prophets clearly represented God's will and were interpreters of the Torah. Therefore, their writings were cherished as sacred. Over the centuries other writings also understood to speak for God had been added. These "writings" incorporated a variety of literature: devotional materials, stories, proverbs, and so on. While the Torah had taken its final form at the latest by 200 B.C.E., and the prophets by 100 B.C.E., the writings were a more fluid group of materials. The value and authenticity of many documents was heatedly disputed. Integral to the question of a proper canon of authentic Scriptures were questions about which writings were authoritative and therefore sacred.

In this context another question arose. Jews of the dispersion, particularly those who had lived for generations under the influence of Hellenistic culture, often lost their ability to read and understand Hebrew readily. Pious dispersion Jews, therefore, translated Hebrew scriptures into a number of Greek versions. The most influential of these was the Septuagint, a work of Jews living in Egypt. Some of the materials in the Septuagint were translated as early as 250 B.C.E. By the first century this work was broadly used among dispersion Jews. It included the traditional sections: Torah, Prophets, and Writings. However, the writings in the Septuagint included works not originally written in Hebrew, but written by Jews in Greek. Many of them reflected late postexilic times and were apocalyptic in interest. They were "original" rather than traditional works. What was to be the status of these works and others like them found in the several Greek translations?

It is not clear how it was decided which works were to be accepted as authentic, but the decision was evidently completed by the turn of the first century C.E. The decision appears to have been influenced by an academy that appeared at Jabneh (Jamnia) on the cost of Palestine after the destruction of Jerusalem. The confusion of the attack on Jerusalem in 70 C.E. led Rabbi Johanan Ben Zakkai to seek permission from Vespasian, the Roman general, to move his academy to Jabneh. Ben Zakkai was the heir to Hillel's school, which had become a dominant academy among Jews. Along with the academy at Jabneh there came the court of the religious community—the successor to the Jerusalem Sanhedrin or ruling religious court. Since the leaders of the old Sanhedrin were no longer in control, the new court was made up of scholars—essentially the members of the academy.[4] This academy/court appears to have determined which books among the various writings would be accepted as authentic Scriptures. Traditionally the date given for the decision is 90 C.E.

The criteria developed to determine authenticity must have included several principles, but the basic consideration seems to have been whether a work could be traced in some manner to the prophetic period or tradition. If it could, it was worthy of acceptance; if it could not, it was rejected. The result was to reduce substantially the number of writings included in the final canon to twenty-four books considered to be ancient "tradition."[5] This scripture came to be known as *Tanakh*, combining the Hebrew first letters of each of the sections: *Torah* (Pentateuch), *Nebi'im* (Prophets) and *Ketubin* (Writings).

The fate of the Septuagint among Jews and Christians is curious. From an early time, the Septuagint was regularly used as the Christian source of the Hebrew Scriptures. This is an understandable development, since Christianity expanded most rapidly among gentiles and among dispersion Jews. The common language among the Christians scattered over the Roman Empire was Greek, so it was natural to use this familiar translation. It became the authentic form of the "Old Testament" or "Old Covenant" (the Christian designation of the Hebrew Scripture) for the church throughout its early centuries.

When the Scriptures were translated from Hebrew to Latin by Saint Jerome in the fourth century, the books incorporated were those found in the Septaugint. This Latin translation, *The Vulgate*, became the basis of Western Christian Scripture. Centuries later, Protestant reformers, noting the difference between the Hebrew versions and Greek versions, and anxious to return to the tradition, omitted from their translations the extra works included from the Septuagint in the *The Vulgate*. These materials were assigned to an Apocrypha, only recently included (and usually as secondary material), by Protestants in translations of the Jewish Scriptures.

Among the Jews, the Septuagint was rejected completely as the movement toward consolidating the tradition became stronger. Perhaps its popularity among Christians also contributed to its rejection by Jews.

The differing Jewish and Christian attitudes toward the Septuagint in the early centuries only reflect wider divergencies in attitudes toward the Jewish Scripture. Christians of the period, following Paul, spoke of the "New Covenant" that Jesus brought; therefore, the Jewish Scripture became for the Christians the "Old Covenant," or testament. Justin Martyr, a Roman Christian writing in the

---

[4] Samuel Sandmel, *Judaism & Christian Beginnings* (New York: Oxford University Press, 1978), p. 138.

[5] In this calculation the Twelve Prophets are counted as one as are the books of Samuel, Kings, Ezra-Nehemiah, and Chronicles.

second century, took the distinction further. In his *Dialogue with Trypho* (Trypho was a Hellenized Jew), Justin attempted to show that the Jews had misunderstood their own Scriptures when they turned them into instructions for righteous living. He argued that the law had been given to the Jews as an instruction in moral integrity and purity of heart rather than a pattern to be observed in a legal fashion. Justin made extensive use of the prophets to show that Jesus was the anticipated Messiah and thereby the consummation and the true character of Judaism. He went so far as to claim that Christians who follow Jesus are really the true Israel—heirs to the promises and the true successors to the Jews.[6] Justin's claim had the effect of making the Hebrew Scriptures Christian at the expense of the traditional Jewish understanding of these same Scriptures. Clearly, in the second century, the two religious communities shared the same scriptures, but interpreted them from radically differing viewpoints.

QUESTIONS

1. What beliefs do Christians and Jews continue to share?

2. For many Christians Judaism is understood to be only a "predecessor" religion to Christianity. Why? What effect does such understanding have for the relationship of modern Jews and Christians?

3. What insights into "tradition" might Jews offer American Christians?

4. Does the Jewish understanding of religion as a "way of life" contrast significantly with most Christian understandings?

5. In beginning the study of Chistianity as a religious tradition, why is it important to consider the interaction between Judaism and Christianity? Explain.

FURTHER READING

The following titles are offered as representative of a wide range of writings on Jews and their heritage.

ABRAHAMS, ISRAEL, *Jewish Life in the Middle Ages.* Philadelphia, Penn.: Jewish Publication Society, 1958.
ARENDT, HANNAH, *Origins of Totalitarianism.* New York: Meridian, 1958.
DAVIES, W. D., Ed., *The Cambridge History of Judaism,* 4 vols. Cambridge, Mass.: Cambridge University Press, 1979.
HESCHEL, ABRAHAM J., *God in Search of Man: A Philosophy of Judaism.* Philadelphia, Penn.: Jewish Publication Society, 1956.
KEMELMAN, HARRY, *Conversations with Rabbi Small.* New York: William Morrow & Co., 1981.
MARGOLIS, MAX and MARX, ALEXANDER, *History of the Jewish People.* Philadelphia, Penn.: Jewish Publication Society, 1953.

[6] Justin Martyr, "Dialogue with Trypho," *Ante-Nicene Fathers,* Vol. I, Chs. 122-25.

MICHENER, JAMES, *The Source.* New York: Random House, 1965.

NEUSNER, JACOB, *Between Time and Eternity: The Essentials of Judaism.* Encino, Calif.: Dickenson, 1976.

____. *There We Sat Down: The Story of Classical Judaism in the Period in Which it was Taking Shape.* Nashville, Tenn.: Abingdon Press, 1972.

____. *The Way of the Torah,* 3rd Ed. North Scituate, Mass.: Duxbury Press, 1979.

OESTERLEY, W. O. E., et al. *Judaism and Christianity.* New York: KTAV Publishing House, 1969.

POTOK, CHAIM, *Wanderings.* New York: Alfred A. Knopf, 1978.

ROTH, CECIL, *Short History of the Jewish People.* London: East and West Library, 1953.

SACHAR, HOWARD, *A History of Israel.* New York: Knopf, 1947.

____. *The Course of Modern Jewish History.* New York: World Publishing Co., 1958.

SANDERS, E. P., *Paul and Palestinian Judaism.* Philadelphia, Penn.: Fortress, 1977.

SANDMEL, SAMUEL, *Judaism and Christian Beginnings.* New York: Oxford University Press, 1978.

SPONG, JOHN SHELBY and JACK DANIEL SPIRO. *Dialogue: In Search of Jewish Christian Understanding.* New York: Seabury Press, 1975.

STEINBERG, MILTON, *The Making of the Modern Jew.* Indianapolis, Ind.: Bobbs-Merrill, 1934.

TREPP, LEO, *Judaism: Development and Life.* Belmont, Calif.: Dickenson, 1966.

WOUK, HERMAN, *This Is My God.* New York: Random House, 1965.

ZBOROWSKI, MARK and HERZOG, ELIZABETH, *Life Is With People.* New York: International Universities Press, 1952.

chapter two
JESUS AND THE BEGINNING OF CHRISTIANITY

SOURCES OF KNOWLEDGE ABOUT JESUS

The Historical Jesus
and The Christ of Faith

Christianity began as a result of the activity of Jesus during the latter years of the first third of the first century C.E. There is much important background information from first-century Judaism that provides vital historical knowledge about Jesus. The Talmud, the works of the Jewish historian Josephus, and the Dead Sea Scrolls that belonged to the Qumran (probably Essene) community provide a wealth of material. By and large, however, the only direct sources about the life and teachings of Jesus are to be found in the New Testament, the Christian Scriptures.[1] Within the New Testament, though Jesus is quoted (rarely) and his action are at times directly or indirectely mentioned in the Epistles (I Corinthians), it is only the fourth Gospels that provide any extended information about him. During the past 200 years, multitudes of scholars have analyzed the Gospels in depth, using all the tools of literary and historical scholarship. One of the major goals of their

---

[1] Some scholars have suggested that some of the noncanonical gospels, like the Gospel of Thomas, found at Nag Hammadi in Egypt in the 1940s, may rest on a body of tradition independent of the sources utilized by the canonical gospels. (See Chapter Seven for discussion of the Christian Gnosticism represented by many of the Nag Hammadi works.) What we certainly do not have is access to significant historical information about Jesus from non-Christian sources.

studies has been to discover as much as can be learned about Jesus as a figure in human history.

By the eighteenth century, one fundamental problem involved in using the Gospels as historical sources had already been noticed by the great German dramatist, critic, controversialist, and scholar G.E. Lessing. The Gospels were written years—the earliest possibly thirty to fifty years—after the events they record. They were written not to give biographical information about Jesus for posterity. Rather, the Gospels were written to proclaim the early Christian community's (or church's) faith in and about Jesus, their belief that Jesus had come into the world representing God, and that he had come to bring redemption to humanity. The Gospels were written to proclaim that Jesus was in some unique way the Son of God and the Savior of the world. Thus, instead of intending to give what a historian would consider biographical or historical information about "the historical Jesus," the Gospels were written to express and interpret the early church's message about the Christ of its faith. Or as the author (or editors) of the Gospel of John wrote toward the end of that Gospel:

> Now Jesus did many other signs in the presence of the disciples, which are not written in this book; but these are written that you may believe that Jesus is the Christ, the son of God, and that believing you may have life in his name.

(JOHN 20:30-31 RSV)

Thus, New Testament scholars as long ago as the eighteenth century came to believe that the historical materials about Jesus recorded in the Gospels had been subjected to arrangemement and to theological interpretation in order to serve the church's primary purpose of winning people to the new faith and strengthening them in it. One of the major goals of much nineteenth-century study of the Gospels was to strip away or delve beneath the ordering of Gospel materials dictated by the church's religious purpose and theological interpretation in the hope of arriving at a solid core of historical data—an outline and explanation of the life of Jesus as it actually occurred and a summary of his teachings.

By the beginning of the twentieth century there had been a proliferation of scholarly and popular "lives of Jesus," many of which had attempted to separate the "historical Jesus" from the early church's proclamation and interpretation of Him. During the first decade of the twentieth century a distinguished German biblical scholar, the many-sided genius (theologian, philosopher, and musician), Albert Schweitzer, wrote a critical study of the "lives of Jesus" that had appeared in the eighteenth and nineteenth centuries. This book was soon translated into English under the title *The Quest of the Historical Jesus.*[2] In general, Schweitzer argued that none of the "lives of Jesus" had succeeded in giving an accurate histori-

---

[2] Schweitzer's book appeared in two different German editions, with some changes of emphasis between first and second editions. These changes need not concern us. The important point for our study is the historical impact of Schweitzer's book.

cal picture of Jesus because they had ignored or overlooked the most important background feature of first-century Judaism, its apocalyptic, eschatological beliefs and hopes. In Chapter One we saw that most of the Jewish religious groups and most Jews of the first century C.E. believed that the present age was/is under the rule of powers of evil. They looked forward to God's inaugurating the New Age in which His will and kingdom would be established. The Greek term *eschaton* refers to the "last time" or "end time." *Eschatology* literally means "discourse about the last things" and is used, particularly in reference to Judaism and Christianity, to designate beliefs and teachings about the end time, the time of transition from the evil present age to the New Age that God will inaugurate. An Apocalypse (literally meaning *revelation*) was a type of literary work very common in the times, which, often in highly symbolic form, professed to give information about the coming of the New Age and the defeat of the evil powers that controlled the present age. *Apocalyptic* refers to any message or view characterized by such eschatological themes.

Schweitzer argued that not only were the beliefs of first-century Judaism generally characterized by apocalyptic or eschatological hopes, so was the message of Jesus. Nineteenth-century European scholars, he thought, tended to regard apocalyptic thought as largely incomprehensible or irrelevant. They believed in continuous historical progress under the inspiration of scientific truth and humanitarian ideals. In writing their lives of Jesus, Schweitzer argued, they had left out Jesus' radical apocalypticism—his belief that the old age was soon to be directly overthrown by God with the establishment of a Messianic Kingdom. In doing so, they had made Jesus a nineteenth-century humanitarian. Some of them, critical of Christianity and ignorant of the all-pervasive apocalyptic background of first-century Judaism, had gone so far as to treat Jesus as a kind of madman suffering from various delusions.

Schweitzer's Jesus of history was, then, a radical apocalyptic preacher who had deliberately gone to his death on the cross with the purpose of provoking events that would lead to the coming of the New Age. According to Schweitzer, the New Age had not come as Jesus had thought it would. Therefore, twentieth-century Europeans could not hold the apocalyptic views that Jesus held—they could barely, if at all, understand them. What they could relate to was the radical commitment of Jesus to something, the transcendent claim of the idea of a Kingdom of God, to which Jesus' life had been dedicated. According to Schweitzer, in encountering the historical Jesus, twentieth-century people can find themselves called to a similar total commitment, even though the content of that commitment will be very different from the Kingdom of God envisaged in first-century Jewish apocalyptic thought. Acting on the results of his own inquiries, Schweitzer abandoned his theological professorship, spent several years qualifying for medical degrees, and devoted the rest of his long life to service as a medical missionary in Africa, committing himself to serve on the basis of Jesus' example.

The immediate impact of Schweitzer's work was very great. It was agreed that apocalyptic and eschatological themes dominated first-century Judaism and the message of Jesus. Even more profound was a further result, which was not really intended by Schweitzer, namely: New Testament scholars became cautious, even sceptical, about using the Gospels as sources of historical knowledge about Jesus. The quest of the historical Jesus was, by and large, abandoned. Schweitzer's historical Jesus seemed as much a figment of his creative imagination to some scholars as did the nineteenth-century portraits of Jesus he had criticized. Some even argued that it is impossible to go behind the "Christ of Faith" of the early church's proclamation to the historical Jesus at all. It was generally conceded that the Gospels do not follow a chronology of the life of Jesus, do not allow us to discover exactly when or where his ministry began, how long it lasted, or what its basic phases were.

Long before the time of Schweitzer, major differences in literary style, content, and details had been noticed between the Gospel of John on the one hand and the three Synoptic Gospels (Matthew, Mark, and Luke) on the other. Many events reported in John did not occur in the Synoptics. The Synoptics followed a common outline different from that of John. Matthew and Luke shared much common additional material, mainly teachings of Jesus not included in Mark, but very different in style and content from the teachings of Jesus as given in John. Often there seemed to be large discrepancies between John's account of Jesus' actions and his ministry and the accounts given by the Synoptics which, with some exceptions, tended to agree with each other. Scholars became extremely cautious about relying on John for historical data—that Gospel had always been regarded as the "spiritual gospel," thought to take a more symbolic than literal approach in its account of the life and teachings of Jesus. Some more recent students of the Gospels have found more in common between John and the Synoptics, although the differences noted above are readily apparent.

By and large, scholars came to believe that Mark, possibly an earlier version than the one we possess, was the earliest of the Gospels, and had been used to provide their outlines and a large part of their content by Matthew and Luke. Matthew and Luke were believed to have used another source, either oral or more likely documentary (called "Q" from the initial letter of the German word *Quelle* meaning "source"). This source was thought to contain materials from the teachings of Jesus as well as stories about him that had been collected but not arranged in chronological order or given connected narrative form. Thus, it was assumed that Mark's gospel, as the earliest, and as the source of Matthew and Luke's accounts, was also the most reliable source of historical information about the shape, length, and content of Jesus' ministry.[3]

After the time of Schweitzer, however, New Testament scholars came to believe that the order and content of Mark's Gospel are as much influenced by theological and religious motives as is John's. For instance, Mark uses an elaborate

---

[3]The actual evidence for the use of Mark by Matthew and Luke, and for their use of a further source, Q, cannot be examined here but is dealt with in all standard introductory texts on the New Testament.

pattern based on number symbolism to organize his account of Jesus' activities. The point is that even Mark's Gospel cannot be used as a very reliable source for the kind of historical information about Jesus that scholars hoped to get.

Two of the most famous New Testament scholars of the post-Schweitzer period were Rudolf Bultmann and Martin Dibelius. Both argued for extreme caution in using the Gospel materials as sources of historical information about Jesus. Both were pioneers in form criticism (or tradition-history), a method of studying units of Gospel material to uncover ways in which original or primitive sayings of Jesus or stories about him were shaped by the needs of the early church. Form criticism tried to show that the stories about Jesus and the teaching materials that appear in the Gospels originally were handed down as brief, independent oral units. Over time, these units were utilized and changed to meet new situations. Even before they were given written form, the oral units reflected the history of their adaptation to new situations, such as the change from Palestinian-Jewish to Hellenistic-gentile settings.

Bultmann, Dibelius, and the other form critics were convinced that the nature of the New Testament materials does not allow a chronological account of the ministry of Jesus, and does not allow a reconstruction of his activities, goals, or motives, much less a psychological portrait of his inner life. Nevertheless, Bultmann and Dibelius each wrote outstanding accounts of the *message* of Jesus, and if one studies these works, one discovers that although both advocate and practice extreme caution in their approach to their subject and their sources, their results are not as negative as some of their critics have claimed.

Since the time of Bultmann and Dibelius, many scholars, although not abandoning the caution of the form-critical movement in identifying original or primitive material relating to Jesus, have tended to be somewhat more confident about the possibility of using the Gospels as sources of historical information about Jesus. In the 1950s there was much talk of a new quest of the historical Jesus. Günter Bornkamm, Ernst Käsemann, Joachim Jeremias, and other New Testament scholars in Germany did pioneering work. In the United States James Robinson, Leander Keck, Norman Perrin, and others made important contributions to the clarification of the possibility of a quest of the historical Jesus old or new. Using form-critical methods, Jeremias and Perrin focused especially on Jesus' parables as historical sources. Although the "New Questers" did not discard the caution or assumptions of Bultmann and Dibelius, they were willing to find much *indirect* evidence in the Gospels that cast light on questions about the attitudes, motives, and goals of Jesus, and about the shape of his ministry, questions that the older scholars had been reluctant to address.

Recently, the question of the priority of Mark has been reopened, although in general Markan priority is still accepted by most New Testament scholars. The existence of the source document Q has been debated. Some studies have shown more connections between teachings and accounts of Jesus' activities in the Gospel of John and those of the Synoptics than were earlier thought to exist. A contemporary Jewish historian, David Flusser, has written:

... it is possible to write the story of Jesus' life. True, we have fuller records about the lives of contemporary emperors, and some of the Roman poets; but, with the exception of the historian Flavius Josephus, and possibly St. Paul, among the Jews of post Old Testament times Jesus is the one about whom we know most.[4]

Almost any assertion made about Jesus on the basis of historical scholarship can be challenged and will be subject to qualification. The following account attempts to give an accurate, probable picture of the historical Jesus. The Christian churches have traditionally asserted most of what will be said here plus much more about the Christ of their faith. One of the beliefs of the New Testament Christians was that after the Resurrection of Jesus and the imparting by him of the Spirit of God to the community of his followers, much more knowledge about him and his mission was made known—revealed by him in his Resurrection appearances or by the Spirit of God to the churches—than had been communicated during his pre-Resurrection ministry (see Luke 24:49; John 16:12-15). Thus, to Jesus' followers this new material and new interpretations, added to material remembered and transmitted about Jesus and his teachings, did not involve invention or falsification. It nevertheless was subject, in theory, to the test of coherence with what the earliest disciples of Jesus remembered and reported.

Nature of the Gospel Accounts

All of the Gospels relate Jesus' actions and the events of his life to various Old Testament prophecies. Typical are the second and third verses of Mark, which, in connecting the beginning of Jesus' ministry with the message of John the Baptist, quote parts of two Old Testament passages, Isaiah 40:3 and Malachi 3:1. Both were clearly understood by most Jews in Jesus' time to be prophecies concerning the coming of the Messiah. All of the Gospels, Matthew at times more explicitly than the others, frequently cite Old Testament events or passages as foreshadowing and foretelling the episodes in Jesus' life. Also, each Gospel uses symbols drawn from Israel's religion and history to make clear that Jesus is the Messiah, and that in him the promises made to the patriarchs and prophets are being fulfilled.

Two of the Gospels, Matthew and Luke, have accounts of the birth of Jesus and the events preceding it. These accounts are very different from each other in detail. The role of Mary, the mother of Jesus, is highlighted in Luke's account, as is the fact that those who learn of the birth of the Savior—shepherds in the fields—are among the humble poor. Luke emphasizes throughout his Gospel that it is a sign of the beginning of the Messianic Age that the good news of forgiveness, healing, and new life is being proclaimed to women, the poor, the outcast, sinners, foreigners, and those without prestige or influence. In Matthew's Gospel, the role of Joseph, the supposed father of Jesus, is highlighted. Joseph is presented as a man of faith like the Old Testament patriarch Abraham, the birth of Jesus is treated as a miracle

---

[4]David Flusser, *Jesus* (New York: Herder and Herder, 1969), p. 7.

even more wonderful than the birth of Abraham's son Isaac, and the events surrounding the birth are implicitly related to other events of Israel's history, including the descent into Egypt and the Exodus, suggesting their repetition and fulfillment in Jesus.

Two of the Gospels, Mark and John, begin with accounts of the baptizing activities of John the Baptist. Matthew and Luke contain accounts of these events too. All of them use several chapters detailing the ministry of Jesus. If one read only the Synoptic Gospels, one might believe that most of Jesus' ministry took place in Galilee. John's Gospel has Jesus' ministry alternate between Galilee and Judea. The time span covered by the ministry seems much shorter in the Synoptics than in John.

After the chapters describing the ministry and message of Jesus—Mark has much less teaching material than the others—each of the Gospels devotes several chapters to an account of the events of the last few days of Jesus' activity: His trip to Judea, his entry into Jerusalem to celebrate the Passover with his disciples, His conflict with the religious authorities, Sadducees and Pharisees, his last instructions to his disciples including a celebration of the Passover with them (here there are very important differences between John and the Synoptics), his arrest and appearance before the Sanhedrin and the Roman Governor Pilate, the determination that he should be put to death, and his crucifixion. (Crucifixion was the method used by the Roman government to punish noncitizens considered to be despicable, criminals guilty of degrading offenses, including insurrection and treason.) There are a number of interesting differences in the accounts of these events from Gospel to Gospel.

This is even more true of the Resurrection accounts, although here, too, the Gospels are in fundamental agreement. Shown as having lost hope at Jesus' arrest and crucifixion, his disciples are told afterwards—"on the third day"—that He has risen from the dead. Then each of the Gospels except Mark, which apparently in its original form ended with an angel's announcement of the Resurrection and the promise that Jesus would soon meet the disciples in Galilee, recounts a number of appearances of the risen Jesus to his disciples. The disciples are told by Jesus, in a variety of ways, that they will be empowered by God and will take the message of salvation to others, even throughout the whole world.

THE MINISTRY OF JESUS

Jesus appears to have begun his ministry in Galilee, the Northern part of Palestine. Galilee, where he conducted most of his activity, was governed by one of the sons of Herod the Great, Herod Antipas, who ruled at the pleasure of the Romans. The southern part of Palestine, Judea, with the Holy City of Jerusalem and its Temple, was under the direct rule of a Roman official. The Sanhedrin, with a majority of its members being Sadducees and the remainder Pharisees, was the supreme Jewish religious council and served as a governing board for Jerusalem and its environs.

The Transcendental Christ Mosaic from Hagia Sophia. Photo by Lessing, used with permission of Magnum Photos, Inc.

Roman intervention was more frequent in Judea than in Galilee, since the Sanhedrin and Temple authorities had only a minimal number of troops at their disposal. The Romans did not allow them to impose the death penalty. Jerusalem as a center of religious pilgrimage for Jews throughout the world frequently was the locale of explosive religious and cultural interaction. Roman rule, including the presence within the walls of the Holy City of non-Jewish troops, was bitterly resented.

John the Baptist

We have seen in Chapter One and in the first section of this chapter that first-century Judaism was to a large degree apocalyptic in outlook. Devout Jews prayed that God would establish His Kingdom during their own times. They attempted to live in ways that would aid and speed the coming of God's Kingdom. To the Essenes (or Qumran community) living in a way that would hasten God's Kingdom meant to withdraw from contacts with non-Essenes, to repent of one's sins, to practice acts of ritual purification (such as frequent ceremonial washing), to live by the precepts of the Torah, and to wait in readiness for God's commands. To the Pharisees, it meant keeping all the commandments of the Torah with sincerity and to the last detail.

At some point before the beginning of the ministry of Jesus, a message concerning the coming of God's Kingdom began to be proclaimed by a man named John. Tradition soon gave John the title Baptist or Baptizer because he called on those responding to his message to be baptized by him in the Jordan River as a sign of repentance for past sins and of the intention to live with an attitude of inner readiness for God's Kingdom.

One of the Gospels, Luke, recounts a tradition according to which John was a cousin of Jesus and was explicitily sent by God to be Jesus' forerunner. In all of the Gospels, John is portrayed as the forerunner of Jesus. Contemporary New Testament scholars treat with caution both the traditions of John's kinship with Jesus, avowal of Jesus as Messiah, and his claim to be Jesus' forerunner. However, nearly all scholars are agreed that John's movement was decisive for the beginning of Jesus' ministry, that Jesus did see John's activity as a sign that God's Kingdom was at hand, and that Jesus was baptized by John at or prior to the beginning of his own ministry. New Testament evidence points to the continuation of John's movement after the work of both John and Jesus had been ended by their executions. It also points to tensions between the two movements and to the joining of Jesus' movement by some of John's disciples both before and after the crucifixion of Jesus (John 1:35-42; Acts 19:1-7).

The message of John was simple, although its interpretation is controversial. John announced that "The Kingdom of God is at hand" and called on people to respond by repentance (sorrow for sins and willingness to lead a new life in accordance with God's will). Repentance and willingness to lead a new life were to be indicated by baptism. It has sometimes been suggested that being baptized by John symbolized willingness to become a Jew all over again, signifying rededication, recommitment, even a kind of rebirth. Thus, John's baptism may have been partially analogous to the kind of ritual purification that a gentile convert to Judaism would undergo. For John, baptism was a once-for-all event. It was not like the repeated ceremonial washings of the Essenes. Some similarities between John and the Qumran community have been noted. However, John did not counsel withdrawal from society or the world, as the Essenes did. Rather, he told converts to await the kingdom's coming while maintaining their new attitude of repentant faith and abiding by the commandments of the Torah to treat others with justice and mercy:

> And the multitudes asked him, "What then shall we do?" And he answered them, "He who has two coats, let him share with him who has none; and he who has food, let him do likewise." Tax collectors also came to be baptized and said to him, "Teacher, what shall we do?" And he said, "Collect no more tax than is appointed to you." Soldiers also asked him. And he said to them, "Rob no one by violence or false accusation, and be content with your wages."

> **(LUKE 3:10-14 RSV)**

In these precepts John differed from the Pharisees. The Pharisees would have agreed with most of what he demanded, but would have added detailed instructions about keeping the ritual parts of the law, particularly the intricate regulations about Sabbath observance. For John, apparently the crucial commandments of the Torah could be reduced to great simplicity and involved one's attitudes and actions toward others.

John's message and activity aroused great excitement. Large numbers of people came to hear him in the rugged country near the Jordan River. Some, no doubt, came out of curiosity. Many received baptism. Many began to refer to John as a prophet. *Prophet* is used in the Old Testament to designate one who is sent by God to deliver a message. Usually the message is intended to bring its recipient to faith or repentance or both, to give a warning, or to give encouragement and guidance in a time of crisis. Sometimes the message is directed to the rulers of Israel, sometimes to the whole of God's people. Sometimes it was addressed to non-Israelites. It is significant that for Judaism in the first century there was a long-standing tradition that prophecy had ceased hundreds of years earlier and that there would be no new prophet until God sent "a prophet like Moses" (spoken of in Deuteronomy 18:15-18), or one who would represent or be the great Old Testament figure Elijah, as forerunner of the Messiah. Thus, the appearance of a prophet would be considered a Messianic sign. Early Christians, and possibly Jesus, identified John the Baptist with Elijah. Naturally the very existence of claims that John was a prophet would indicate to Herod Antipas and the Romans a threatening Messianic movement was building and, therefore, raised suspicions about John. John apparently compounded his difficulties by strongly criticizing Herod's lifestyle and activities. John was arrested and imprisoned by Herod, and eventually was put to death.

Jesus paid high tribute to John the Baptist. He saw John's work, as has been noted, as a clear indication of the nearness of God's Kingdom. In this sense there is no doubt that Jesus considered John to be his forerunner. Though it is difficult to characterize fully the content of John's message, and very difficult to see what he intended the full significance of baptism to be, his emphasis on the nearness-at-hand of the Kingdom of God connects his message very closely with that of Jesus. The major difference seems to have been a nuance, or what the philosopher Whitehead sometimes described as a small difference that makes all the difference. The central proclamation of both John and Jesus was the same: "The kingdom is at hand; repent and believe." For John, this meant that the kingdom was so close that there was nothing that people could appropriately do but wait for it with repentance and faith. For Jesus it meant that the Kingdom was already present, and that the New Age was breaking into the old and conquering it. One who repented and had faith did not need to wait for the kingdom to come, but could already enter it—immediately.

The Message of Jesus

This was in fact the message of Jesus—that the hoped for Kingdom of God was breaking in and available to those who would receive it by obedient faith.

Signs.   Jesus apparently began and largely carried out his ministry in Galilee, which was ruled by Herod Antipas, a son of King Herod the Great. It was not until later, when Herod Agrippa ruled briefly over a reunited Palestine (still under Roman control) that the majority of Jews were willing to accept a member of the Herod family, originally of Idumean (non-Jewish) stock, as being Jewish. Herod Antipas was not a popular ruler, though there was a party of Herodians who depended on and supported him. Subject to Roman approval, he ruled Galilee and a part of the area across the Jordan River called Perea.

Jesus began his ministry by announcing the beginning of the new age, the Kingdom of God. The kingdom was not present in its fullness. It was not yet visible to all, it was visible only to those who had *faith*, but it *was* present and would come in its fullness. Its presence was entirely the gift of God. Its visible triumph would be the work of God. Nevertheless, now that it was present and available, all were invited to enter—to receive it in their lives as God's gift. All that was required was the ability to discern its presence by faith—a kind of trustful insight or openness—and repentance—a willingness to let one's life be shaped by it. Since technically *Kingdom of God* meant a condition or realm in which God's will is accomplished, this meant that willingness to enter God's Kingdom implied willingness to let one's life be shaped by God's will.

Jesus addressed his message to all Jews, but especially those who for one reason or another would not have been qualified or fit to be received into the kingdom. This group included social and religious outcasts. Galilee, with a much larger gentile population than other parts of Palestine, offered large opportunities for ritual and ideological contamination. Also, many ordinary working people, even if they avoided contacts with foreigners, might not be trained in the intricacies of Pharisaic Torah interpretation, or might find keeping the detailed Pharisaic laws virtually impossible or impractical. Women, who were not trained in the Hebrew Scriptures, were segregated from men both in Temple and synagogue services. Then there were those persons who were outcasts because they collaborated with the Romans or Herod—tax collectors, for instance. There were also moral outcasts like prostitutes, and those who were religiously unclean because of spiritual or physical conditions, the insane, thought to be possessed by evil spirits, and lepers.

To all these, Jesus announced the availability of God's presence in their lives. He is reported to have healed lepers and the insane and sent them to the religious authorities to be pronounced ritually clean (Luke 17:11-19). He is reported to have healed many others suffering from a variety of afflictions. Jesus himself interpreted these cures as signs of the presence of God's Kingdom. Since the blind were being made to see, the deaf to hear, the lame to walk, since lepers were being cleansed and the unclean spirits being cast out of the possessed, the power of God's Kingdom was being made evident to all who had eyes to see (Matthew 11:2-6). His critics, especially some of the Pharisees who opposed him, admitted the miraculous cures but claimed that Jesus was using the power of the Evil One, of Beelzebul or Satan, to accomplish them. Jesus' response was that they were signs of the healing power, of the victory, of God's Kingdom. If they were done by God's power—"by the finger of God" (Luke 11:14-23; cf. Exodus 8:19)—then clearly God was establishing His reign. If they were done by the power of Beelzebul, then since the evil, contrary to its nature, was doing good, the Kingdom of Evil was bringing about its own collapse. Thus, God's rule was being established.

Jesus also saw the simple fact of his proclamation of the presence of God's Kingdom—the mere fact that the good news of God's loving gift was being proclaimed to the poor, to those in need and without hope—as a sign of its presence.

He also frequently pronounced forgiveness of sins to individuals (Mark 2:1-12). That sins were being forgiven was seen by him to be a sign of the kingdom. His opponents took it as such: They blamed him for claiming to do what only God could do, and accused him of blasphemy.

Jesus saw his healings, his message of hope to the poor, and his willingness to pronounce forgiveness to sinners, as signs of God's present activity in establishing the Kingdom. Also, many of his acts had clearly symbolic meaning. They could be taken by Jews only as intentional Messianic signs. Although caution should be used in believing some of these to be actual historical acts of Jesus, many contemporary scholars are convinced that there is solid evidence for at least the following signs. Jesus attracted followers or disciples from among whom he selected twelve—soon actually called The Twelve—for special training and for leadership (a Messianic sign indicating the coming restoration of Israel through these leaders of its twelve tribes). He apparently sent his disciples out, having empowered them with the Spirit of God, to preach and heal (another sign of Messianic times, that the Spirit of God would be active in peoples' lives again and that the "lost sheep" of Israel would be sought). He called his disciples and others, who frequently were outcasts, together to eat in a meal of celebration (one of the signs of the New Age was a banquet which those inside the kingdom would share).

Such symbolism provoked hostility from many religious Jews. Some of the Pharisees appear to have been sympathetic to his mission. However, Jesus attracted strong criticism and opposition from most Pharisees because of his association with sinners (*before* they had proved themselves worthy of God's Kingdom) and because he was thought to relax the commandments of the Torah, especially those regarding Sabbath observance and ritual cleanliness.

Many of the laws concerning cleanliness referred to the distinctions between clean and unclean foods in the Pentateuch and to laws about preparation of food including ritual cleansing of oneself and of utensils used for preparing and serving food. Jesus, though he did not violate or teach the violation of Pentateuchal laws, did teach that it was inner attitude that mattered to God rather than ritual cleanliness. One could not be defiled by the food one ate, or by omitting ritual. One could only be defiled by one's own personal attitudes, by the thoughts of one's heart (Matthew 23:25-28).

Nor did Jesus teach disregard for the laws about keeping the Sabbath. These laws demanded that no work be performed from sundown Friday until sundown Saturday. There were various exceptions. To save life or prevent serious damage to health or property, work might be done. Also, Pharisaic scribal tradition (in Jesus' day an expert in interpretation of the Jewish laws and scripture was called a scribe) had created much detailed and specific interpretation as to what counted as work and what counted as justifiable exception. (Was it work, for instance, to clean one's teeth on the Sabbath or could this, under certain conditions, be counted as a necessary function, like eating?)

What Jesus taught and did concerning Sabbath observance had essentially two aspects. First, he by and large disregarded the newer Pharisaic specifications and interpretations of Sabbath requirements, staying with the older, simpler, more open traditions. Sometimes he criticized the Pharisees for their zeal to make clear what the law required, saying that they were loading the people down with unnecessary burdens. Second, he taught that the true keeping of the Sabbath is a matter of one's attitude toward God, oneself, and one's fellow human beings. "The Sabbath is made for man, not man for the Sabbath." Jesus claimed the authority—and was criticized for doing so—to interpret God's intention in giving laws related to the Sabbath and other laws, including those related to marriage and divorce. Also, he was criticized for healing on the Sabbath in nonemergency situations, when the person could just as well have been healed later. His response was that the failure to do good to one's neighbor is not a neutral act when it is a question of sharing the benefits of God's Kingdom; it is a way of doing evil (Mark 3:1-6). Thus the Sabbath is made for doing good. Jesus claimed—another Messianic sign—the authority to interpret what true fulfillment of the law entails (Matthew 12:1-8; Mark 2:27).

Thus, many contemporary scholars believe that Jesus intended his ministry as a proclamation, through signs, of a dawning messianic age. They have debated whether Jesus (1) proclaimed himself to be the Messiah, or (2) believed himself to be the Messiah. Some contemporary theologians have argued that both of these questions are irrelevant from a theological point of view. They are certainly not irrelevant as historical questions. But they are very difficult to answer. The Synoptics, at various points, suggest that Jesus either directly or indirectly claimed to be the Messiah or at least acquiesced when others gave him the title and role of Messiah. The Gospel of John attributes to Jesus not only the Messianic claim, but the claim to be one with God ("I and the Father are one" John 10:30). All of these passages, though, are among those about which New Testament scholars urge caution, since they may be post-Resurrection interpretations read back into Jesus' historical ministry.

At one point in the Gospel of Mark, Jesus is reported as having repudiated the very concept of a Messiah who will be the "son of David"—presumably a military Messiah expected to reestabish the political glories of Israel (Mark 12:35-37). But this does not mean that Jesus rejected the idea of a Messianic Age—we have seen that he proclaimed its dawning presence—or of a Messianic figure, an agent of God who would bring the Kingdom in its fullness. The Synoptic Gospels frequently attribute to Jesus the use of the term "Son of Man." The Son of Man was a traditional figure of Jewish apocalyptic thought, a heavenly being who would defeat the powers of evil and establish God's reign. Apparently Jesus did speak often of the Son of Man in this sense. Scholars are divided as to whether he used the term to refer to himself or to a Messiah for whom he was preparing the way. The Synoptics clearly understand Jesus' use of the term to be a reference to himself.

Many of the New-Quest scholars argue that even if Jesus did not make direct claims to being the Messiah, the authority he assumed—in his preaching, teaching, healing, forgiving sins, and the importance he attributed to his ministry and message—makes at least an indirect claim to Jesus' Messianic significance. There is solid evidence of his disciples' beliefs and hope that Jesus was the Messiah. There is even evidence that they quarrelled with Jesus over the interpretation of what he should do if he were the Messiah. Often they seem to have tried to shape his acts and attitudes in accordance with what they thought to be appropriately Messianic. There is some evidence that at least two of his disciples had been members of a Zealot organization: Simon, called "the Zealot" and Judas called "Iscariot." It is possible that these and others became members of Jesus' movement hoping that he, the Messiah, would lead a victorious Jewish army against the Romans and perhaps against the Sadducees. There is evidence that at various times during his ministry certain of Jesus' followers forsook him when it became clear he did not intend his movement to become a Zealot revolutionary uprising (John 6:60-69). Judas is reported to have betrayed Jesus to Temple authorities.

Certainly Jesus is pictured as having sympathized with critical attitudes that many in his society had toward rule by Rome, the Sanhedrin, and Herod. However, he taught that the kingdom would come by God's activity, not by human efforts. He also taught that one should forgive and love one's enemies, return good for evil, and not respond to violence and coercion with violence and angry resistance. In fact, to be righteous according to the law as Jesus interpreted it meant to be as perfect in love as God. God loves and does good to everyone, good and evil alike (Matthew 5:38-48). This attitude set Jesus apart both from Zealots and Essenes (who taught that one should love the children of light and hate the children of darkness). Some recent writers, apparently partly influenced by one aspect of various liberation theologies of the present, have argued that Jesus did indeed lead a Zealot movement against the Romans and the Sadducees, and that at the defeat of this uprising he was executed by the victorious oppressors. Oscar Cullman has argued impressively against such a view.[5] It must be noted that the oppressors of Jesus' day apparently took no comfort from his nonviolent approach, for they viewed his liberation movement as a threat to order and established custom.

One of the most dramatic of the Messianic signs reported of Jesus is the cleansing of the Jerusalem Temple. All of the Gospels report this event. The Synoptics place it at the end of his ministry. John's Gospel places it, perhaps for symbolic significance, at the beginning.

In the large outer court of the Jerusalem Temple, much activity occurred. Temple worship was oriented to the ritual sacrifice of animals. Animals to be sold for sacrifice were kept in the courtyard, and sold there to worshippers. There were also money-changers in the courtyard, since only the sacred Temple coins could be used for Temple fees and taxes. The courtyard was the only part of the Temple that gentiles were allowed to enter. A traditional Messianic sign was that with the coming of the Kingdom of God, gentiles would flock to Jerusalem to worship the true God. In Jesus' day many gentiles *were* attracted to Judaism; a few became converts, more became God-fearers—persons who remained gentile but worshipped the God of Judaism—and some came to Jerusalem. At the cleansing of the Temple, Jesus and his disciples occupied the outer court of the Temple, driving out the money-

---

[5] Oscar Cullman, *Jesus and the Revolutionaries* (New York, Evanston, and London: Harper & Row, 1970). But compare S. G. F. Brandon, *Jesus and the Zealots* (New York: Charles Scribner's Sons, 1967). Also see William R. Farmer, *Maccabees, Zealots and Josephus* (New York: Columbia University Press, 1957).

changers and animal keepers. Jesus is reported to have said in justification of this act:

> Is it not written "my house shall be called a house of prayer for all nations?" But you have made it a den of robbers.

(MARK 11:17 RSV)

Again, many scholars urge caution as to how much information the accounts of the cleansing of the Temple give about the strictly historical career of Jesus. Naturally, the early Christian church would find this a highly appropriate act on Jesus' part, both because of the church's later highly successful mission to gentiles and its somewhat strained relations to the religious institutions of Judaism. First-century Jews, the Essenes for example, believed that the cleansing of the Temple would be one of the Messiah's most important acts. Malachi 3:1 was widely held to be a Messianic prophecy relating to just such an event. But it seems highly likely that Jesus did cleanse the Temple as reported by the Gospels and probably, as the Synoptics have it, near the end of his ministry. Such an act would cohere with the other signs of his ministry to which he himself called attention. And Jesus' action in the Temple may reasonably be taken to have been the precipitant, the occasioning cause, of his arrest and crucifixion.

Parables.   One of Jesus' most characteristic methods of proclaiming and interpreting the message of the kingdom was the use of parables. Often a parable is defined as a very short story that clarifies one major point by comparing an ordinary, everyday event or incident and a more difficult truth or reality.

Jesus told many parables, all concerning the Kingdom of God. All of the Gospels contain parables, although they are less frequent and harder to recognize in John than in the Synoptics, and there are fewer of them in Mark than in Luke and Matthew.

Many of the parables concern the importance of recognizing and taking advantage of God's offer of His Kingdom. For instance, one parable in Matthew (13:44) tells of a man who, walking through a field, discovers an enormous treasure. He reburies the treasure and rushes off to buy the field. The point is not that one would be justified in using a deceptive method to acquire property, but that one should act immediately and do everything needful to accept the treasure of God's Kingdom. Another parable in Matthew (13:45-46) concerns a merchant and connoisseur of pearls who owns a marvelous pearl collection. One day he sees a pearl so much superior to any and all he has ever seen that he sells *all* of his other pearls to raise enough money to buy this one.

The parable may be saying that the merchant values the pearl because he believes he will ultimately make a larger financial profit from it than from all of the others he owns combined. This would not change the point of the parable, which concerns the matchless worth of the Kingdom of God to the individual who participates in it. So membership in the Kingdom of God is worth far more than anything and everything else we may have thought of value—belonging to the Kingdom is a value so great to those who possess it that even if they have nothing else that will be enough.

Some of the parables are intended to show that things appear to be very different to those within the kingdom than to those outside. Thus in Matthew (20:1-16), workers who have worked all day complain because their employer rewards those who have worked only a short time with as much as he does them. The owner's reply has the implication that what he is freely giving to some does no injury to the others, since none are getting less than they need or deserve. Thus belonging to God's Kingdom is certainly the gift of God, unearned, and no one should think of herself or himself as being more worthy of God's love, or being worthy of more of God's love, than others are. The love and status that all have who belong to the kingdom will be more than enough.

One of the most famous parables, the story of the Good Samaritan, occurs only in Luke's Gospel (10:25-37). It is used by Jesus to answer a question asked by a scribe (a lawyer) about what is required if one is to fulfill the commandments of the Torah. The encounter with the scribe and the question about the law occur in Matthew and in Mark as well as in Luke. Although the setting and details differ, in each of the Gospels the encounter revolves around the question: Who is righteous in God's sight? In Matthew (22:34-40) a lawyer asks Jesus which is the greatest of the commandments and receives the answer of Jesus that there are two, or that the great commandment has two aspects, wholehearted love of God and love to one's neighbor. Only in Luke is the Good Samaritan story used to give a further answer to the question. In Luke, the lawyer begins the discussion not by asking about which commandment is greatest, but with the question, "What shall I do to inherit eternal life?" The implication of Jesus' response in each of its Gospel settings is that being able to answer *either* question means knowing who belongs to God's Kingdom, that is, who fulfills the commandments. The commandments are to love God with one's whole heart, soul, strength, and mind, and to love one's neighbor as oneself. One who knows God's love—one who belongs to the kingdom— will be able to love God and neighbor in this way.

In Luke's Gospel, the lawyer and Jesus agree that to fulfill these commandments means participating in God's Kingdom, fulfilling the Law. But the lawyer asks: "Who is my neighbor?" That is, "How can I know whether I have kept this part of the law or not?"

Jesus responds by telling the story of a traveller who is beaten, robbed, and left for dead. He is ignored by a priest and Levite. Keeping the external laws of ritual cleanliness—they would risk being defiled by coming in contact with the dead or dying man—is more important to them than fulfilling God's intention that one should help those in need. The man is, however, helped by a Samaritan. The parable would have been offensive to many of Jesus' listeners. Samaria, the home of the Samaritans, lay on the west bank of the Jordan, separating Judea from Galilee. Normally Jews avoided even traveling through Samaria. Samaritans were looked upon with hatred and contempt—they were outside the law, and could not fulfill it because they were religiously unclean. They accepted the Pentateuch, but none of the rest of Jewish Scriptures, worshipped God in their own temple, not the

Temple of Jerusalem, and for centuries had been enemies of the Jews. Yet the Samaritan is the one who fulfilled God's Commandments. He is the one who loved his neighbor. He is the one seen to be already in the Kingdom.

Other parables, such as the story of the Prodigal Son, which also occurs only in Luke's Gospel (15:11-32), and several shorter ones, comment on God's attitude toward sinners, explain Jesus' concept of his ministry, and contain criticism of the attitudes of some of the religious leaders of Israel. One of the shortest of these (Luke 15:8-10) is the story of a woman who possessed ten coins. She lost one. She looked for it with great zeal, rejoicing when she found it. Thus, God wants to rescue sinners, the outcast, the lost. He does not need to seek those who are already found, like the Pharisees, who *are* already members of His kingdom if they sincerely accept it. Certainly he loves them too. (Jesus criticized only Pharisees he judged to be insincere, those who put the external keeping of the law above the inner meaning of it, or who obeyed the external law for reasons of prestige, social acceptance, or financial or psychological security.) Thus, also, Jesus directed his mission mainly to those who were "lost."

Important collections of Jesus' Parables are found in the following Synoptic locations: Mark 4; Matthew 5-7; 13; 21-25; Luke 10-16; 18-19. There are many implicit parables in Jesus' teachings, that is, comparisons so brief that they are not stories but nevertheless have the nature or character of parables. For instance, his saying to his hearers, "You are the salt of the earth, but if salt has lost its savor it is no good and fit only to be thrown out and trampled under foot" (Matthew 5:13). This could easily have been made into a story.

Crucifixion.　The Gospels give a number of details about the arrest, trial(s), and crucifixion of Jesus. It is clear that many of the Pharisees opposed him, believing that by teaching laxity toward the law he was retarding the coming of God's Kingdom. It is clear that the Sadducees and Herodians perceived his potentially Messianic movement as a threat to the stability of their rule and of their not always harmonious relations with the Romans. Jesus was arrested and given a hearing before the Sanhedrin. It is likely that some of the Pharisees opposed his arrest, and were not informed of the hearings or trial until Jesus' execution was a *fait accompli.* Apparently, Jesus appeared before the Sanhedrin on charges of blasphemy. It appears that statements Jesus was alleged to have made about the Temple were cited—a prediction of its destruction would have been blasphemous (Mathew 24:2). Possibly some accusations were based on alleged claims of being the Messiah and sayings and actions for which Jesus had claimed direct authorization from God. At any rate, Jesus apparently was found, whether officially or informally, guilty of blasphemy and was sent to the Roman governor with the request that he be found guilty under Roman law of treason—revolutionary activity or claims—and that he be executed. Much has been written about Jesus' appearance before Pilate and much still remains cloudy and in doubt about the nature of the hearing and its outcome. What is clear is that Jesus was crucified at the order of the Roman governor and at the hands of the Roman soldiers after having been sent to them by members of the Sanhedrin.

RESURRECTION

Earlier in this chapter mention was made of the accounts of Jesus' Resurrection appearing in the Gospels. These accounts are very intricate, weaving together various strands of tradition. What seems most clear is that the disciples, most or all of whom had believed Jesus to be the Messiah, were frightened, shocked, and devastated by his arrest and crucifixion. They probably remained in hiding, fearing arrest as co-conspirators. Later, they were told that some of the women who had been followers of Jesus had learned from a divine source that Jesus had risen from death. Then the risen Jesus began to appear to and among the disciples. The disciple Peter (or Simon), a fisherman who had been leader of the Twelve, apparently was the first to experience an actual appearance of the risen Lord (Luke 24:13-35).[6] Others, usually in groups, also experienced such appearances. One written account by an eyewitness, Paul, is found in the New Testament in I Corinthians, Chapter 15.

Thus the early Christian movement was born of the conviction, attested by experience, that God had raised Jesus from the dead. A contemporary New Testament scholar, Stuart Currie, once remarked that the question "Who must Jesus have been for God to have raised him from the dead?" stood at the origin of all Christian theology. Jesus' original disciples were convinced that they knew at least part of the answer to that question. They had believed before his death that he was the Messiah, the Christ of God, sent to bring in the New Age, to "restore the Kingdom to Israel" (Acts 1:6). Now, on the basis of their Resurrection experiences, they were convinced that this was true, and that the New Age was indeed, as Jesus had said, begun. They believed that now it would come, inevitably, in its fullness.

Early Christian tradition, recorded in the first two chapters of the New Testament Book of Acts, reports that Jesus told the disciples to remain in Jerusalem until they received the power of the Spirit of God. The earliest Christian community was made up entirely of Jews. Many of them had been Jesus' disciples throughout his ministry. Others were post-Resurrection converts. They continued to practice Judaism. They worshipped at the Temple. A large group of them lived communally in Jerusalem, and presented the message of Jesus as the crucified and risen Messiah to other Jews, teaching that in his life, death, and resurrection Jesus had fulfilled the Messianic hopes of Judaism, inaugurating the New Age. It was very much against accepted Jewish belief that the Messiah might be rejected, much less crucified (this would have made him ritually unclean, accursed). But by the Resurrection, God had vindicated him, had shown that Jesus was indeed Messiah and Lord. Now God wanted to bring all Jews into the Kingdom by means of Jesus. This was the message of the disciples to their fellow Jews.

The early disciples also believed, at least in theory, that the message of Jesus was relevant to gentiles too. However, they seem to have had no idea at first of reaching out in mission to non-Jews, either in Palestine or elsewhere. The spread of

---

[6] See Willi Marxsen, *The Resurrection of Jesus of Nazareth* (Philadelphia: Fortress, 1970).

Christianity to non-Jewish regions and peoples began almost, it seems, by accident. Persecution by Jewish religious authorities of Hellenistic Jewish Christians (beginning with the death of the first Christian martyr, Stephen) drove these Christians out of Jerusalem, into Samaria. There they began to make converts. Reports of this activity with its results surprised the Palestinian Christian Jerusalem leadership who gave it their blessing (Acts 8).

Somewhat later, both Jewish and gentile converts began to be made in the Syrian city of Antioch, one of the largest cities in the Roman world. Here, the followers of Jesus were first called Christians. And it was from Antioch that some of the first and most important organized missionary efforts to take the message about Jesus to Hellenistic Jews and gentiles in the Asian and European parts of the Roman Empire originated.[7]

QUESTIONS

1. What do New Testament scholars mean by the term "the historical Jesus?" Explain why many New Testament scholars have made a distinction between "the Jesus of history" and the "the Christ of faith."

2. What do you consider to be the significance of the work of Albert Schweitzer as New Testament scholar?

3. Explain and relate the terms "eschatology," "apocalypse," and "apocalyptic thought."

4. Explain the use of the term "Kingdom of God" in first-century Judaism.

5. Compare and contrast the teachings about the Kingdom of God of the Pharisees, Sadducees, Essenes (Qumran Community), Zealots, John the Baptist, and Jesus.

6. Expalin the importance of *signs* and *parables* in Jesus' ministry.

7. Explain how their belief in the resurrection of Jesus affected his disciples.

FURTHER READING

BORNKAMM, GÜNTER, *Jesus of Nazareth*. New York: Harper & Brothers, 1960.
BULTMANN, RUDOLF, *Jesus and the Word*. New York & London: Scribners', 1934.
____. *The History of the Synoptic Tradition*. New York: Harper & Row, 1963.
COLWELL, ERNEST CADMAN, *Jesus and the Gospel*. New York: Oxford University Press, 1963.

[7]Recent study of the Gospels has focused on 1) analyzing distinctive features contributed by their authors as editors of the material utilized from earlier oral and literary sources (redaction criticism) and 2) locating the gospels within literary genres current in the ancient world. Luke-Acts has been usefully compared with and classified as a type of historical writing of the time and Matthew studied as belonging to the category of encomium biography (a biography written in praise of a famous person). Such studies have contributed to understanding of the nature of the gospels and have shed further light on questions related to their use as historical sources.

DIBELIUS, MARTIN, *From Tradition to Gospel.* New York: Scribners', 1965.
_____. *Jesus.* Philadelphia, Penn.: The Westminster Press, 1949.
FOLEY, GROVER (trans.), *What Can We Know About Jesus? Essays on the New Quest by Ferdinand Hahn, Wenzel Lohff and Günter Bornkamm.* Philadelphia, Penn.: Fortress Press, 1969.
FLUSSER, DAVID, *Jesus.* New York: Herder and Herder, 1969.
GRANT, FREDERICK C. (trans.), *Form Criticism.* Chicago; New York: Willett, Clark & Company, 1934, a translation into English of Rudolf Bultmann: *The Study of the Synoptic Gospels* and Karl Kundsin: *Primitive Christianity in the Light of Gospel Research.*
JEREMIAS, JOACHIM, *Jerusalem in the Time of Jesus.* Philadelphia, Penn.: Fortress Press, 1968.
_____. *The Parables of Jesus.* New York: Scribners', 1963, Revised Edition.
_____. *The Prayers of Jesus.* Philadelphia, Penn.: Fortress Press, 1978.
KECK, LEANDER E., *A Future for the Historical Jesus.* Nashville, Tenn. and New York: Abingdon Press, 1971.
KEE, HOWARD CLARK, *Jesus in History.* New York: Harcourt, Brace, Jovanovich, Inc., 2nd ed., 1977.
LESSING, ERICH, *Jesus: History and Culture of the New Testament A Pictorial Narration.* New York: Herder and Herder, 1971.
MARXSEN, WILLI, *The Resurrection of Jesus of Nazareth.* Philadelphia, Penn.: Fortress Press, 1970.
MEYER, BEN F., *The Aims of Jesus.* New York: Oxford University Press, 1979.
McKNIGHT, EDGAR V., *What Is Form Criticism?* Philadelphia, Penn.: Fortress Press, 1969.
PERRIN, NORMAN, *The Kingdom of God in the Teaching of Jesus.* Philadelphia, Penn.: Westminster Press, 1963.
_____. *Rediscovering the Teaching of Jesus.* New York: Harper & Row, 1967.
_____. *What Is Redaction Criticism?* Philadelphia, Penn.: Fortress Press, 1969.
ROBINSON, JAMES M., *A New Quest of the Historical Jesus.* London: SCM Press, LTD, 1959.
SANDMEL, SAMUEL, *We Jews and Jesus.* New York: Oxford University Press, 1973.
SCHWEITZER, ALBERT, *Out of My Life and Thought.* New York: Henry Holt and Company, 1933.
_____. *The Psychiatric Study of Jesus.* Gloucester, Mass.: Peter Smith, 1975.
_____. *The Quest of the Historical Jesus.* New York: Macmillan Co., 1948.
SHULER, PHILIP L., *A Genre for the Gospels: The Biographical Character of Matthew.* Philadelphia, Penn.: Fortress Press, 1982.
ZAHRNT, HEINZ, *The Historical Jesus.* New York and Evanston, Ill.: Harper & Row, 1963.

chapter three
EARLY AND MEDIEVAL CHRISTIANITY

The emergence of Christianity as a viable, dynamic religion within the cultural context of the Roman Empire included an extended gestation period yet resulted in Christianity's spectacular rise to a position of prominence in Mediterranean and European culture.

CHRISTIANITY AND ITS CULTURAL MILIEU

The Roman Empire

In his fourth-century B.C.E. conquest of much of the known world, Alexander The Great initiated a movement toward political and cultural unity previously unknown in the Western world. This unification of peoples became a fundamental element in the civilization that achieved full fruition in the Roman Empire (31 B.C.E.-400 C.E.). Expanding the consolidation of the Greek city-states under his father, Philip of Macedona, Alexander defeated Persia, ending its two-hundred-year rule of Mesopotamia and surrounding territories. Ultimately Alexander controlled Greece, Macedonia, Egypt, Palestine, the Mesopotamian Valley civilizations, and portions of India. Trained by Aristotle and imbued with the cultural splendors of Hellas (Greece), Alexander's greatest contribution may have been his missionary zeal to carry into conquered territories Greek culture, philosophy, and language.

Divergent political systems, languages, and religions of separate peoples were subordinated to an overarching cultural pattern that for centuries influenced civilizations of the region. Alexander's dream of a united Greek world was cut short by his premature death (323 B.C.E.) and the division of his conquest into three Greek kingdoms (The Ptolemaic—Egypt and Africa; Seleucid—Mesopotamia, Palestine, Asia Minor, and India; and Antigonid—Macedonia and Greece). Some aspects of the dream were not permanently lost, however, as they reemerged during Rome's conquest of the area.

The alliance of the Aetolian League of Greek city states with Rome in 212 B.C.E. began Rome's eastward expansion, culminating with the defeat of the Ptolemaic Greek kingdom by Julius Caesar in 48 B.C.E. The consolidation of imperial power was completed by Octavian at the battle of Actium in 31 B.C.E., resulting in Rome's rule of most of the territory controlled by Alexander, as well as the Western Mediterranean. Rome was to maintain control of this vast empire until the fourth century of the common era.

Alexander's dream of a homogeneous culture, modified by the pragmatism of the Roman emperors, created in the Empire a civilization that surpassed any which had preceded it. Land and sea routes built to quickly move army legions and goods served as the means for encounter of divergent cultures and peoples. The *Pax Romana* (Peace of Rome) superimposed on those within the Empire meant that whole generations of persons were freed from the debilitations of wars that had preceded the Empire. Roman law served as a model for local custom and provided an appeals system for Roman citizens, bringing uniformity of law to diverse populations. The use of Greek as the language of commerce, literature, and much of international affairs provided a common means of communication and served as the basis of cultural and intellectual exchange previously unimagined. Migrations of Romans into the territories and of other peoples into Rome itself created a fluid, cosmopolitan culture. Rome's administration of its territories allowed the continuation of national rulers and cultures as long as they did not threaten Roman sovereignty. Local and international interests could exist side by side. The price paid for these advantages included political subservience, heavy taxation, military rule, and the imposition of a rigid social pyramid in which Roman rulers and citizens enjoyed social privileges resting on an often brutal system of slavery.

Changing Values in the Empire

In the cultural matrix, traditional patterns of meaning and value were called into question and modified significantly through the long centuries of Greek and Roman rule. Ancient Greek philosophies were based on popular interest in the nature of the universe and the place of humanity in it. The greatest of the philosophers, Plato and Aristotle, offered elaborate constructs that still influence Western thought. During the later Greek Hellenistic period, Platonic ideas came to prominence even though Alexander had been a student of Aristotle. Plato's concept of an ideal nonphysical, eternal realm incorporating real values (in contrast to the

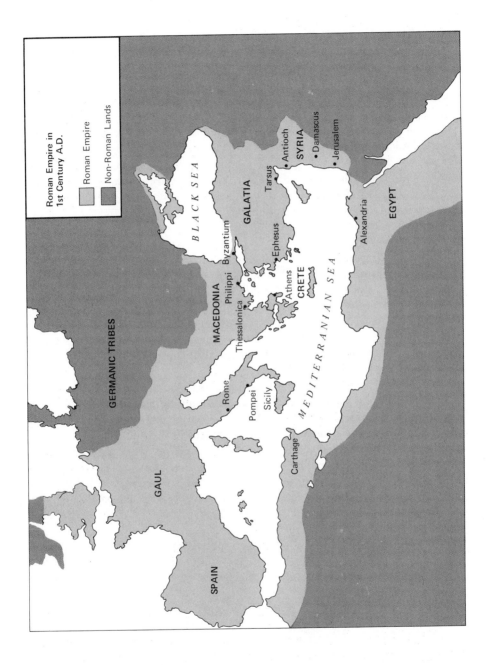

Roman Empire in
1st Century A.D.

■ Roman Empire
■ Non-Roman Lands

GERMANIC TRIBES

GAUL

SPAIN

Rome

Pompei

Sicily

Carthage

MACEDONIA

Thessalonica

Philippi

Athens

BLACK SEA

Byzantium

GALATIA

Tarsus

Ephesus

CRETE

MEDITERRANIAN SEA

Antioch

SYRIA

Damascus

Jerusalem

Alexandria

EGYPT

relative, imperfect values of the physical realm) was to influence much subsequent Greek and Roman thinking. The need for humanity to attune itself to the Good(s) of this ideal realm—justice, truth, beauty, and goodness—lay in the background of Greco-Roman thought. The appeal of these concepts came to renewed prominence in an Empire where universal, or international, ideals dominated local cultures. By the time of the Roman Empire, other philosophies had also become popular. Plato's negation of the values found in the physical world did not sufficiently answer the needs of many.

Stoic thought became the popular philosophy of many leaders in the Roman Empire. Stoicism affirmed the universe to be a harmonious whole in which Divine Fire was the unifying element. This divine fire, expressed in *logos*, or Reason, was found in all reality. Humanity, in whatever status, slave or master, was an expression of reason. Therefore, all were to live in their predetermined roles carrying out their prescribed duties to the best of their abilities. Virtue was fulfilling one's duty. There was no place in this philosophy for personal immortality. One found meaning in living as reason ordained.

Epicureanism offered yet another view of the universe. Conceiving of the universe as atoms randomly joined to produce life, Epicurus suggested there was no immortality and that the gods were not relevant to human existence. He was convinced that humanity's fear of the gods had produced false perceptions and expectations of the universe. Virtue was the eradication of fear and the display of affection for one's fellows. Happiness would be the result of acceptance of life as it is, without illusions, without excessive demands, hopes, ambitions, or fears.

Such philosophies fitted well the practical orientation of many in the Roman educated classes. They were not, however, satisfying to many people, and as the Empire became cosmopolitan alternative world views, particularly from the East, gained popularity. There was widespread acceptance in the early empire of Persian forms of astrology, although astrology was certainly not derived solely from Persian sources. Based on the hypothesis that the stars and their motions control the destinies and events of humanity, astrology with its horoscopes and diviners provided a popular frame for understanding and decision-making. Underlying Stoicism, Epicureanism, and astrology was the basic belief that the destinies of individuals and nations were controlled by impersonal forces—reason, chance, or fate. The life experienced by many in the Roman Empire made these philosophies appealing.

Roman Religious Patterns

Religions oriented primarily to agricultural productivity and survival were modified as Greek and other cultures came to be centered in cities. Local gods provided security and prosperity even within the city-states. As the empire transferred power to an international entity, local gods and their cults began to lose much of their appeal. Persons who had found meaning in the local religions now found themselves questioning their traditions and looking for answers of a more universal nature.

Roman religion had both public (civil) and private (family and personal) aspects. Most of the Greek Olympian pantheon of gods had been, by the time of the Empire, identified with the gods of Rome, serving as the basis for public religious ceremonies throughout the Empire. Every major city had temples dedicated to these deities. In addition, Roman policy tolerated local religions as long as they did not threaten the interests of the Empire. The religion of the Roman state and those of its component ethnic groups fulfilled complementary religious functions.

The Egyptian and Eastern tendency to bestow divinity on their kings, combined with the Western tendency to honor heroes quickly, led to the development of emperor worship. Augustus (Octavian), like Alexander before him, accepted the accolades of the East proclaiming him a divine deliverer. Nevertheless, he made no claims to divinity in Rome itself. However, by the time of the spread of Christianity (100 C.E.) the cultic patterns of emperor worship were widespread. The acceptance of emperor worship became a political expresson of loyalty to the Empire.

Public worship had as its object the well-being of the state and Empire. The emperor, as the most powerful official in the Empire, was understood to stand and act as a representative or intermediary for the whole people to insure security, well-being, and prosperity. At death, the spirit (genius) of the departed emperor was believed to become divine and to continue to exert watchful care over the commonwealth. Some of the emperors proclaimed themselves divine while they were still living. Worship of traditional gods served and continued to serve many of the same functions, but the cult of the Empire provided unity on an Empire-wide basis, and therefore took on a political as well as religious function.

However, many persons cut off from traditional ties found that the established civic religions, including Emperor worship, did not meet their personal needs. Increasingly, individuals looked for more from religion—for a source of meaning, guidance, and protection in this life and afterwards—than the state religions could give.

These needs were met at the common level in many ways. Most popular were a number of religions designated as "mystery religions" by modern scholars. For the most part these religions were grounded in ancient fertility rites wherein the natural cycle of death and rebirth was reenacted to insure health and prosperity. By the time of the Empire they had lost much of their original nature as civic fertility cults. They were transformed into religions that made the mysteries of the universe available to participants. Although numerous, many of them shared several characteristics. Each claimed its adherents, through the acquisition of a secret or mysterious knowledge or rite, would participate in the controlling powers of the universe. Participants were thereby distinguished from their neighbors and elevated above them. One was no longer simply a part of the state or ethnic community. Many of the mysteries claimed that through participating in the rites the participant actually became divine, transcending the limitations of normal life. The mystery religions incorporated elaborate rites of initiation and stringent rules of behavior.

Very important was the element of redemption, a guarantee of eternal life. Among such religions were worship of Isis and Osiris, originating in Egypt; Dionysian and Orphic cults from Thrace (modern Bulgaria); the Eleusinian mysteries from Greece; and the religion of the Great Mother from Asia Minor. Mithraism from Iran normally is considered one of these religions, although it did not share the exact patterns of fertility myth that the others do. While arising in the Eastern sections of the Empire, these religions spread throughout the Roman Empire during its first centuries.

The worship of Isis and Osiris serves as an example of the mystery religions. This religion was initially related to the agricultural life of the Nile valley. After centuries of development, the religion became increasingly preoccupied with the mystery of death and became popular throughout much of the cosmopolitan Greco-Roman world. Osiris, a divine king and compassionate ruler of Ancient Egypt, enjoyed the companionship and love of his sister and consort, Isis. Killed by his jealous brother, Osiris's body was dismembered and cast into the Nile which distributed it through the world. Osiris in the state of death became the god of the underworld. In her sorrow and grief, Isis sought the body of Osiris and buried each part as she found it. By her actions, she revived Osiris so that he assumed a dual role as god of the living and the dead. Isis became the agent of life. An initiate into the religion reenacted the suffering and death of Osiris, thereby overcoming death. In Rome, the worship of Isis as agent and symbol of life overshadowed the role of Osiris in the religion.

The worship of Isis and Osiris offered a means of dealing with both life as it was experienced, good and bad, and with death, since the believer was assured of a secure life beyond the present one. The religion was known for its elaborate and rich ceremonies, which provided distinct roles for a devoted, almost monastic, priest as well as the lay adherent and occasional temple worshiper. The attraction of the cult was its provision of a role and place for the individual, and its attempt to deal with death, in a culture where public religions seldom promised hope beyond the sustaining of the state and its benefits.

Another popular religious alternative in Roman culture was Gnosticism, a complex syncretistic fusion of widely differing religious and philosophical insights with varied cultic practices. Gnostic patterns, of which there were many, existed throughout the Empire, often reflecting various Greek philosophies. The movement was especially influenced by Oriental dualism. This dualism separated the universe into a (good) spirit world of light ruled over by a benevolent and loving divine Principle and a (bad) physical world of darkness created and controlled by the Demiurge, a divine, but evil being, and his representatives. These two worlds were populated and related by a graded hierarchy of beings. Humanity, according to the Gnostics, was one form of these beings, joining the physical evil world with a divine spark or spirit from the world of light. Gnosis (knowledge) of humanity's entrapment in the physical world and the pathways to freedom from it was offered by the religion, often through a savior figure.

Gnostic contact with Christianity resulted in a variety of attempts to incorporate Christ into Gnostic patterns as the revealer of knowledge about the universe, or savior. However, Christ could not be understood by the Gnostics to be a historical figure, for that would mean that he was also contaminated with the evil physical world. For the Gnostics, Christ remained a spiritual or mythical figure. Gnosticism, because of its powerful images of salvation, became a significant and attractive religion, and a particular threat to Christianity, when it claimed Christ for its own purposes.

Judaism in the Empire

The religious policies of the Empire allowed a vast array of religions to flourish, but few produced the separate and distinct cultural communities found among the Jews. By the first centuries of the common era, Jews had been scattered through the Empire for several centuries. Their monotheistic religious beliefs, their high ethical standards, and their unusual dietary and worship practices distinguished them from their neighbors. In Babylon, where there continued to be a large Jewish community, they were separated not only by religious and ethical practice but also by living in separate sections of the city. Elsewhere, Jewish communities often gathered around synagogues, due to the prohibitions of Sabbath travel. This frequently resulted in voluntary ghetto living. Therefore, Jews often comprised a city within a city.

Although separated in religion and ethical practice, Jews were nevertheless integrated into the economic life of the Empire, often serving as traders and craftsmen in their respective cities. Occasionally, some rose to positions of power and distinction. Through the centuries, many had gained Roman citizenship.

Within these communities, the Judaism that survived was largely molded by the Rabbinic traditions continued in synagogues and academies. Patterns of study and interpretation molded out of Pharisaical precedents concentrated on interpretation of the Torah. Interest in establishing the canon of the written Torah (noted in Chapter One) did not lessen interest in the Oral Torah—that dynamic pattern of interpretation drawn from the precedents of the past. Over the years two terms came to designate the separate patterns of Torah. *Mitzvah* (commandment) normally meant any law that was explicit in the Scripture. *Halacha* referred to law derived through Rabbinic decisions—Rabbinic law dependent on Oral Torah.[1] This Oral Torah eventually achieved written form as Rabbinic decisions were collected into *Mishna* which in turn was commented on in two forms of *Gemara* (Palestinian and Babylonian). Because these were the product of study in various academies, they incorporated differences of opinion and judgment. As such they became the foundation for continual refinement and new applications of ancient teachings. Together the Mishna and Gemara make up the two parts of the *Talmud*, or commentary on the Torah. The study of Talmud became, in advanced rabbinical academies and schools, a complex process of legal reasoning, where every possible

[1] Sandmel, p. 103-4.

situation that might confront the law was discussed and every possible answer sought. As new social and religious situations arose, the "living" Torah, in the hands of the rabbis who had meticulously studied the possibilities and guidance found in the Talmud, offered solutions adequate for the time and its questions. Through the centuries, this intense concentration on law and the logic of its application led the Jews to achieve high levels of education and knowledge.

CHRISTIANITY AND THE ROMAN EMPIRE

In the complex, dynamic Greco-Roman world, beauty and brutality lay side by side. Cultural idealism and cruel self-interest fashioned starkly contrasting political and social patterns, while religions appealing to differing needs complemented one another. Christianity, entering this world only slowly, distinguished itself from other patterns of life and cultic community, yet it ultimately became a fashioner of much of the culture that succeeded that of Rome.

Christianity as a Jewish Sect

The earliest Christians, as noted in Chapter One, were Jews living in Palestine. Acceptance of Jesus as their Messiah and rejection of traditional interpretations of the Jewish law distinguished the followers of Jesus from other Jewish groups both within Palestine and among the dispersion Jews. Between Christians and traditional Jews conflict was early and bitter. Nevertheless, for their Roman overlords and most of their contemporaries, the recognizable differences appeared to involve internal disputes of a minority community in which religious idealism had always caused contention. Christianity began, then, as a Jewish sect.

A significant, if uneasy, alliance between Rome and Jewish Palestine existed from the early Maccabean period when Judas Maccabeus established a cooperative relationship with the Romans during Rome's early forays into the Eastern Mediterranean. This alliance was strengthened until in 63 B.C.E. Pompey, a Roman general, taking advantage of an internal dispute in the royal household of Israel, annexed Palestine as a Roman territory. The incorporation of Israel into the Empire as an ally meant the Jews were not enslaved. This had a significant religious consequence. The Jewish faith was given the status of *religio licita* (a legal religion) in the Empire. As long as Jewish practices did not threaten Roman interests, Jews were free to follow their own beliefs and patterns. Certain concessions were also made for the Jews on the basis of their unique belief in one God. They were not required to worship the emperor, although as long as their Temple was in existence, sacrifices for the Emperor and the well-being of the Roman people were to be offered to their God.

As a Jewish sect, the earliest Christians enjoyed the same religious privileges. However, as Christianity spread and matured, it lost more and more of its Jewish character. As noted above, by the middle of the first century, Paul and others had carried Christianity throughout much of Asia Minor, into Greece and even to Rome. It was also spreading eastward and southward. Its appeal was largely to gentiles. By the beginning of the second century, Pliny (ca. 112), a Roman governor of Asia Minor, sought the advice of the Emperor Trajan about what official treatment should be accorded the Christians without referring to their Jewish connections. A major consequence of the Christian shift away from Judiasm was the acqusition of an ambiguous legal status. If they were not Jews, Christians were not able to claim Jewish religious privileges. As a new religious group, whose practices distinguished them from their neighbors and whose refusal to worship the Emperor raised questions of their political loyalty, they were subject to suspicion, hostility, and persecution. Christinity became then an illicit religious group with no legal protection or status.

Persecution of Christians

The initial community of Christians was drawn from the lower economic and social classes. Few Jewish leaders were drawn to the community in Jesus' lifetime, though there were exceptions (John 3:1, 7:50). As the religion moved from Palestine into the gentile world, the appeal continued to be largely to those of lower social status. Christianity offered to these people an all-powerful God in a world where a myriad of gods vied for attention. It brought salvation to the individual and gave one a place in the community. It also conquered the fear of death, offering hope for eternal life (Romans 8:31-9). An ethic of love based on God's love of all persons, whatever their social status, helped make it an attractive religious alternative.

In a rigidly defined social structure that offered little mobility this aspect of Christianity was particularly appealing to the lower classes. Paul's letter to Philemon, a slaveholder, and the addressing of Luke and Acts to the "most excellent Theophilus" may suggest that by the middle of the first century, Christianity was becoming known among those of status and position. Nevertheless, through the first several decades, Christianity only slowly won to its ranks persons of significant political and social position.

Among Roman officials, Christianity must have closely resembled the mystery religions as it offered individual salvation on the basis of voluntary commitment and initiation into a closed community, which carefully guarded its beliefs and practices. Its separation from Judaism and its position in the Empire both legally and socially meant that Christianity enjoyed few, if any, social advantages in its first centuries. Yet it quickly emerged as a religious option in an extremely complex world.

Although Judaism and Christianity took significantly different paths and were separated early, the identification of the two lingered in the understanding of the Roman populace and officials. The position of the Jews deteriorated after the revolts of 66-73 and 132-135 C.E. Jews were looked on with suspicion as revolutionaries whose beliefs and attitudes threatened the state. Christian identification with the Jews meant that some of that same suspicion fell on Christians.

Active persecution of Christians by Rome was sporadic and largely local in the first century. Suspected of arson himself, Nero in 64 C.E. accused the Christians of burning a large section of Rome. In addition, he charged that they were guilty of "hatred of the human race" (Tacitus, *Annals*, XV, 44). Though severe, the persecution which resulted from Nero's accusations seems to have been short-lived. Late in the century (95 C.E.), Domitian, as a part of an effort to consolidate the Empire, insisted on the renewal of ancient public religious sacrifices. He also required "taking an oath by the Emperor's genius," a form of emperor worship. Jews and Christians suffered in the new stringent policies, but extensive persecution did not emerge. The correspondence of Pliny and Trajan indicates that in 112 C.E. Christians were required, as were all other groups, to make sacrifices to the ancient gods. If unwilling to do so, they were punished, sometimes with death. They were not, however, to be sought out. Hadrian's rescript in 124 C.E. guarded Christians from random accusations. Persecution depended largely on local enforcement of general Roman religious policy and the attitudes of local officials. Major territorial persecutions did occur under these conditions, but persecution was occasional rather than systematic.

Marcus Aurelius, a Stoic committed to the traditional state religion and believing that the security of the Empire depended on the ancient gods, instigated the first reasoned and systematic persecution of the Christians in 165 C.E. He saw the Christians as a threat to the state. In the reign of Septimius Severus, an edict was promulgated (202 C.E.) proscribing conversion to either Judaism or Christianity. This was an obvious attempt to limit the expansion of these religions. By this date, Christianity was found throughout the Empire. It was perceived by the Emperor to be a threat, since Christian refusal to worship the emperor, as well as the growing organizational strength of the movement, raised fears of a "state within the state."

A declining military situation and threats to the stability of the empire from the North led to repeated attempts to stabilize the Empire. This was to be accomplished by purging it of recent innovations and returning to the ancient ways, particularly traditional religious practices. The Emperor Decius (250 C.E.) instituted an Empire-wide persecution of those who would not conform—largely Christians. Without the ability to enforce the edict militarily it did not accomplish its intent, but Christians did suffer in the renewed persecution that continued under Decius' successors. Leaders were killed, possessions confiscated, some Christians reduced to slavery, and Christian worship outlawed. Enforced unevenly and, therefore, more severely for some than others, this persecution had run its course by 260 C.E. and from that time until the turn of the century Christianity enjoyed unprecedented freedom and expansion. It was no longer simply a religion appealing to the lower classes; its adherents extended into the highest ranks of society. It was now one of the major religions of the Empire.

Another attempt to revive ancient Rome came under the Emperor Diocletian (284-305 C.E.). Traditional Roman practices and virtues were to be sought and guaranteed by the rebuilding of temples and restoring the worship of Roman gods.

All were to sacrifice to the ancient gods, and Christians came quickly to be persecuted. Scriptures were surrendered, churches dismantled, honors and citizenships were suspended. Again the extent of persecution depended on the provincial authorities, but real attempts were made to eradicate Christianity. These failed, and Constantine, the ruler who rose to power during the struggle following the reign of Diocletian, saw the religious persecutions as a major detriment to the unity of the Empire. Constantine and Licinius, his co-ruler for a period, issued an Edict of Toleration (313 C.E.). The edict granted the right of all citizens of the Empire to follow the "religion which to each of them appeared best." The effect of the edict was to grant Christians legal status and at the same time enlist Christian support for the Empire.

Constantine's actions on behalf of Christianity appear to have been largely political in motivation, but his sympathy and interest went much further. Tradition has it that in his early military struggles, he took as his sign of battle the cross and invoked the Christian God's help. More importantly, he gave his support to the expansion of Christianity, built churches, offered state support for church councils and actively participated in the religion. He accepted baptism as a Christian on his deathbed. Christianity in his reign became the predominant religion within the Empire, although it was some fifty years before it officially became the state religion.[2]

Christianity in the Late Roman Empire

The transition of Christianity from one sect of a minor Eastern religion to the official religion of the Empire was not rapid by some standards (300 years), but for it to triumph at all was no mean achievement. The worship of one God where many were available, the elimination of a sacrifical system of worship based on agricultural and patriotic traditions, the acceptance of new ethical standards and ideals for the masses, and the consolidation of religious practice and polity into one general pattern meant that religion became a cohesive and central aspect of culture rather than one of its divisive elements. Christianity now assumed a position as one of the major molding factors of Western civilization.

The acceptance of Christianity as the state religion brought several changes to the religion. With the cessation of persecution, martyrdom was no longer a premier form of holy life. Large churches were built, with an attendant need for expanded clergy and elaborated liturgy. Theological issues among Christians now affected the unity of the Empire. In its new situation, Christianity shifted from being a voluntary group, one among many in society, to one of society's central coordinating forces. This new role meant that in its deliberations and actions the church was obliged to consider the interests of the society at large. Political issues now became

---

[2]For an extended discussion of the early relationship of Christianity to Rome see W. H. C. Frend, *Martydom & Persecution in the Early Church* (New York: Doubleday and Co., 1967).

concerns of the church and influenced its decisions. Christianity and the Empire were inexorably intertwined.

Political and social developments within the Empire prompted major adjustments in Christianity. Constantine, like Diocletian and others before him, recognized that the Empire could no longer be controlled from a western capital far removed from the rich and crucial eastern provinces. Consequently, he established a new imperial capital in the ancient city of Byzantium, renaming it Constantinople. Rome remained the western capital, but the establishment of a new center in the East inevitably meant tensions and separation between the two sections of the Empire. Effective control moved to the East, and Rome declined in imperial significance. Political changes of this magnitude inevitably affected the Christian community. The Church at Constantinople, serving as the church of the emperor, rose in significance until it rivaled Rome and overshadowed other eastern churches.

Acceptance of Christianity as the official religion by the Roman Empire significantly changed Judaism's status in Western society. Judaism's relatively small numbers compared to the expanding Christian community made its minority status permanent. More importantly, Christian exclusiveness questioned all other religions. Jews, for the Christians, were a particular engima, for in the Christian understanding the Jews had condemned themselves by their refusal to accept Christ as the Messiah. During the century that followed Christian establishment, the situation of the Jews deteriorated significantly. The court with its patriarch (See Chapter One) was disbanded (425 C.E.). Jews lost much of their ability to enforce discipline among themselves, their rights to build synagogues were restricted, and they were not allowed to participate in religious taxes collected within the Empire.

Early Church Organization

Paul's letters to Christian communities suggest that the earliest churches were similar to Jewish synagogues. Local Christians were leaders in worship and administration. Leadership developed on the basis of ability and dedication; generally the churches were dependent on their own resources. Christianity tended to spread first to the cities, and by the second century larger cities might be represented by several congregations. While bishops emerged early as central leaders in the local churches, they were often assisted by presbyters, deacons, teachers, "prophets," and others. As the movement grew, the bishop tended to become the authoritative leader. His responsibilities might include oversight of several congregations within a city or territory. The correspondence of Paul and that of Ignatius (c.a. 35-115), martyred bishop of Antioch, indicate early connections between various churches, particularly through their leaders and traveling evangelists. But systematic organization beyond the local church level appears to have been slow to develop. Churches in major cities emerged with the passage of time as central churches, giving leadership and support to churches in outlying territories. Consequently, the bishops of principal cities such as Antioch in Syria, Alexandria in Egypt, Ephesus in Asia Minor, and

Rome in Italy became powerful leaders of the Christian movement. Questions of belief or organization that broadly affected the Christian movement were often decided through the gathering of local bishops into representative synods or councils. Constantine recognized this pattern of representation when he convened the first ecumenical, or universal, council of the church, the Council of Nicaea, in 325 C.E.

Differences between the churches were many, and reflected the great variety of peoples scattered through the Mediterranean world who were attracted to Christianity. Cultural differences were perhaps not as crucial, however, as were the questions of belief that arose within the church: What is the nature and role of Jesus in humanity's relationship to God (Paul's letters and Hebrews)? Was Jesus essentially divine or human? What were the implications of the answers to these questions for humanity and its salvation? What is the relationship of Jesus as the Son of God to God the Father? What writings should be recognized as authoritative, as being Scripture? What is their function? Does a person have some role to play in his or her own salvation or is salvation entirely the result of God's action unmerited by human beings—dependent solely on His grace? What is the nature of grace and how is it conveyed to humanity? Defenders of almost every possible answer to these questions were found in the early church. These controversies are discussed more fully in Chapter Seven.

Synods and councils were used to give answers to these and other questions. Occasionally no agreement could be arrived at and differing answers were given in distinct sections of the church. Through a series of seven ecumenical councils beginning with the Nicene council and stretching through the centuries until the seventh council in 787 C.E. (the second Nicene) the Church formulated "orthodox" beliefs in which the major questions were answered.[3] Councils were by their very nature representative and did not satisfy all participants or those they represented. Therefore, their rulings were not always universally accepted. Nevertheless, the orthodoxy approved by these councils became the standard of Christian belief. Acceptance of particular beliefs contributed to consolidation of the Christian community, especially after Christianity became the state religion. It would be a mistake, however, to assume that the church ever enjoyed total unity, either in doctrine or polity.

Early heretics (persons who held divergent or unorthodox beliefs) often gathered those of similar opinions into rival or alternative Christian groups. Arius, an Alexandrian priest, was condemned by the Nicene Council of 325 for his understanding of Jesus the Christ as a being divine but subordinate to God the Father. His followers nevertheless continued for a number of centuries to provide an important pattern of Christianity among the Teutonic tribes of Europe, which were eventually incorporated into the Orthodox or Catholic communities. The ecumenical Council of Chalcedon (451) determined that Christ is of two natures, divine and

---

[3]These councils were Nicaea I (325 C.E.), Constantinople (381), Ephesus (431), Chalcedon (451), Constantinople II (553), Constantinople III (681), and Nicaea II (787).

human. Several groups that could not accept the formulations of this council rejected its decisions and became Monophysite Christians. Monophysites believed that there is only one nature of Jesus, the divine nature. The native Egyptian (Coptic) Church, the Abyssinian or Ethiopian Church, and the Syrian Jacobites are all groups that espoused the Monophysite position and continue today as separate Christian communities. The Armenian nation was the first to convert to Christianity and the first to form a national church (in 294 C.E.). Armenians also rejected the decisions of Chalcedon and are considered to be Monophysite. Such groups often remained localized and comparatively small in numbers but have persisted throughout Christian history. Separated from the main body of Christians, they not only hold distinctive doctrines but have developed their own liturgies and ecclesiology. As these variant groups and others indicate, Christianity never experienced monolithic unity; dissent and differences continued to exist.

The vast majority of Christians, nevertheless, accepted the decisions of the Ecumenical Councils and remained a unified community intermeshed with the late Roman Empire. Christian belief was incorporated into the philosophical and theological bases of later civilizations. Concurrently, Christian practice and ethical codes significantly influenced social and cultural developments.

Eastern Christianity

Christian identification with and influence on culture are especially evident in the Eastern Empire, where after the time of Constantine, church and state were effectively interwoven to form a distinct Christian pattern. As noted above, the early development of the church was localized. Individual Christian communities emerged from the work of missionaries, spreading first from Palestine, later from Syria, Asia Minor, and Egypt. The pattern of local leadership, wherein local bishops became the central leaders of the church, remained the dominant structure throughout the eastern Mediterranean and Asia. By the fourth century, the churches in certain political and social centers had risen to leadership in their regions and throughout the church. The churches of Rome, Antioch in Syria, Alexandria in Egypt, and, by the third century, Jerusalem in Palestine were looked to for leadership. However, local bishops were considered to be peers. This relationship is attested to by the practice of convening regional synods attended by bishops of that region (as well as ecumenical councils) for making doctrinal and policy definitions within the church. The Church at Constantinople, located in the new imperial capital, quickly joined the other premier churches in a role of leadership. In the East, churches depended for their significance on numerical strength, traditional leadership, and political connection. Apostolic foundations were not crucial.

The Roman Church, depending on its location in the ancient imperial capital and its claim to apostolic foundation by Peter and Paul, quickly became the premier church in the Western section of the Empire. It was looked to by other churches to give definitive guidance on questions of doctrine and practice. The pre-eminent authority of Rome and its bishop was never accepted in the Eastern churches. The second Ecumenical Council included a canon stating that Constantinople, as the "new" Rome, should be second in rank to Rome, with its authority closely approximating that of Rome. This assertion was expanded as the Council of Chalcedon (451) reaffirmed the rank of Constantinople and defined its specific territorial authority.

In the East, while Constantinople had premier authority along with Rome it was understood to be authority gained through honor and not through autocratic power. The Church at Constantinople did not "rule" the East. Only councils of bishops carried final authority. Such was to be the continuing pattern.

The growing rivalry between Rome and Constantinople was not only politically based but included divergencies in theological emphasis, liturgical practice, ecclesiastical structure, and patterns of church-state relationships. These slowly divided the two Christian communities. These forces finally culminated in an official break in 1054 C.E. (See Chapter Five for expanded discussion of the Eastern Church and its characteristics).

The rise of the Islamic faith in the seventh century brought Christians and Jews another religious relationship of great consequence. Muhammad (570-632 C.E.), the Islamic prophet, consciously related both Judaism and Christianity to his religious message. Proclaiming a radical monotheism in which adherents were to submit to the will of Allah, Muhammad understood the *Koran*, like the Jewish Bible, to be the word of God intstructing His people in all areas of their lives. His claim that the Arab nations descended from Abraham meant that Judaism and Christianity, which were also related to Abraham, were not to be treated as idolaters as were all other religious groups. They were part of the "peoples of the Book," and therefore would enjoy special status.

When Palestine and other areas of the Mediterranean were overrun by the Muslims, Jews and Christians were allowed to continue to practice their faiths, although they were required to pay a heavy tax for the privilege. Animosity between Muslims and Jews began early and occasionally became acute, as during Muhammad's later life. Nevertheless, when the Muslims became rulers of much of the old southern Roman Empire, Jews attained important political and social positions in the administrations of the Muslim Caliphs (rulers).

The Muslim sweep across the eastern Mediterranean and Asia in the seventh and eighth centuries greatly reduced Christianity in the east. The influence of Antioch, Jerusalem, and Alexandria was lost, as the Muslims limited the scope of Christianity to that of a hereditary non-evangelistic ethnic religion. Constantinople, although often threatened, was able to retain its independence until its final capture by the Turks in 1453 C.E. The Church in Constantinople continued to serve as a symbol for Eastern Christianity throughout this long history, and even under the Turks retained its honorific position as the premier church in Eastern Christendom. Because Constantinople superseded ancient Byzantine culture, the Eastern Christianity that emerged there is often known as Byzantine Christianity.

Although its position rose and fell with the political vicissitudes of the period, Eastern Christianity, largely under the leadership of Constantinople, carried on an active missionary campaign. The Balkans (Rumania and Bulgaria), much of the Middle East, and, most important, Russia, were Christianized. After the fall of Constantinople, Moscow claimed to carry on its tradition as the "third Rome." Through the centuries, as national states materialized, the Eastern Church developed national churches governed by their own chief bishops, often known by the ancient titles of Metropolitans or Patriarchs. At present there are fifteen of these churches.[4] While politically independent, they are nevertheless interdependent theologically, and in polity and liturgy. Because they define orthodox faith and practice in terms of their acceptance of the seven Ecumenical Councils, they are normally referred to as Eastern Orthodox Churches.

EARLY MONASTICISM

Monasticism, as it arose in the early Church, offered an alternative Christian life style and emphasis. Judaism began to display ascetic patterns after its encounter with Persian and Greek cultures. Even so, Judaism, stressing wholeness of life in all its forms, incorporated major ascetic patterns of withdrawal and denial only in radical and exceptional forms (*i.e.*, the Essenes and the Qumran community). Early Christianity, however, was exposed to the Greek dichotomy between body and soul, which exalted the spiritual life of the soul. Patterns for seeking a "higher" spiritual life emerged early, and numerous New Testament passages were used to support a life distinguished from that of the surrounding society (Matthew 5:48, 6:19-31; Mark 10:21; John 4:24). Although patterns varied, extensive fasting, prayer, and contemplation as well as virginity, celibacy, and poverty were considered by many in the first few centuries to be signs of devotion and dedication. These qualities served as examples for ordinary Christian believers. As noted, martyrdom also came to be revered and was often accompanied by ascetic practices.

St. Anthony of Egypt (251?-356 C.E.), often known as the father of monasticism, after becoming disillusioned with the world and its evils, sold his substantial estate and withdrew into the desert to devote himself to solitary contemplation of God. Although a hermit, he did not cut himself off from communication with others. Consequently his self-discipline and holiness became widely known and his advice and counsel were sought by many interested in the contemplative life. Others came to him for instruction and advice concerning theological issues (*e.g.*, Athanasius relative to the Arian controversy). He formulated a rule for the spiritual life to be used by the relatively unstructured community of hermits that gathered around him.

---

[4]The Church of Constantinople (Istanbul, Turkey), the Church of Alexandria, The Church of Antioch, The Church of Jerusalem, The Church of Russia, The Church of Georgia, The Church of Serbia, The Church of Romania, The Church of Bulgaria, The Church of Cyprus, The Church of Greece, The Church of Albania, The Church of Poland, The Church of Czechoslovakia, and The Church of America.

Martydrom ceased in the fourth century as Christianity became the Roman state religion. Its image as the ideal, or higher, form of Christian life was inherited by monasticism. Many laymen in the fourth century were convinced that Christianity was being compromised by its union with the state, so they abandoned society for the contemplative life, living in small groups as hermits.

The ordering of this movement into cenobitic (community) monasticism largely depended on the work of Basil of Caesarea (338-379 C.E.). Basil, having studied eremitic (solitary) monasticism in Syria and Egypt, settled as a hermit close to Caesarea. Although he was called from the contemplative life to be a bishop and became actively involved in the life of the church, Basil remained close to many who were pursuing the spiritual life. Monasticism at this point was largely a lay movement. Basil provided the small communities of monks in his area with priestly leadership, and in other ways linked the monastics to the church from which many had effectively separated themselves. More important for the subsequent development of monasticism, Basil formulated a series of questions and answers relative to the contemplative life that became the "rule" for Eastern monastic life. Under this rule monks were to live communally, submitting in obedience to the community and its decisions. Liturgical prayer was practiced and manual labor incorporated, but ascetic concentration was seen as the means of perfect service to God. Poverty and chastity were required of all participants. The monastic community was also to provide for the poor and offer education to youth, with the assumption that some might then seek the monastic life. Contemplation was to remain, however, the central focus, as it has been in the monasticism of Eastern Orthodoxy until the present time.

In the next century, monasticism remained a viable option and generally expanded, but only with loose order and form. John Cassian (c.a. 360-435 C.E.), trained in the East and sent as an emissary to Pope Innocent I, remained in the West and founded two monasteries. He also drew up a rule for the monastic life. Jerome (347-420 C.E.), secretary to Pope Damasus for a period, founded several monasteries in Palestine, urging others to abandon the corrupt world. Jerome combined the monastic life with that of scholarship, translating the scriptures into Latin in a work known as the Vulgate that became the standard Bible in the West.

Western medieval monasticism was, however, more directly dependent on the work of Benedict of Nursia (c.a. 480-550 C.E.). Beginning as a hermit, Benedict gathered around himself a community of monks. Eventually he established twelve monasteries of twelve monks each near Rome and the famous monastery at Monte Cassino. He formulated for these communities a rule that reformed the loose and often undisciplined contemplative life of many in the West. Based on rules formulated by Basil, Cassian and others, it was an inclusive directory of the individual spiritual life for the monks, and a pattern for the administration of the monastery. Centered on the sacramental Divine Office, it included instructions for prayer, work, and spiritual readings. All possessions were to be abandoned by the individual monks, but the community could have possessions to be used for the benefit of the poor and needy. Ruled by an abbot selected by the monks, the monastery was under the supervision of the local bishops. Rejecting extreme forms of asceticism, Benedict's rule provided clearly defined patterns of discipline.

This rule became the order for most monasticism throughout the West. Its allowance for communal property and its insistence on service made Western monasticism more oriented toward social service, missions, and education than was the case in the East. In the West, clergy were often urged, if not required, to experience some form of the monastic life. Church leaders of both East and West were drawn from the ranks of the monks.

Basil and Benedict, in shaping Christian monasticism, significantly contributed to Christianity, for it was the monastic life of both the East and West that served as the pattern for Christian idealism and service. Life in the monastery often provided the discipline, devotion, and training that molded the spiritual dedication and service of church leaders. Monks were frequently the theologians of the church, bishops were sometimes called from the monastic life for service in the world, and priests were trained in the monasteries. As we shall see, in the West the monasteries became the preservers of religion, education, and art through the centuries of social disintegration that followed the destruction of Roman civilization.

WESTERN CHRISTIANITY

The rise of the Church at Rome to a preeminent position among the churches of the West was a natural process. Located in the capital of the Empire and established early, Christianity in Rome could be appealed to by the Apostle Paul for its help in his missionary activities. Peter's traditional relationship to the church added to its prestige. By 95 C.E., Clement, bishop of Rome, claimed that Rome carried special responsibility and oversight for the Church at Corinth in Greece. Early appeals were made to Rome for assistance and guidance. Irenaeus, bishop of Lyon in France, writing against heresy, suggested that all churches should look to Rome for authoritative interpretation of doctrine. By 254 C.E., Stephen, bishop of Rome, asserted his authority over other bishops, even though this assertion was not accepted by many outside the West. The extent to which the authority of the Roman church and its bishops was accepted by other local churches varied, but clearly grew throughout the first several centuries of the common era.

The removal of the imperial capital to Constantinople recognized the military and political practicality called for if the Empire was to continue, and it profoundly affected Rome's role in Western civilization. Rome, even though it continued to be the western capital of the Empire, found its political influence curtailed and degenerating. Sacked by the Visigoths (Germanic tribesmen) in 410 C.E. and never adequately defended by the Eastern Empire, Rome, along with most of the west (Italy, Carthage, Spain, Gaul, and Britain), slipped into political and cultural oblivion. The process was gradual and occasionally emperors such as Justinian (527-565 C.E.) attempted to reconsolidate the Empire, East and West. These brief periods of resurgent imperial control and power were the exception rather than the rule. As the Empire faced challenges to its power and position in the East, its involvement in the West continued to wane.

In the cultural and political vacuum left by the western imperial decline, one of the few surviving stable and well-organized institutions was the Christian Church. In the West, the system of autonomous local bishops had been supplemented by territorial bishops, resulting in territorial organizations related to and, in some sense, subservient to the church in Rome. Lines of authority and communication were intact within the church, whereas they had distintegrated in the Empire. The church offered the people not only spiritual solace and hope, but also structured patterns of life in a deteriorating society.

Gregory and the Church at Rome

The changing role of the church is apparent in the leadership of Gregory I, bishop of Rome 590-604 C.E. With a background as a civil officer of the city of Rome, Gregory abandoned the monastic life when he was called on to assume the duties of bishop. He raised an army and defended Rome against the Lombards (another Germanic tribe). He established civil order, collected taxes, and provided for the welfare of the citizens. Although technically still responsible to the Emperor in political matters, Gregory extended the church's role beyond its traditional function as a religious institution. It became a civic organization dealing with every need of the citizen. While the church was not to retain or seek such a role during every period, Greogry's tenure shows the significant role of the church in the West. Therefore, it is readily understandable why the church was to be a principal element in the shaping of medieval Europe.

Gregory also illustrates the role and importance of the monasteries in the West. When he abandoned civil service to pursue the religious life, he dedicated himself to the spiritual life separated from the world and its interests. When leadership was needed in the face of cultural crisis, he was willing to leave the monastery, but he carried the disciplined spiritual interests nurtured in the monastery into his work in church and society.

Gregory's assumption of civil powers in a time of crisis, while it was unusual, fits a significant western pattern of church-state relationships. Weakened imperial power in the West meant the role of church hierarchy relative to that of political leaders developed with different emphases from those of the East. Ambrose, bishop of Milan, 374-397 C.E., defied civil encroachment in the internal affairs of the church and refused communion to the Emperor Theodosius for a malicious act of vengeance against citizens of Thessalonica. Such action on the part of a bishop suggested that the church, as custodian of the spiritual and moral life of its members, could and should oppose the acts of the civil authorities when they ignored or defied the teachings of the Christian Gospel.

Augustine, a student of Ambrose and Bishop of Hippo in Africa, elaborated this position into the classic statement of western theory relative to church and state in the *City of God*. Written as a response to the barbarian sack of Rome, this work suggests there are two cities, an eternal or heavenly city, and an earthly, limited city. In the earthly city, because of humanity's love of self, there can be only relative good. Here, the state has the important function of guaranteeing peace and order, essentially of protecting persons from themselves and others.

Political rulers are necessary and they are divinely authorized to carry out their responsibilities. The heavenly city is an ideal city where God's love reigns supreme. In it, one concentrates on God rather than self. For Augustine, the heavenly city was comprised of those who through God's grace had been granted such love. The heavenly city can only be *fully* evident in heaven. The church, however, because it attempts to follow God's will and because it is comprised of those who have been granted God's grace and love, gives some evidence of the heavenly city on earth. In the church one finds pilgrims who live by faith. The church is not pure; in it the heavenly and earthly cities are commingled.

Augustine's understanding assumes that for all history both cities are present and necessary, but the role of the church is that of helping the world to find the knowledge and love of God, defining morality, checking injustice, and administering the sacramental means by which God's grace is conveyed to the world. Obviously, the church incorporates within itself the moral and spiritual conscience of the state, so its function is ultimately superior to that of the state. Practically, bishops and secular rulers share coordinate powers, but it is the office of the bishop that is of ultimate significance. Augustine's imagery became the pattern for medieval European church-state relations. While few kings and emperors in the West submitted passively to control by the church, the prestige of the church in moral and spiritual realms gave it immense influence that often translated into political power. For a short period, Gregory mixed the two powers, but he based his understanding on the ideas of Augustine, as did most of his successors.

The Holy Roman Empire

Although Gregory was momentarily successful against the invasions of the Lombards, Italy and western Europe continued to be victims of successive Germanic tribal invasions, with little political and social stability for centuries. Pope Stephen II, faced with renewed Lombard attacks, appealed to Pepin, ruler of the Franks, a rival Germanic tribe that had settled in Gaul in the fifth century. Pepin successfully defended Rome, granting to the Pope political control of the "Papal Estates." Pepin was responding to Stephen's earlier granting him the title of "Patriarch of Rome." These events effectively meant that the ancient claims of political control in the West still residing in the emperor at Constantinople were being circumvented.

In the next generation a more formal break with the Eastern Empire occurred when Charlemagne, Pepin's successor, was crowned (800 C.E.) by Pope Leo III as the Emperor of the Holy Roman Empire. The new empire was a recognition of the Eastern Empire's loss of power in the west and the creation of a rival Western Empire understanding itself to be the true successor to ancient Rome. The designation of this new Empire as *Holy* illustrated the interconnection of the state and church in the West. Charlemagne was certainly not dependent politically on the church, but his coronation by the Pope implied that the church held the spiritual and moral right to invest rulers with their powers. Western Europe was to struggle with the meaning and political significance of that claimed right for centuries to come. However it might be interpreted at any one historical moment, in medieval Europe it meant that the church and its teachings were inexorably bound to all of life, including its political, economic, and educational aspects. The reestablishment of a Western Empire further contributed to the separation of the Eastern and Western churches.

Charlemagne's extensive political control throughout much of Europe quickly dissolved under his successors, retarding the development of the new Empire. The European feudalistic period that followed Charlemagne brought yet another facet of the church's relationship to society to the fore. Based on a system of rights in which occupancy and land tenure were exchanged for military protection and service, feudalism increased the importance of land and territorial rights. Over the centuries, through gifts and acquisitions of buildings and institutions, the church and its monastic orders had become vast landowners. Integrated into the feudal system, the church's bishops and abbots became equivalent to the lords and dukes of the secular realm. They were endowed with political and economic power within their territories in addition to spiritual responsibilities for the people. A major basis of the medieval church's immense wealth was its holdings in land (in some areas by the late medieval period as much as a third of the land was controlled by the church). The relationship of the church to the land also led in ensuing centuries to extremely complex relationships between leaders of church and state, with the church holding important political rights and privileges and political leaders seeking church offices because of their political significance.

Established to succeed the ancient Roman state in the West, the Holy Roman Empire never achieved the solidarity of political control nor the stability of the earlier Empire. The new Empire was at best an uneasy collection of political entities that succeeded the European tribal communities. The rise of European economic fortunes based on feudalist land reform and greater social stability beginning in the ninth and tenth centuries led to new religious, political, and social patterns.

THE MEDIEVAL CHURCH

At its height, the medieval synthesis of Christian faith and life welded together every feature of existence. Structurally, the church provided organization and contact beyond tribal and ethnic lines of separation. By the beginning of the tenth century, the forms and patterns of medieval Christendom were clearly discernible.

The initial unity of the Holy Roman Empire had depended on the personal leadership and power of Charlemagne. When this political unity disintegrated upon his death, stability only slowly returned with the rise of a more locally oriented

feudalism. Social organization in feudalism depended on property and its protection; nevertheless, community relationships remained the organizing principle in
the new structures. In full flower, feudalism and its gallantry gave a picture of
magnificent pageantry. Such richness was slow to develop but signified the extent
of change in the period.

A high degree of cultural unity emerged in the medieval period based to a
large extent on the church. In the early medieval period, the prestige of the church
centered in the spiritual power of the apostolic successor to Peter, the Bishop of
Rome (commonly known as the Pope), and made it the unifying agent of the
culture.

The central role of the church in local communities resided in its sacramental
functions derived from the apostolic authority of the Pope. In the sacraments, one
achieved unique contact with God, and through them one experienced His grace. In
their role as celebrants of the sacraments, priests held a preeminent place in the
organization of the local society.

Symbolic of the importance of the church in medieval society was the rise of
cathedrals beginning in the late tenth and early eleventh centuries. Architecturally
the most massive buildings of the time, they sometimes required centuries to build
and incorporated the best of the culture's art and building techniques. They also
served important community purposes, being the only places for mass assemblage
of the people in a local area. Around them grew centers of commerce, and with
their schools they became centers of education.

The ninth and tenth centuries witnessed an undulating struggle for political
power between the papacy and the imperial leaders. Augustine's concept of church-
state relations still provided the basis for understanding the relation of spiritual and
secular institutions, but the secular power of the church became increasingly real.
Conflict was inevitable, particularly as the church became more engrossed in land
ownership. This struggle accompanied the rise of feudalism, and the church experienced periods when secular interests prevailed over spiritual concerns. Church
offices took on secular powers and functions through involvement in the feudalistic
property patterns. Secularization of church offices often led to the corruption of
their basic spiritual intent. During these centuries, European economic life improved as a mercantile economy slowly emerged.

The position of the papacy was strengthened under the leadership of Popes
such as Gregory VII (ca. 1021-1085 C.E.) who, in an attempt to renew the spiritual
life of the church, forbade lay investiture—the practice of kings investing bishops
with their secular offices, thereby effectively choosing them. Although unsuccessful
in eliminating the practice, the principle of papal dominion was reinforced through
Gregory's action. Innocent III (1160-1216 C.E.) proclaimed the right of the Pope
to intervene in secular matters on the basis of his powers of moral control over
rulers. Innocent was able to enforce such claims to a greater extent than any pope
before or since. Boniface VIII (ca. 1234-1303 C.E.) reached the height of papal
claims in asserting the absolute power of the papacy in all affairs, secular and

sacred. Unable to enforce these claims, Boniface actually experienced reductions in his secular powers. Nevertheless, in his claims, built on those of Gregory and Innocent, the papacy envisioned itself, based on its spiritual prerogatives, as the ultimate power in medieval Europe.

The majesty, power, and beauty of the medieval church can still be seen in is massive cathedrals representing the best of craftsmanship, art, and learning of the period. In the high Middle Ages, Thomas Aquinas (1225-1274 C.E.) also articulated the church's wonder by formulating theology into the "Queen of the sciences," synthesizing all knowledge under the capstone of faith in his *Summa Theologica*. Christianity had clearly become the religion of Europe and was seen as the spring from which all of life flowed. While Aquinas's work symbolizes the magnificent idealism of the period, it also suggests the extent of Christianity's penetration and domination of the culture.

The Crusades

The claims of Gregory VII, Innocent, and Boniface to secular power based on spiritual prerogative objectified the trend within the church to put secular interests before, or at least on a par with, spiritual interests. The wealth and power of the church and its consequent focus on political and economic status within the society led many to view it as abdicating, if not abandoning, its central spiritual function.

Consequently, the eleventh century saw genuine attempts to reform the secular excesses of the church. Significant spiritual renewal resulted from these efforts (see Chapter Four). Prominent in this renewal were forms of popular piety expressed, among other ways, through pilgrimages. Numerous sites of spiritual significance within Europe became the focus of local pilgrimages. As the economic situation of Europe improved, the Holy Lands also assumed an important place as pilgrimage sites.

The Turks (Muslim in religion) effectively closed Asia Minor and then Jerusalem to pilgrimage late in the tenth century—at the same time they were threatening to overrun Constantinople. An appeal from Alexius I of Constantinople to Pope Urban II for assitance in resisting the Muslims led to the promulgation of the First Crusade in 1095 C.E. Urban understood its purpose to be to save Constantinople and, more important, to secure Jerusalem for pilgrimage. Conversion of the infidel Muslims was assumed to be a goal. Urban's spiritual interests were matched with his insight that a crusade offered an opportunity to quell the incessant feuding between Europe's private armies by uniting them in a holy war against non-Europeans. It also offered opportunity for expansion of European feudal power into the East, with its immense economic possibilities.

According to the moral theology of the church during the period, God had given to his apostles and their representatives (Pope, bishops, and priests) the power to require penance for certain sins. Their sacramental responsibilities also meant they could withhold the sacraments with their accompanying grace from those

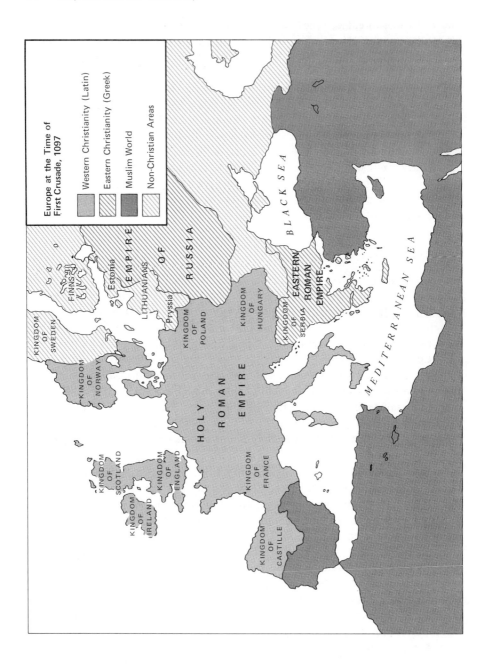

Europe at the Time of
First Crusade, 1097

Western Christianity (Latin)
Eastern Christianity (Greek)
Muslim World
Non-Christian Areas

BLACK SEA

MEDITERRANEAN SEA

EMPIRE OF RUSSIA

KINGDOM OF SWEDEN

FINNS

Estonia

LITHUANIANS

Pryssia

KINGDOM OF POLAND

KINGDOM OF HUNGARY

EASTERN ROMAN EMPIRE

KINGDOM OF SERBIA

KINGDOM OF NORWAY

HOLY ROMAN EMPIRE

KINGDOM OF SCOTLAND

KINGDOM OF ENGLAND

KINGDOM OF IRELAND

KINGDOM OF FRANCE

KINGDOM OF CASTILLE

considered to be immoral. Within the context of these powers, Urban, in his call for a crusade, declared that the journey would, for those who participated from devotional and holy motivation, release a participant from the usual penitential practices. In addition, he promised that those who died in the attempt would receive full remission of sins. What Urban offered the crusaders was remission of penance and of sin itself in exchange for extraordinary service to God and His Church. The principle invoked by Urban—remission of sin and penance for that sin in exchange for extraordinary service—lay at the base of the later system of indulgences to which Martin Luther so strenuously objected.

At first successful, the crusades degenerated into expeditions of plunder and pillage, even including the capture and sack of Constantinople by Western Christians. Often in the later crusades the original religious motivation became secondary, and secular interests supposedly abandoned in Holy War dominated the crusades.

The cultural contacts with the Eastern world that the Crusades provided were, however, to have most important consequences. By reopening commerce between the East and West, which came as a consequence of the crusades, the West was exposed again to ancient Greek and Roman art and learning. In addition, it was introduced to Arabian art, medicine, science, and philosophy. The European Renaissance of the high Middle Ages (twelfth and thirteenth centuries) as well as the later Renaissance of the fourteenth and fifteenth centuries directly depended on these encounters with eastern and ancient culture. The cultural impact of these encounters is incalculable.

The late Middle Ages saw the flowering of a European Christendom in which all of life was related to the religion. The pietistic renewals seen in pilgrimages were matched by reforms within the monastic movements. The rise of transnational mendicant orders of friars responsible directly to the Pope strengthened the papacy. Universities, such as those at Bologna, Paris, Cologne, and Oxford, emerged during the twelfth and thirteenth centuries. The earliest faculties were clerics, even though the universities were eventually to take education from under the aegis of the Church. Even as Aquinas was writing, both conservatives and radical thinkers questioned his theological assumptions, and reformers were calling into question the power and authority of the church and its officials.

Judaism in Medieval Culture

Before turning to the reform movements that changed Western Europe from a medieval culture to a modern one, it may be useful for the understanding of modern relations between Christianity and Judaism briefly to consider Judaism in medieval Europe.

Judaism had spread throughout the Roman Empire, reaching into England, France, and Germany, before the Christian era. Through the Dark Ages (500-800

C.E.) and the early medieval period, European Jews, while socially and occasionally politically restricted, were a tolerated, sometimes respected, minority. Largely occupied as merchants and traders, Jews carried on lively contact with traders of the Mid- and Far East. Refining interpretation of the Torah, they circumvented prohibitions against usury and became the bankers of the Middle Ages, since usury was prohibited to Christians.

The relationship of Jews and Christians changed as the Christian West emerged from the cultural and economic Dark Ages in the eleventh and twelfth centuries. The threat of heresy within the Christian societies of Europe (See Chapter Five) led to the establishment of the Inquisition, an offficial body of the church designed to detect and eliminate false teaching. In time, the Christian Inquisition throughout Europe turned to the Jews in its quest for heresy and false belief. The Jews, since they did not accept Jesus as the Messiah, had always been an anomaly for Christians. To Christians of the time it seemed obvious that the Jews had embraced false teachings. It is not surprising that the Inquistion became an instrument of Jewish persecution at a time when Christian heresies were also being persecuted. Many Jews were put to death for their beliefs, and others lost their homes and possessions.

Persecution intensified during the period of the Crusades to a point where the Lateran Council of the Western Catholic Church (1215 C.E.) ruled that Jews must wear identifying yellow badges and live in separated, walled ghettos. The results were general degradation in status, restrictions in occupation, and finally expulsion from a number of nations: England in 1290 C.E.; France in 1309 C.E.; Spain in 1492 C.E. Jews were even blamed by many for the Black Death or plague. These expulsions and later pogroms (massacres) of Jews in western Europe may have served as psychological if not historical prototypes for Germany's modern Holocaust.

Spanish Judaism developed along unique lines. Tolerated by the Muslims who controlled Spain for centuries, Jews made important contributions to the life of the community. They participated with Muslims and Christians in the academies of Cordova and Toledo, centers of Western learning. A central task in these centers during the Middle Ages was the integration of Aristotelian philosophy into the theologies of each of the religions. In this milieu emerged Maimonides (1134-1204 C.E.), perhaps the greatest of the medieval rabbinical scholars. His commentary on the Mishnah synthesized Jewish thought and Aristotelian philosophy. Other works equally expressed concern for the fusing of new learning and ancient religious tradition as contained in the Talmud.

Spanish Judaism was not exempt from persecution, however. Jews were ultimately driven from Spain first by a Berber uprising and ultimately by the Christians after they had regained control of Spain. Many escaped north into Europe where they were absorbed into European Jewish communities or, like Maimonides' family, returned to Palestine.

QUESTIONS

1. Why is it important to study the relationship of Christianity to its cultural setting in any period of history?

2. What significant changes in the self-understanding of Christianity occurred when it became the official religion of the Roman Empire?

3. Within the Roman Empire at the time of Christianity's formation what functions did religion fulfill in the society? What were some of the principal religions?

4. Why may it be said that Christianity began as a Jewish sect? What caused it to become an independent religion?

5. What are the principal characteristics of Eastern Christianity?

6. How and why does Western Christian thought and structure differ significantly from that of the Eastern Church?

7. What characteristics of medieval Christendom distinguish it from modern Christianity?

8. What was the position of Judaism in the Western medieval culture?

9. What characteristics of Monasticism were attractive to the members of the early church? Why was it particularly significant in Western Christianity?

FURTHER READINGS

The following titles are offered as representative works detailing the history of Christianity.

BETTENSON, HENRY, *Documents of the Christian Church.* New York: Oxford University Press, 1963.

BROWN, PETER, *Augustine of Hippo.* Berkeley, Calif.: University of California Press, 1967.

CADOUX, C. J., *The Early Church and the World.* Edinburgh: T & T Clarke, 1955.

CHADWICK, HENRY, *Early Christian Thought and the Classical Tradition.* New York: Oxford University Press, 1966.

CONZELMANN, HANS, *History of Primitive Christianity.* Nashville, Tenn.: Abingdon Press, 1973.

DANIEL-ROPS, HENRY, *Cathedral and Crusade, 1050-1350.* New York: E. P. Dutton & Co., Inc., 1957.

DANIELOU, J. & H. MARROU, *The First Six Hundred Years.* New York: McGraw-Hill Book Company, 1964.

DAVIES, W. D., *Christian Origins and Judaism.* Philadelphia, Penn.: The Westminster Press, 1962.

FREND, W. H. C., *Martyrdom and Persecution in the Early Church.* Garden City, N.Y.: Anchor Books, 1967.

GRANT, F. C., *Hellenistic Religions.* New York: Liberal Arts Press, 1953.

KNOWLES, DAVID, *The Middle Ages.* New York: McGraw-Hill Book Company, 1968.

LIETZMANN, HANS, *The Founding of the Church Universal,* trans. B. L. Woolf. New York: Charles Scribner's Sons, 1938.

RUSSELL, J. B., *A History of Medieval Christianity,* New York: Thomas Crowell Company, 1968.

WALKER, WILLISTON, *A History of the Christian Church,* New York: Charles Scribner's Sons, 1970, 3rd Edition.

chapter four
CHRISTIANITY AS A WORLD RELIGION

Christianity's rise to preeminence in the northern Mediterranean and throughout Europe was not without its difficulties. The long night of the Dark Ages saw little development of the religion or the rest of culture in the West. From the seventh to the fourteenth centuries, Christianity was constantly threatened by Muslims along its southern frontiers. Reduced in its influence in the East, Christianity's triumph in the West brought with it the dangers of social identification and the loss of spiritual vitality. Throughout the millennium from 500-1500 C.E. there were those within the church who, critical of its wealth and secularity, sought to remind the church of its spiritual functions and responsibilities. A number of individuals, groups, and movements sought reform of various abuses within the Christian community and to return the church to primary concern with spiritual matters. Reformers in the Middle Ages most often were found in the ranks of the monks.

WESTERN MONASTIC REFORM

With its roots in the need for an alternate life style, monasticism can be credited with sustaining the spiritual life and much of civilization during the Dark Ages of incessant wars that dominated the sixth to the ninth centuries. In that period, which culminated in the rise of feudalism, the monasteries became landlords of vast territories and holders of benefices. This led ultimately to wealth. Thus, intricately involved with the political and social life of the church, many monasteries found spiritual interests overshadowed by their secular interests. Discipline declined in the Benedictine monasteries, which had become scattered throughout Europe.

In 910 C.E. William, Duke of Aquitaine, founded a new monastery at Cluny in southern Burgundy (France). The intent of the founder was to restore the Benedictine rule in its ancient form within this monastery. The contemplative life with its spiritual discipline was again to be the center of monastic life. This return to discipline produced renewed piety among the monks and eventually among those outside the walls of the monastery, who looked to the monks for spiritual guidance. In order to guarantee that the monastery would be free from outside influences, William established new rules. The monastery was to be free of secular rulers and influence. To achieve this, it was to elect its own abbot without interference from either the local bishop or prince. It was ecclesiastically directly responsible to the Pope, rather than the local bishop. This move away from local control symbolized an important reform, since it made monasteries that joined in the movement autonomous, and, because of their direct relationship to the Pope, it made them transnational in character.

Seen as sources of spiritual renewal in a period of spiritual lethargy, these reforms were soon adopted by other monasteries, some 300 houses throughout Europe made similar reforms. They were supervised by priors trained at Cluny, who gave the movement stability and centralized its reforms. Because this renewal of piety was not limited to life within the monasteries, many concerns for spiritual life were translated into reforms within the "secular" church, as Cluniac monks accepted bishoprics and other positions of power outside the monasteries.

Often in reform movements the vitality and ardor that brings success eventually wanes. Such was the case with the Cluniac reforms. By the end of the eleventh century, Cluny, having itself grown wealthy, relaxed its discipline and fell into patterns resembling those that had called forth its own reforms. Robert of Molesme, disillusioned by this situation, founded a monastery at Citeaux, France, in 1098 C.E. Again calling for the return to strict Benedictine patterns, the new monastery sought, in contrast to Cluny, simplicity in all matters. Wearing undyed habits (from which they drew their name of "white monks") Robert's followers built houses in isolated places, erected plain churches, and used ordinary unadorned vestments. Manual labor was given prominence, and strict dietary patterns, along with a rule of silence, were enforced. Known as the Cistercians, the order spread rapidly with Citeaux serving as the general chapter house and exerting discipline and control over all monasteries which joined the movement.

The Cluniac and Cistercian reforms are examples of major reform movements within the church. There were many others, which took a variety of forms. The rise of the mendicant friars took monasticism out of the monasteries and made it a preaching, service movement (see Chapter Eight). Calls for spiritual renewal sometimes led to heresy, as among the Cathari (see Chapter Five). The need for reform is persistent, particularly in the institutional and theological structures of any religion.

Reform movements that bring change and vitality eventually settle into standardized patterns of behavior and thought and new reform movements rise to replace them. Western Christianity has experienced this pattern of renewal constantly throughout its history. With the coming of the Renaissance in the late medieval period, however, changes in thought, learning, and culture arose that could not be met by traditional patterns of renewal.

PROTESTANT REFORMS

The Renaissance, reaching full bloom in the fourteenth and fifteenth centuries, opened insular Europe to new knowledge, art, and conceptions of reality. On the basis of the new knowledge, traditional assumptions were questioned. The nature of the universe, the size and form of the earth, the relationship of God to humanity (human free will relative to God's will), and, very importantly, the institutional bases for social, political, and spiritual authority were all reformulated. Major cultural change was in the making. Feudalism had slowly given way to the nationalistic interests of nation states. Spain, France, England, and a confederation of German states emerged as nations progressively limiting and threatening the Holy Roman Empire.

Throughout the fifteenth century, cultural changes intensified pressures on the church and its tradition. Among these were the discovery of the New World by Portugal and Spain; the invention of the printing press, making information more readily available to an emerging European middle class; abandonment of the church as the focus of knowledge and art by some intellectuals and the continued rise of national political entities with their separatist interests. Renaissance scholars and artists raised major objections to the traditional evaluation of humanity and its abilities. Generally, they asserted that rather than humanity's being limited by its sinful self-centeredness, it was capable though free will of unlimited achievements. Humanity's dependence on God was not denied, but a much more optimistic attitude was taken by some toward humanity and its possibilities.

As culture opened to new forms of thinking and organization, the church experienced increasing attacks on its traditional moral and spiritual leadership of society. As early as the 1370s, John Wycliff, an English clergyman and scholar, raised questions about the authority of clerics, suggesting that they held their offices as stewards of God. If they were not faithful stewards, they should be removed. Carried to its extreme, this position questioned the traditional authority of the priests and bishops, including that of the Pope. Wycliff further assumed that the scriptures constituted a basic religious authority superior to that of the church and, therefore, should be in the vernacular languages of the people. Acting on this assumption, he translated the Bible into English. Although Wycliff's suggestions were welcomed by some, they were strongly resisted by the church, which posthumously condemned Wycliff as a heretic. John Hus, a Bohemian cleric and professor, applying many of Wycliff's ideas, led a popular revolt against the authority of the church and its moral corruption. Hus lost his life for his beliefs. He was burned at the stake in 1415, condemned by the Council of Constance.

Wycliff and Hus voiced criticisms that were being raised against the backdrop of major scandal within the church. The Councils of Pisa and Constance had been called to settle an unprecedented problem within the church—rival popes. Under French influence, the seat of the pope had been removed from Rome to Avignon in 1309 to escape the control of local Roman politicians (who had controlled elections of the popes) and to impose French control. Rival popes were chosen in 1378—one Roman and one French. The ensuing struggle for power and the disorganization created by rival authorities were part of the setting for the critiques of Wycliff, Hus, and others. The Council of Constance settled the Papal dispute by reestablishing one pope, but it could not quiet the questions that had been raised about authority and about many of the practices within the church.

The catalyst for permanent modification of medieval Christendom came, nevertheless, from the conviction of an obscure German monk, Martin Luther, that the people of his city were being duped by a commonly exploited money-raising practice within the church. Urban's offer to the Crusaders of remission of sin and its penance had by the sixteenth century evolved into an intricate system of "indulgences." Elaborating on the Aquinian concept that the church had been given responsibility for the storehouse of grace attributed to the merits of Jesus and the saints, the church extended that grace on an ever-widening basis in the form of indulgences for the remission of the punishment for sins. For example, by the time of the late crusades, one could, by paying the expenses of a crusader, receive the benefit of the crusader's service by participating in his remission of penance. In Luther's period, the idealism of Urban had become basically a commercial exchange. One could purchase for oneself or one's dead loved ones remission of punishment in purgatory. Luther's call for a university debate on the validity of the system, in the form of Ninety-Five Theses tacked to the church door at Wittenburg on October 31, 1517, had consequences that neither he nor anyone else could have imagined. His questions struck a responsive chord, and within three years he had become the center of a full-scale reform movement.

Luther's critique of indulgences struck at the heart of traditional church authority. By questioning the power of the Pope and his representatives to grant indulgences, Luther raised the more fundamental question of the relationship of humanity to God. Did that relationship primarily depend on the individual's faith and trust in God or did it depend on the sacramental grace conveyed through the church? Luther's answer was that one was saved or justified before God through faith—direct dependence on God. Luther's authority for this revolutionary teaching was his interpretation of Scripture. The effect of these arguments was to shift the locus of authority in religion from the church and its representatives, the priests, to an individual's faith based on his or her own interpretation of the Scriptures. Although Luther, frightened by the immediate consequences of his arguments, did not advocate a position allowing totally individual interpretation of the Scripture, his concepts contributed significantly to a modern western attitude wherein religion is essentially a matter of personal commitment dependent on individual interpretation.

Luther, while protected by German princes, was excommunicated from the Roman Church and succeeded in establishing an independent Christian denomination. His work did not take place in a vacuum. As indicated above, many were calling for change within the church. Concurrent with Luther's work, Ulrich Zwingli established a Swiss reformation incorporating many of the same ideas. John Calvin molded the Swiss reform into a pattern that was to influence the English Reformation greatly. Within a decade, numerous groups took reform into their own hands and established autonomous Christian churches. Henry VIII, king of England, motivated by political and personal interests, declared himself "supreme sovereign" of the Church in England, effectively rejecting the political claims of the Pope and Empire upon his nation. While not intending to change the polity or theology of the church materially, Henry's separation from the Roman Church opened England to many of the reform ideas current on the continent.

By the end of the century, the Protestant Reformation had effectively shattered the patterns of medieval Christendom. Central to this reform was rejection of the church as the final religious authority. In its place stood the Scripture, interpreted with the aid of the Holy Spirit. Religion was not dependent on priests nor was the ideal Christian the cloistered monk. Religion was to be the unhampered, direct experience by the individual of God in his or her life, though most of the reformers, including Luther and Calvin, insisted on the necessity of preaching and sacraments as God-ordained means of grace within the necessarily communal life of Christians.

The Renaissance and Reformation brought some improvement in the status of the Jews in Western Europe. The Renaissance's reevaluation of the nature of humanity based on intellect and personal ability meant some humanists were more appreciative of Judaism, particularly its tradition of learning. The new attitudes toward knowledge and Scripture led scholars to seek out Jewish teachers to instruct them in Hebrew in order that the Scriptures might be translated from their original languages.

However, improvement was slow and limited. Some Christian leaders proclaimed that no genuine Christian would seek to learn anything, even Hebrew, from Jews, since the Jewish religion seemed to these Christians to be thoroughly renegade, literally an instrument of the devil. In his early reforming period, Martin Luther sought Jewish help. When Jews failed to accept the proclamation of Jesus in its new Protestant form, Luther, in his later years, turned on the Jews with vehement anger.

In order to establish its own thought and practice, Protestantism formulated its teachings into standardized patterns that soon assumed the force of law in many communities. Catholic forms of church governance were replaced by Protestant forms. Liturgical innovations became accepted practice within the churches. Theological innovations were formulated into credal and confessional statements with which members were expected and often required to agree—the Augsburg Confession (Lutheran), the Geneva Confession (Calvinist), the Articles of Religion (English). In the struggle to formulate clearly subtle theological differences, Protestant theologians argued fine points of theology, much as had the schoolmen of the medieval period. Protestant patterns of Christian life lost their distinctiveness when they became the standards expected of the whole community. Consequently, as these new forms of Christianity settled into accepted patterns, there was a tendency for the Reformation to lose its dynamic quality and return, at least for many ordinary people, to a situation in which religion was merely a matter of form without empowering vitality.

Because of its very nature as a diverse and fragmented movement that allowed for constant renewal and reorganization, Protestantism always experienced change and innovation. However, such change was never the threat that Protestantism itself had been to the medieval church. Renewal movements were constantly arising. The several branches of the sixteenth- and seventeenth-century Puritan movement in England were originally concerned with purifying the English church of its continuing "Romish" patterns, particularly episcopacy and Catholic liturgical rituals. Of real importance for the Puritans was a disciplined and vital Christian life motivated by vigorous and lively preaching. Although it failed to gain control of the church permanently, Puritan innovations and discipline did affect large sections of the English people. Nevertheless, this invigorating movement, having experienced substantial success, found itself settling into standardized forms that by the eighteenth century had lost their vitality.

Protestant renewal often attempted to restore the dynamic nature of personal religious life in both faith and practice. P. J. Spener, a late-seventeenth-century German Lutheran pastor, helped revitalize Christian life for the ordinary Christian by stressing personal religious experience. Using small support groups, Bible study, and enthusiastic preaching, this movement became known as Pietism. Through its preaching, development of religious support groups, and educational endeavors it was to have a significant influence on later German theology. Through groups coming under its influence, such as the Moravians, it also spread to America.

In the eighteenth century, England experienced a similar movement in the Evangelical Revival. Led by John and Charles Wesley, but not limited to their particular organization (Methodism), the revival was concerned with ministering to those no longer related to the church or those who had lost any sense of vital Christian life. In America, an associate of the Wesleys, George Whitefield, and Jonathan Edwards were leaders of still another movement to revitalize the Christian tradition. Known as the Great Awakening, it shared many of the concerns and patterns of Pietism and the Evangelical Revival. These movements have continued to serve as patterns for continuing spiritual renewal among Protestants.

WORLD WIDE EXPANSION

Among the effects of the religious divisions in Europe was a new relation of church and state. Because the church has been intimately involved in political patterns of Europe, religious change meant the old spiritual domination of church over state had come to an end. The protection of Luther by northern German princes and that of Calvin and Zwingli by the republican Swiss states, along with the actions of Henry VIII in England, signaled the development of national churches. Protected by the political entities but no longer enjoying spiritual powers over the state, except in Geneva, many Protestant churches became state churches. Even in Catholic countries, the church's spiritual power relative to the state, affirmed and yet resisted for centuries, was now substantially curtailed.

The Protestant Reform served as a renewal agent for all of Western Christianity. Responding to the Reformation during the sixteenth century, the Roman Church in the Council of Trent moved against the major abuses of power and the corruption that had gripped the church. It redefined its position, taking a largely traditional and conservative posture in theology and polity, but consolidating its work both to defend itself against Protestantism and to evangelize the New World that Europeans were aggressively colonizing. While much of northern Europe was no longer related to Roman Catholicism after the Reformation, it retained its role in southern and western Europe and remained the largest, most unified Christian body. This position was enhanced by the colonization that followed the Reformation.

Protestantism, freed from the restrictions of tradition, eagerly moved into experimentation in theology and polity while joining in colonial evangelization. The discovery of the New World in the fifteenth century led to colonization of these areas by European countries seeking both economic opportunity and territorial expansion. Often, these colonial endeavors were understood to be divinely sanctioned. Portugese and Spanish conquistadors were accompanied by Christian missionaries, usually Franciscans or Jesuits. Lasting settlements were most often those of the missions still evident throughout the southwestern United States and throughout Latin America. Dutch and English colonists supported and established Christian missions wherever they went. North America was a particularly fertile ground for Protestant dissenters unable to find the religious freedom they sought for themselves within the European Protestant states.

Colonization normally meant the imposition of European culture on the conquered territories. As a result, Christian missions tended to export European forms of Christianity, allowing little openness or congenial contact with native religions.

Where direct colonization did not take place but expansion brought trade with a variety of cultures, Christian missionaries also accompanied the traders. China, Japan, and India all received Christian missions. In these trade areas, the Christian position was much more that of a foreign religion competing with native religions. Evangelism of these areas depended on Christianity's ability to attract voluntary commitments in societies dominated by long-established, often complex, religious traditions.

By the late seventeenth century, Christianity was certainly a world religion. It was scattered throughout the then-known world. In much of the world, its several forms (Protestant, Roman Catholic, Orthodox, and their varieties) aggressively evangelized the native populations.

NEW PATTERNS WITHIN CHRISTIANITY

Scripture, Reason, and Science

The Reformation's image of the Bible, rather than the teaching office and tradition of the Church, as the basis of religious authority led many to look at the Bible with new eyes. Among Protestants, the Bible, as the divine word of God, was looked to as the primary source of authentic religious and moral truth. Anglicans, Lutherans, Reformed churches, and other Protestant groups looked to Scripture as the basis of authority for all teachings, even if the variety of their interpretations clearly separated them from each other. The establishment of the Scriptures as the premier religious authority prompted the succeeding generations in some Protestant groups to view the Bible as a body of truth directly revealed by God, inerrant and consistent in all its teachings. Rigid orthodoxy, with a new literalistic and legalistic attitude toward Scripture, was often the result.

At the same time the Scriptures were being elevated to this sacrosanct position among some groups, new intellectual currents were leading others to look at religion from a very different perspective. In the seventeenth century, John Locke, applying ancient but rediscovered principles, insisted that mankind had no knowledge except that obtained by sensory perception and then formulated into knowledge by discursive reason. Knowledge was not obtained from authoritative teachers and officials, but discovered by the individual making use of sensory experience and rational reflection on it. Such a teaching had broad implications for the human understanding of political states, religious authority, and individual freedom.

In this same period, Isaac Newton, drawing on more precise observation of astronomical data and using newly invented mathematical techniques, reformulated the whole scheme of physical science with a theory of universal gravitation and his three laws of motion. The new science, especially its adoption of the Copernican theory of the revolution of the earth around the sun and rejection of the accepted earth-centered model of the universe, caused tensions between the secular and religious authorities. Many thought the earlier theories were taught in the Bible. Earlier Galileo had been censured by the Inquisition for teaching the new astronomy as established fact rather than a mere hypothesis. By the time of Newton, most educated churchmen, especially in Protestant countries, were ready to embrace much of the new science as a natural manifestation of the wisdom the Creator had displayed in His creation of the physical universe.

The impact of these and other discoveries produced a "scientific revolution," which included the claim that all areas of knowledge were to be examined by humanity's critical reason, drawing on tools of mathematical analysis and observation of the world. Humanity's critical powers came to be the new source of authority. They were also the basis of thought and action. The eighteenth century saw the fruition of these ideas in the Age of Reason or Enlightenment. Lockean and Newtonian principles and methods led to many innovations in the understanding of the physical world and, with practical technological applications, produced the Industrial Revolution. Accompanying these were economic and political innovations culminating in modern democratic principles of government and production-oriented economic systems geared to the maximum utilization and exploitation of natural resources.

When these theories were applied to religion, as they inevitably were, revolutionary ideas emerged. Lockean principles meant that each person was responsible for his or her own religious experience and knowledge. Religion, like all other areas of life, was based on individual experience and was to be participated in voluntarily. It could not be prescribed or enforced by the state and its officials—the pattern of religious authority that had emerged after the Protestant Reformation. This principle, supplemented by the reforms relative to authority instigated by the Reformation, forms the basis of modern religious freedom. At the height of the Enlightenment the theories of Locke and Newton led to reason becoming the basis of all authority. Even divine revelation and Christian Scriptures were to be judged on the basis of whether they could be reasonably explained and understood.[1]

Intent on doing away with superstition in religion, Deistic thinkers sought to retain the highest ethical teachings of Christianity but jettisoned any idea of God other than that of a creator no longer actively involved in the world who rewards the good and punishes the wicked beyond this life. The traditional authority of the church and the renewed authority of the Scriptures were both spurned. Deism, unsuccessful in attracting a large following except among such intellectuals as Voltaire in France and Jefferson in North America, ultimately fell into disfavor. Nevertheless, it signaled in the religious field a primary shift in thinking that was to be permanent in Western society. No truth, religious or otherwise, was to be accepted on the basis of traditional authority. Scriptural teachings and church doctrines were to be subject to the same scrutiny as any other presumptive or proposed truths.

While such a scientific evaluation of religion and its truth was not immediately popular among the ordinary members of Christian communities, some leaders of the church recognized that the changes in intellectual patterns brought by the Age of Reason could not be avoided. They had to be appropriated within the religious sphere. The result was major reevaluation in the nineteenth and twentieth centuries of traditional Christian patterns of thought, doctrine, and practice (see Chapter Nine).

Central in this reevaluation were changes in attitude toward the use of the Scripture. The subjection of the Bible to textual, literary, and historical criticism—using the tools of reason—substantially altered the understandings of what truths the Bible contained. The historical materials of the Bible were compared to other historical sources from the ancient world. Biblical history was not accepted simply on the basis of the scriptural record, but coordinated with other historical information. Where inconsistencies occurred, the Biblical record was subjected to question. Literary patterns were carefully studied, using the same methods as those used to study Homer and other ancient documents. These methods produced questions

---

[1] Titles of some books produced in this period are illustrative of this position: Locke's *The Reasonableness of Christianity* (1696), Toland's *Christianity Not Mysterious* (1724), and Tindal's *Christianity as Old as Creation* (1730).

concerning the Mosaic authorship of the Pentateuch. The Pentateuch came to be understood to be the compilation of materials from different authors and communities written over several centuries. The authorship of several of Paul's letters was questioned because their style and content differed from works accepted as authentically his.

As a result of these and many other similar inquiries, Scripture was understood by many to contain religious truth (truth relative to the nature of God and His relationship to mankind) couched in the language, beliefs, assumptions and world view of its human authors. Thus, in the works of theologians such as Adolf Harnack (1851-1930), the kernel of abiding religious insight was sought with the assumption that it at times lay concealed in an otherwise very human document. This view of the nature of Scripture contrasts markedly with the notion that the Scriptures were a direct inerrant revelation of God's word to be accepted without question.

Changes in attitude toward and appreciation of the Scriptures were accompanied by theological modifications of traditional concepts. The expanding vision of humanity and its ability to understand and control the universe was incorporated into the theological tradition known as Liberalism. Liberalism accepted the intellectual strides of the eighteenth and nineteenth centuries to be a God-given expansion of humanity's vision and a continuing appropriation of natural human abilities. As a result it tended to be receptive to new knowledge. Instead of seeing such knowledge as a threat to tradition, Liberalism understood it to provide opportunities for new and creative encounters with the wonders of God's creation and plan for humanity (see Chapters Two and Six).

Liberals were confident in humanity and its possibilities under God's direction. They also stressed the importance of personal encounters with God, described by Friedrich Schleiermacher as "religious feeling" or "affections." Reason was important and necessary to understand religion, but religion itself depended directly on religious experience. Among Liberals, the central reality of Christian faith lay in the event of Jesus. In Jesus was revealed the highest example of true humanity, humanity as it should be, and in this event was expressed God's forgiveness of human sin. Jesus and his teachings concerning love became the focus of Liberal teaching. Jesus' teachings were to be applied not only in personal life but in the life of the whole community. The social gospel that grew out of Liberal theology was a direct, if idealistic, attempt to apply the teachings of Jesus to society—to establish the Kingdom of God on earth through the use of humanity's God-given intellectual abilities and moral discipline. With these ideas Liberalism helped adapt Christianity to the new intellectual climate giving the religion continuing relevance amidst massive change.

Expansion, Ecumenicity, Pluralism

The West's expanded vision of humanity and its abilities to understand and control the world brought in the nineteenth century a new wave of geographical exploration and further development and application of scientific theory. A new colonialism arose, directed toward Africa and Asia in particular. Renewed and expanded Christian mission programs were a part of an optimistic vision. Early in the twentieth century, young American missionaries set out to convert the world to Christ within their own generation. Obviously, many western Christians at that time envisioned Christianity as the only authentic religion. The success of Christian missions varied throughout the world, but by the mid-twentieth century Christianity in its various forms could claim the largest number of adherents of any of the world's religions.

Missionary efforts brought an acute awareness to Christian leaders that the divisions of Christianity were a liability for the faith. In the evangelistic work of winning the world to Christ, Christian denominations directly competed against each other. In an effort to coordinate their work and share responsibilities, a series of fraternal meetings were held from the 1850s into the twentieth century. These meetings led to official delegates from various denominations gathering in the World Missionary Conference at Edinburgh in 1910. Cooperation on the mission field was only one area of interest in Christian fellowship and unity across denominational lines. Youth meetings spanning denominational lines emerged and organizations transcending such lines were founded (*e.g.*, Young Men's Christian Association, 1844). Federations were formed to promote Christian "Life and Work", cooperative Christian service, and common ethical action. Coordinated discussions of "Faith and Order" issues faced the crucial areas of doctrinal and polity differences. Out of these common concerns grew the World Council of Churches (1948) with the objective of achieving a greater degree of Christian unity. Although limited in its ability to establish unity because of diverging interests and because major groups, notably Roman Catholics, did not join, it has provided a forum for continuing discussion and a means to act jointly in missions and social work.

Twentieth-century events have at times greatly modified attitudes toward religion and Christian concepts about other religions. Two world wars and other recent conflicts shattered Liberal idealism and replaced it with more traditional and realistic evaluations of humanity's capabilities. Neo-Orthodox or neo-reformation theology gives greater credence to humanity's sinfulness and its dependence on God's grace.

This century has also thrust the West into intimate contact with all of the world, including much more dynamic and direct contact with other religions. Economic developments and technological advances have added to this worldwide contact. As a result, many religions now vie for the commitment of peoples whose perspective is no longer limited to their own geographical or ancestral regions. Religiously, the world has become pluralistic. Christians, particularly in areas where Christianity is a minority or mission religion, now tend to recognize truth and value in non-Christian religious traditions and their teachings. This does not mean that Christians have given up their own claim to the unique revelation of God in Jesus Christ, but it does mean that perspectives in which other religions are viewed have been significantly modified in recent times.[2] Representatives of some of the world's major religions, such as Buddhism and Hinduism, have pointed to similarities between elements of their own practice or teachings and those of Christianity.

The present pluralism of religions, the Protestant Reformation's legacy of change, the contributions of the Enlightenment, and the scientific revolutions of recent history have all contributed to the modern attitude that religion is a private, voluntary aspect of life often only tenuously related to daily existence. Such an attitude contrasts greatly with that of the medieval Christians, for whom religion penetrated all of existence.

The rise of Christianity from a sect of Judaism to a worldwide religion claiming adherents in every portion of the globe and displaying a great variety of forms has been slow but steady. The development has not, however, been smooth and direct. Modern Christianity is an extremely complex family of traditions, organizations, and institutions incorporating great diversity in belief, practice, and life styles. Chapters Five, Eight, and Nine will expand on some features of this complexity.

MODERN JUDAISM

The emergence in the past two centuries of Judaism as a major religious community in Western civilization speaks to its tenaciousness and stability in a culture where it has survived persecution for centuries. Its close connection to Christianity through these centuries and its significant position in the world today make the development of Judaism since the Reformation an important part of Christian history.

The epoch-making reforms of Western European civilization that followed the Reformation crystallized in the eighteenth century Enlightenment. Although variously dated, modern Judaism is usually connected to the movements toward social and political emancipation that accompanied the Enlightenment. The American and French revolutions, with their insistence on freedom of thought and practice, symbolized the period. Jews were freed from French ghettos in 1791. Discriminatory laws and other disabilities were reduced in severity, and limited citizenship was granted to Jews in several Western European countries. Freedom of movement spawned the first significant Jewish emigration back to the Holy Land.

The movements of the Enlightenment prompted ventures into new fields for Jewish intellectuals. Jewish intellectual pursuits through the Renaissance and Reformation periods had continued to be narrowly religious. There were a few exceptions, such as the philosopher Benedict Spinoza (1632-1677). Spinoza, however, was expelled from the synagogue for his ideas. The expansive mood of the

[2] See the "Declaration on the Relationship of the Church to Non-Christian Religions," *Documents of Vatican II* (New York: Association Press, 1966), p. 660f.

eighteenth century allowed significant Jewish contact with the intellectual pursuits of the age. Moses Mendelssohn (1729-1786) could investigate the relationship of Judaism to other religions and remain an accepted member of his Jewish community. Mendelssohn concluded that while Judaism was indeed a revealed religion it was at the same time only one manifestation of a universal religion of reason. Such a formulation suggests that some Jews readily embraced the rationalism of the time.

Generally, the intellectual leaders of the European Enlightenment displayed a new openness toward and interest in Judaism. There was wider acceptance of Jews in the academic, medical, and legal professions. Nevertheless, European churches continued their policies of condemning Judaism and its threat to Christians. Popular opinion, ingrained for centuries, changes slowly.

During the period of the Inquisition large numbers fled to the East—into Poland and Russia. Although welcomed by Poland's rulers, Jews were considered a threat to the church and their status was one of constant change. Many were ultimately massacred in a civil war (1648), and the eighteenth-century partition of Poland left many Jews subject to Russia. Anxious to keep Jews out of Russia itself, the government created the *Pale* where they lived in isolation from the rest of society. Jews in Russia continued to suffer traditional restrictions and occasional active persecution. The new openness toward Judaism produced by the Enlightenment did not, therefore, substantially affect Eastern Euopre.

Jewish Parties

The Enlightenment brought major changes to West European Judaism. Freedom of movement, thought, and practice created tensions within the Jewish community, where life had been controlled and sustained for centuries by ancient Jewish law interpreted by the Rabbis. Adjustment to the modern world created three distinct Jewish parties, or groups, in the nineteenth century.

French and German Jews participating in the Enlightenment turned intellectual inquiry toward their religion. The result was Reform Judaism, which essentially moved away from dependence on the Torah for organization of daily life and limited the use of Hebrew language to certain scriptural readings. Conservative German Jews resisted these innovations. Recognizing that change in the modern world was necessary, they nevertheless sought to maintain traditional Jewish patterns, including the use of Hebrew for worship services. Known as the Conservatives, this title became that of the centrist party. Neither of these groups, dependent as they were on the intellectuals of the time, attracted the majority of European Jews.

Another response to reform movements led to a new orthodoxy (a term used by the reformers to refer to those who resisted change). By and large this group, aware that religious rule of secular life was no longer possible, separated religion and culture. These Orthodox Jews were to keep all of the traditional laws, including those of diet, but allow acculturation in their secular lives. Each of these groups found a place in the new Judaism and were part of the large emigration to America during the nineteenth century.

The development of Jewish parties also meant the adoption of differing attitudes toward Christian institutions. Reform Judaism tended to use as its model the progressively changing Protestant Christian Churches, with the expectation that by making such progressive adjustments, Jews would become accepted participants in the large society. Conservative and Orthodox groups, on the other hand, insisted on their distinctive religious patterns, and continued to distinguish themselves in more fundamental ways from their non-Jewish neighbors.

Behind all modifications of Jewish life remained the basic religious differences between Jews and Christians. Christians generally continued to think that Jews should accept Jesus as their Messiah as interpreted by Christian theological traditions. Jews continued to reject Christian beliefs, particularly those about the role of Jesus as the unique revelation or manifestation of God. Suspicion by Christians that Jews somehow subverted and undermined "Christian society" provided occasions for tension, confrontation, and even persecution in Western Europe, although for the most part to a less severe degree than in earlier centuries.

While Reform was dominant among Jews in late nineteenth-century America, Conservative congregations were also strong, especially among the later West European immigrants. Among them, worship, dietary practices, and teaching methods were modified less radically. Orthodox congregations comprised the smallest of American Jewish parties until the massive East-European immigration of the late nineteenth century.

East-European Jewish immigration, beginning in the 1880s, far exceeded the previous migrations. These Jews, who were generally poor, settled on the industrialized East Coast where they formed their own ethnic communities. They brought to America a Judaism much less affected by the changes of the eighteenth and nineteenth centuries. They insisted on strict Torah observance, but adopted the patterns of Western European orthodoxy, separating religion and secular life. To maintain their religious heritage they created a system of parochial education: The *Yeshiva*, or academy, taught traditional rabbinical methods wherein religious education dominated all other subjects. Modern orthodoxy later incorporated many of the earlier Reform changes, but the centrality of Torah study, the religious use of the Hebrew language, and dietary codes are still held to be indispensable.

A hallmark of American culture, diversity, is exemplified by American Jews. At the same time cooperation between American Jews is evident in many social and philanthropic organizations which cut across Reform, Conservative, and Orthodox lines. In all branches, accommodation to American culture has prompted major changes. The rabbi has become preacher, pastor, and administrator. Although Talmudic study is still emphasized, it is no longer the rabbi's central focus. Practice of ancient law varies widely, but is seldom (even in the most conservative communities) enforced as it was in previous centuries.[3]

---

[3] Much of the information in the present section depends on the insights of Leo Trepp, *Judaism: Development and Life* (Belmont, Calif., The Dickinson Press, Inc., 1966), pp. 47ff.

American Jews have not suffered the religious restrictions of their European forefathers. Judaism has been one among many religious choices in America. The prejudice and bias mainfested in America was often ethnically oriented. Animosity frequently arose between recently arrived competing ethnic groups as well as between established Americans and the immigrants.

Such *ethnic* animosity has, however, not guaranteed the absence of *religious* prejudice. American Christians often imported the biases of their own immigrant forefathers, sharing their suspicion of Jews and of the Jewish religion. The natural distinctions between the two religions were not lost in America. While this did not mean legal barriers for Jews, it did contribute to mutual suspicion, distrust, and, occasionally, to persecution. Such groups as the Ku Klux Klan significantly increased anti-Jewish sentiment, especially during the post-World War I period when America had emerged as a world power and many Americans became frightened about increasing "foreign influences" in American society. Such anti-Semitic feeling did much to stimulate major Jewish leadership in American organizations and movements intent on protecting civil and religious freedoms in America.

Zionism

The intellectual and social ferment brought about by the eighteenth and nineteenth centuries renewed among Jews an age-old hope for the restoration of political and cultural freedom by a massive return to the land of Israel (Zion). In the later nineteenth century, suggestions were made that Jews should seek self-emancipation from their place in European and other societies. Other Jews came to believe that no people could be truly creative without having a land of their own. Such ideas found full flower in Theodore Herzl (1860-1904). Herzl was an Austrian newspaperman who became convinced that even the influences of the Enlightenment could not overcome the anti-Semitism of Europe. Political and religious freedom had not overcome the latent hatred that led to anti-Semitic acts. Herzl's solution was to seek a free Jewish state or homeland. He organized a Jewish Congress in 1897 to promote his ideas. The congress launched the project to establish a free state of Israel.

Eastern European Jewish refugees had been settling in Palestine for some time. But the Turks, who controlled the territory until after World War I, resisted the establishment of an independent Jewish community. The dissolution of the Turkish Empire brought the Balfour Declaration of 1917, in which the Allies promised a portion of Palestine to the Jews. Because of conflicting interests in the post-war period, this promise was not brought to fulfillment, although settlement continued. Only after World War II was Herzl's dream implemented. Responding to Jewish political pressure and the horrors of the German holocaust, the United Nations established an independent Israeli state in Palestine in 1948.

Zionist nationalism, as envisioned by Herzl and others, was only partly religious. *Cultural* Jews (those more interested in Jewish ethnic heritage than religious tradition) as well as *religious* Jews were interested in the establishment of a state where political, cultural, and religious freedoms could be preserved by Jews without depending on others. The major influence on modern Israel's religious development was drawn largely from Eastern Europe. The opportunity for freedom meant a return to strict orthodox observance of Torah. With the establishment of a Chief Rabbinate in Israel, some attempt has been made to exert authority throughout the world. Religion has been incorporated into state observances, and religious holidays are officially observed. Nevertheless, as in many modern states, active religious observance is limited to a minority of the population. In fact, the phenomenon of a strict religious minority enjoying considerable political power in a state that is largely secular has created tensions within the Israeli community.

The Zionist movement and the creation of the state of Israel has been understood among some Christian evangelical and fundamentalist groups to be the fulfillment of scriptural prophesy. Believing that prophesies forecast the renewal of Israel and its religion as a precondition to the second coming of Christ, these groups have become an important part of the political support of Israel in America. Most liberal Christians have supported Israel for humanitarian reasons. However, the aggressive Israeli expansion and continuing failure to deal sympathically with the plight of Arab refugees in the Mideast by recent Israeli administrations has led some Christians to question Israel's intentions and good faith. Clearly, Zionism remains a focal point for many Jews throughout the world and at the same time an enigma for others.

QUESTIONS

1. What were the major contributions of Monasticism to the development of Western Christianity?

2. Why may it be said that Monasticism replaced martyrdom in the life of the church? What distinctions arose within the religious life of the church because of the rise of Monasticism?

3. In what ways did the critiques of the church and its practices made by Wycliff, Hus, and the Humanists contribute to the setting for the Reformation?

4. Why may it be said that the Protestant Reformation shifted the basis of authority within Christianity? What became the new authority in Protestantism?

5. How did the new emphasis on individual interpretation of scripture and personal experience of religion affect the development of Christianity in the post-Reformation period?

6. The Protestant Reformation turned out be a very fragmented movement without central unity. Why was this true? What effect did that have on modern Christianity?

7. How did the eighteenth-century Enlightenment bring another shift in the concept of authority? What has been the effect of that shift?

8. What effects have the intellectual changes and scientific developments of the past two centuries had on Christianity in Western Culture?

9. Account for the fact that in the modern world Christianity must again be considered one among many religions as it was in its beginnings within the Roman Empire.

10. What developments within Christianity itself contributed to its spread throughout the world?

11. Major changes have occurred in the position and treatment of Jews in the West since the Enlightenment. Are these changes basically positive or negative? What has been their result in modern culture?

FURTHER READINGS

The following titles are offered as representative works detailing the later history of Christianity.

AHLSTROM, SYDNEY E. *A Religious History of the American People.* New Haven, Conn.: Yale University Press, 1972.

BAINTON, ROLAND H. *The Reformation in the Sixteenth Century.* Boston, Mass.: Beacon Press, 1972.

____. *Here I Stand.* Nashville, Tenn.: Abingdon Press, 1950.

BEN-SASSON, H. H. and S. ETTINGER, Eds. *Jewish Society Through the Ages.* New York: Schocken Books, 1973.

BROMILY, G. W. *Zwingli and Bullinger.* Philadelphia, Penn.: The Westminster Press, 1953.

BURNS, E. M. *The Counter-Reformation.* Princeton, N.J.: Princeton University Press, 1964.

CALVIN, JOHN. *Institutes of the Christian Religion.* tr. J. T. McNeill. Philadelphia, Penn.: The Westminster Press, 1960 2v.

CLEBSCH, W. A. *From Sacred to Profane America: The Role of Religion in American History.* New York: Harper and Row Publishers, 1968.

CRAIG, G. R. *From Puritanism to the Age of Reason, 1660-1700.* Cambridge, Mass.: Cambridge University Press, 1960.

DICKENS, A. C. *The English Reformation.* New York: Schocken Books, Inc., 1964.

DILLENBERGER, JOHN and CLAUDE WELCH, *Protestant Christianity.* New York: Charles Scribner's Sons, 1964.

HANDY, ROBERT T. *A Christian America.* New York: Oxford University Press, 1971.

____. *The Social Gospel in America, 1870-1920.* New York: Oxford University Press, 1966.

HILLERBRAND, HANS. *The Reformation.* New York: Harper and Row Publishers, 1964.

JEDIN, H. *A History of the Council of Trent.* St. Louis, Mo.: Herder and Herder, Inc., 1957. 2v.

KNOWLES, DAVID. *Christian Monasticism.* New York: McGraw-Hill Book Company, 1969.

LITTELL, FRANKLIN. *The Origins of Sectarian Protestantism,* New York: The Macmillian Company, 1968.

LUTHER, MARTIN. *Luther's Works,* Ed. by J. Pelikan and H. Lehman. St. Louis, Mo.: Concordia Publishing House, 1955. 55v.

MAHLER, RAPHEL. *A History of Modern Jewry.* New York: Schocken Books, 1971.

MANSCHRECK, CLYDE. *A History of Christianity in the World.* Englewood Cliffs, N.J.: Prentice-Hall, Inc., 1974.

MCNEILL, J. T. *The History and Character of Calvinism.* New York: Oxford University Press, 1954.

NEILL, STEPHEN. *A History of Christian Missions.* Baltimore, Md.: Penquin Books, 1964.

NEUSNER, JACOB. *The Way of Torah: An Introduction to Judaism.* North Scituate, Mass.: Duxbury Press, 1979.

ROUSE, RUTH and STEPHEN NEILL. *History of the Ecumenical Movement: 1517-1948.* Philadelphia, Penn.: The Westminster Press, 1952.

SPINKA, MATTHEW. *Advocates of Reform from Wycliff to Erasmus.* Philadelphia, Penn.: The Westminster Press, 1963.

TREPP, LEO. *Eternal Faith, Eternal People: A Journey into Judaism.* Englewood Cliffs, N.J.: Prentice-Hall, 1962.

WORKMAN, H. B. *The Evolution of the Monastic Ideal.* London: Epworth Press and The Methodist Publishing House, 1927.

chapter five
UNITY AND DIVERSITY IN CHRISTIAN INSTITUTIONS: TRADITION, POLITY, AND LITURGY

At the core of Christian faith is the belief that God uniquely reveals His nature and love in Jesus Christ. This belief enlightens and directs how Christians view God, themselves, the world, history, and Scripture. Christians are unified in their belief that in Jesus God reveals Himself. Yet there are significant differences of interpretation among individual Christians and among the groups they have formed about what this means. There is both unity *and* diversity in Christian belief (see Chapter Seven for a discussion of theological issues).

This same phenomenon is present when Christians incorporate themselves into churches, religious communities, and other groups and organizations. Their unity is seen in similar institutions and the bases of worship, yet their diversity is also expressed in church policy, liturgy, and the practice of the Christian life. Also, because these institutional forms of religious faith are to some extent, even when understood to be divinely ordained, human constructs, they inevitably reflect the historical changes of their social and cultural contexts.

The present chapter investigates major aspects of unity and diversity found among Christian communities, focusing on forms of liturgy, organizational polity, and Christian life rather than theological differences which of necessity will occasionally be noted. Limitations of space dictate a selective discussion of representative groups.

EAST AND WEST:
DIVERGENCE IN A COMMON FAITH

Discussion of the similarities and differences between Eastern and Western Christianity often concentrates on the division of the Roman Empire in the fourth century and its aftermath, the separation of Christianity into two major church bodies in the eleventh century. The contrast between these two forms of Christianity is, however, much more complex than those that can be related to political and institutional separation. Differing patterns of thought, polity, and worship contribute to their distinction.

Eastern Orthodoxy is, as noted in Chapter Three, a title referring to Christians whose churches are presently found throughout Eastern Europe, the Eastern Mediterranean, and the Middle East. The term *Orthodox* indicates their acceptance of the doctrinal formulations of the first seven Ecumenical Councils in contrast to others in their geographical regions who rejected these councils' rulings. Divided today into a number of national churches and voluntary organizations, they are unified in their characteristic beliefs and practices, which arose early in Christian history.

Western Christianity has traditionally been referred to as *Catholic,* or universal, denoting its early claim to be representative of the universal Christian faith. Because of the premier position of Rome in its history, the Christian community that arose in the West is also referred to as *Roman Catholic.* Dominating Western culture from the fourth century until the sixteenth century, it continues, as we have seen, to be the largest unified body of Christian believers. With Eastern Orthodoxy, this branch of Christianity accepted the first seven councils as defining Christian belief, yet also accepted later Western councils that continued to reformulate theology, worship, and practice.

In its first four centuries, Christianity developed in a patchwork fashion across the Roman Empire. It enjoyed unity of essential belief, it resisted heresy, and it established similar patterns of worship and practice. Persecution by and distinction from its surrounding community tended to insure unity and mutual support. Nevertheless, regional differences of thought, worship, and practice were distinguishable from the earliest period of the church. The late third and fourth centuries witnessed increasing divergence over theological issues, and organizational policies began to differ significantly with the establishment of Christianity as the religion of the Roman Empire.

Concept of Humanity and Salvation

At the height of its power, the Roman Empire imposed significant unity on many divergent peoples, but distinctions between communities as variant as the Persians, Egyptians, Greeks, and the Romans themselves always remained. As Christian groups were formed in each area of the Empire, distinct forms of Christianity tended to reflect the practices and thought of the local communities. Major distinctions between Eastern and Western Christianity were in large part dependent on differences between Greek and Roman patterns of thought. Roman practicality, seen in thought patterns oriented toward precise definition and efficiency, insisted on clarity of concept and expression. On the other hand, Greek interest had always been philosophical; the nature of universal truth in all of its intricacy was far more important than whatever practical application it might have.

Tertullian, a third-century Western theologian, had little interest in the philosophical and theological speculation popular with his Eastern contemporary, Origen. Tertullian was very concerned about defining Christian faith and morals in clear, rational, logical terms. Tertullian's concern with the logical and practical was typical of Western thought. Theological speculation, a sense of mystery, and an appreciation for the mystical were not absent, but they did not have the same emphases as these matters had in the East.

It is not surprising, therefore, to find that the understanding of humanity and its salvation differs substantially between the East and the West. Among the Orthodox, humanity is only *fully human*, or complete, when it is in communion with God. The natural state of humanity is to be in God. One is free only when he or she is in communion with God. Humanity, having chosen to reject this full communion, has fallen into slavery to itself and the world. The utlimate result of this rejection is death—an unnatural state. Sin is understood, following the Platonic tradition, as a separation from God in which the image of God becomes unclear and humanity lives in an unnatural state. Through sin, humanity loses the freedom to be fully human and like God. On these assumptions, the Orthodox understand Jesus' role to be the restoration of humanity's full freedom, the freedom to be in full communion with God. By participating in and then rising from death, Jesus restores the original state of humanity. He deifies humanity by restoring its original communion with God.

Roman theology, taking its imagery from the framework and patterns of Roman law, understood the fall of humanity as the assertion of selfish will against God's intent to create a world of love. Humanity is therefore responsible for its hereditary, sinful condition and cannot be fully human in it. Humanity's rebellion not only doomed individuals to a condition of selfish alienation, but also brought guilt from which there could be no release without punishment or retribution. God's gracious act in sending Jesus was to take upon Himself the guilt of humanity, making retribution for sin and restoring the possibility of the unity of love with God, humanity, and the redeemed world. Through God's self-giving, known as his Grace, God's intent in the creation is again possible. Jesus, embodying and exemplifying God's love in his life, death, and resurrection, triumphs over humanity's sin and removes its guilt. The pattern of thought here is juridical: The removal of guilt is central. This has not been all, by any means, that Western Christianity has seen in the Atonement (what God has done in Christ for humanity) but it became the *dominant* theme. The heavy emphasis on legal and judicial imagery in Western Christianity's interpretation of salvation came to differ substantially from the more mystical concept of deification found in the Eastern Church.

The Sacraments and Worship

Because of these respective understandings of the nature of salvation, it is natural that the sacraments should occupy the central place in worship for both the Eastern and Western churches. Through the sacraments, a believer experiences contact with God and receives His grace, which restores the believer to proper relationship with God. In both churches, the Eucharist occupies a most significant place among the sacraments. Liturgical patterns concentrated on this sacrament (in contrast to the central role of preaching in most Protestant worship patterns).[1] Elaborate and beautiful liturgies have emerged over the years to assist the worshipper. Also, in both churches the mystical aspects of the sacramental experience have been stressed.

In the East, liturgy has normally been in the vernacular languages of the local churches. Several differing but similar liturgies have developed. In the West, the liturgy continued to be celebrated in the Latin language until the Second Vatican Council (1962-1965), giving the liturgy a universal form throughout the church. With Vatican II, the Roman Church also embraced vernacular languages and allowed modifications in liturgical patterns.

With all their similarity, there are significant differences in the understanding of the sacraments in these two branches of Christianity. In Orthodoxy, the sacraments, reflecting Jesus' role and sacrifice, are the means by which restoration of humanity to its God-like image is available to individuals. Reestablishment of community with God conveyed through the liturgical forms of the sacraments brings humanity to fulfillment and completion. In view of this restoration, Christian experience is most complete when congregations are gathered in worship. Worship becomes the most essential Christian act for the Orthodox. In the Western church, worship also is central, but there are subtle differences in understanding. The Western emphasis on human guilt and the sacrificial role of Jesus in taking upon himself humanity's rightful punishment for sin means that each time the Eucharist is celebrated it becomes a sacrificial act rectifying human guilt. The focus here is on human guilt and its eradication by God's grace, rather than on the deification of humanity, also by grace, which is the central theme in the Orthodox understanding of the sacrament.

In both churches, the role of worship has been enhanced through the construction of beautiful church buildings and the use of elaborate works of art. For centuries, the most significant art of both regions was incorporated into churches, forming an essential element in worship services and the education of believers. Because the East experienced a strong protest relative to the veneration of statues and pictures in worship, Eastern art has concentrated on two-dimensional representations of Jesus and the saints, resulting in a distinctive Byzantine art form, the icon. The extensive use of statues and pictures in the West has continued through-

---

[1] Both traditions recognize seven sacraments: Baptism, Confirmation, Reconciliation (confession and penance), Eucharst, Marriage, Anointing (of the sick), and Ordination (to the ministry).

out its history. Art in both sections served an important educational function, with stories from scripture and church history presented visually in periods of broad-scale illiteracy among believers. Even in modern, visually oriented cultures such use remains important.

Ministry

The emphasis on the sacraments within both traditions has required that the churches develop a stable, trained, and honored priesthood. Priests are, by their sacramental and pastoral roles, distinguished from the laity. Individual contact of the believer with God through personal faith and devotional experience was not rejected. Nevertheless, ordination to perform sacramental rites gave the clergy special significance, for they became the mediating agents of God's grace. Preaching or proclamation of the Gospel was also understood to be an important part of the function of the priesthood normally requiring special training and gifts, contributing to their distinction from the laity.

Patterns in the two branches do, however, differ. In the East, priests and deacons may be married, although they may not contract a marriage after ordination. Bishops may not be married and are drawn from the monasteries, in accordance with a continuing high evaluation of monasticism. In the West, from an early period the church's hierarchy sought to impose celibacy, originally found in monasticism, on all clergy because of the importance and demands of their office (see Paul's admonitions, I Cor. 7:32ff). This effort was not entirely successful until the medieval period, but continues today within the church.

As noted in Chapter Three, the role of the bishop, assisted by priests and deacons, as spiritual leader of the local congregation developed early. Through the centuries, this role remained part of the ideal image of the bishop. A bishop was responsible for the faith of the congregation—not only in its sacramental patterns but also in its spiritual, intellectual, and moral expression. Doctrinal and moral questions were determined by the bishop. As geographical territories were added to the jurisdiction of the bishops, their local image was modified, but the understanding of their role remained the same, even though other functions were added. They became the agents of tradition and succession, since they were responsible for training and ordaining priests. As larger questions of doctrine, polity, and practice arose, bishops in a particular geographical locality joined with their peers in other churches to form councils and synods. The bishops of provincial towns or capitals who often presided at these synods came to be called metropolitans (archbishops). These patriarchs held a loose jurisdiction over local churches in their area, even though all bishops were understood to be equals. In the East, the essential nature of these early developments continued, so that while certain churches and their bishops became preeminent, such leadership was understood in a collegial framework. This understanding of the place and position of bishops and patriarchs continues today.

In the West, while the image of the bishop was based on these ancient patterns, the functions of bishops significantly changed. The juridical pattern of thought present in Western theology is evident in its concepts of the priest and the bishop. As early as Irenaeus (c. 130-202), there emerged the idea of transference of power and true teaching from the apostles of Jesus to their successors, the bishops. Later known as apostolic succession, this concept of leadership in the church has several significant features. First, power and authority resided in the office and in the person who occupied the office rather than in the congregation at large. Second, the concept incorporated an emphasis on the passing of truth and authority from one generation to the next, emphasizing the authority both of the transmitting persons and the transmitted tradition.

Complementing these concepts, which took form over the centuries, was the Western church's tendency to pattern itself after the Roman Empire. Officers of the Empire held supreme power in office, although they were subservient to superiors and responsible for subordinates. This hierarchical pattern was adopted by the Western church. The bishop of Rome (the Pope) was equivalent in power within the church to the emperor in the Empire. Cardinals, archibishops, bishops, and finally priests all held sacramental power and teaching responsibilities appropriate to their positions, each subservient to his superior in the faith. The claim of the Church of Rome to Apostolic foundation as well as its emerging importance in the West (see Chapter Three) led eventually to the claim that the Pope is God's representative on earth with universal dominion over the Christian faith. Such claims seemed highly credible in the West on the basis of the Roman hierarchical system. As a consequence of these ideas, clergy have enjoyed, until recent times, almost total authority and control in the church. Vatican II attempted to enlist more participation of the laity in the governance of the church.

The closely disciplined structure of theology and practice inherent in this pattern of authority and tradition focused in the one office of the Pope did much to make the Western church one unified body in structure, doctrine, and practice. It also contributed greatly to Western Catholicism's ability to shape European culture during the medieval period.

The monasticism of the two churches displays differences of emphasis, suggesting some of the contrasts between the churches. From its beginning, eastern monasticism followed the patterns and rule of St. Basil. One joined the monastery in the East to separate oneself from the world and its concerns. The contemplative life of spiritual meditation on God and His love was and is a monk's goal. Consequently, while the monasteries have some educational functions, especially among the clergy, they are not understood to be service agencies of the church. Bishops are drawn from the ranks of the monks because of their spiritual fervor and insights— for it is the spiritual role of the bishop that is most important in the East.

Western monasticism also made contemplation a central point. Nevertheless, other functions attached to monastic life significantly modified it. Under barbarian rule (fifth to the eighth centuries), monasteries served as the preservers and depositories of civilization. From this role they became agencies of social conservation.

They also provided teachers for the cathedral schools and early medieval universities. These duties, added to those of contemplation, led to the establishment of monastic orders whose principle functions were to serve the world as educators, preachers, missionaries, and social servants. Much of the spread of western Catholicism as a worldwide church must be credited to monastic *orders*, which accompanied the colonial and economic expansion of Western Europe. The practical orientation of monasticism in service areas reflects the general concern of the Western church with the practical, worldly aspects of Christian life.

Church and State Relations

Concentration on worship and the spiritual life has kept Orthodoxy from having extensive interests in political and social questions. In its early pattern of close affiliation with the secular rulers of the Roman Empire Orthodoxy generally chose to allow these rulers an important role in church matters. Consequently, state rulers tended to take an active role in church administration and organization. The church essentially became a department of the state, often subservient in secular matters to the emperors and kings. It is not surprising then that among the Orthodox, laypersons may hold significant administrative positions, often becoming leading theologians; in some parts of the church they have traditionally participated in the election of bishops.

These structural patterns served as the foundation on which Orthodoxy's characteristic pattern of church and state was built. Churches are generally state or national churches except in areas such as America where religious institutions are formed as voluntary associations. Because of the close association of Orthodoxy with the state and its primary concern with the spiritual life, it has seldom questioned the moral, social, or political abuses that may exist in its cultural setting.

The relationship of church and state in the West has, on the other hand, displayed a much more tumultuous history (see Chapter Three). The claim of the Pope to preeminent spiritual power occasionally meant the assertion of political power as well. Ideally, in Augustine's scheme, church and state complement each other, but balance of power and influence is always imperfect and fleeting. Generally, the Western church has not been subservient to the state, but has understood its position to be at least equal to that of the state, particularly in moral matters. Therefore, the church has taken seriously its responsibility for society in the West, shaping the social, moral and, occasionally, the political norms of the Western states. Often it has served as a critic of culture when society has failed to appropriate or follow its definition of Christian moral norms.

Eastern and Western Christianity, arising from the same historical sources, do indeed share a common faith, many doctrines, and numerous practices, yet, their divergences are many. Most of these reflect their grounding in different cultural patterns, which have created distinct practices and structures.

ASPECTS OF PROTESTANTISM

A galaxy of groups and communities make up the third major branch of Christianity. Commonly referred to as *Protestants*, these grew out of the sixteenth-century protest, led by Martin Luther, against the moral and spiritual decadence of the late medieval Catholic church. Unified in their criticism of Catholic abuses, the motivations of Protestants for wanting change were often diverse. Modifications by Protestants of traditional theology and practice quickly led to many separate groups varying widely in thought, organization, and practice, shattering the unity of Western medieval Christendom. Diversity among Protestants has contributed to the modern fragmentation of Christianity, yet it has also brought with it immense expansion as many Protestant groups have sought adherents throughout the world. This diversity makes it necessary to comment selectively on distinctive aspects of Protestantism represented in some of the major groups.

Lutheranism

Martin Luther's initial protest concerned the manner in which indulgences were being sold among the German peasants (see Chapter Three) but was based on

Martin Luther preaching: a detail from the Cranach altarpiece. Reprinted through the courtesy of Lutherhalle Reformationsgeschichtliches Museum, Lutherstadt Wittenberg, Germany.

much more profound theological issues. In studying the Scriptures for his lectures at the University of Wittenberg, Luther had become convinced that humanity's relationship to God was not based on the mediated grace offered by the church through the sacraments, the common assumption of the time, but on personal encounter with God's love and faith in His saving act in Jesus. Luther's understanding of faith moved him away from basic concepts accepted in his day. The medieval Catholic definition of faith reflected the teachings of Thomas Aquinas—faith meant the acceptance of that which one could not know by sensory experience. This included the revealed mysteries taught through the doctrines and traditions of the church. In contrast, Luther, studying Paul and following the lead of Augustine, came to define faith as an inner awareness of, need for, and dependence on God. Faith is trust, as distinguished from intellectual acceptance. This shift from cognitive and rational acceptance to affective and existential trust threatened traditional authority, for it placed individuals in direct contact with God, and removed them from dependence on clerical mediation of God's grace. It also reemphasized the Paulinian understanding that humanity is not "justified" before God by what it does, but through faith (meaning trust) in God. Justification by faith in contrast to justification by works (participating in the sacraments, penance, and so on) became the clarion call of Protestants.

Because Luther had arrived at his understanding through his personal study of the Scriptures, he insisted that Scriptures were the primary source of contact with God's truth. In the scriptures, God speaks directly to humanity and through the guidance of the Holy Spirit makes known to the individual His eternal truth. In light of this insight, Luther could claim that Scripture was the sole authority in the life of the Christian whose truth was only supplementally interpreted by the tradition of the church passed from one generation of clergy and hierarchy to the next. Practically, Luther emphasized the importance of preaching and the sacraments within the church as mediating the Biblical message. Luther's shift in the understanding of the place of Scripture had two important consequences. First, Luther was convinced that Christians should be able to read the Scriptures in their own languages, and he translated the Bible into German. This set the pattern for the vernacular translations of Scripture throughout Protestantism.

Secondly, Luther assumed that anyone could find truth in the Scriptures. Therefore, they were not solely dependent on either the interpretations or the mediation of priests. In fact, for Luther there was a "priesthood of all believers" in which all believers were responsible before God for themselves and their neighbors. The degree and quality of one's religious life was not to be identified with particular religious vocations (the priesthood or monasticism). All vocations were to be practiced *religiously*. This second concept did much to blur the distinction between clergy and laity that had been so important in Catholic tradition. Luther's attitude toward the priesthood also recognized the humanity of the priests and caused him to promote clerical marriage—rejecting the idea that the celibate life is the highest or most Christian form of life.

The success of Luther's revolt against Roman Catholicism, dependent to a large extent on his political protection by a German prince, Frederick the Wise, led ultimately to the disestablishment of the traditional medieval relationship of church and state. The church in Germany came under the protection of the particular state in which it might be found. This arrangement was made possibly by the decision that each German prince should decide whether Protestantism or Catholicism would be the religion of his state. While northern Germany became Protestant, much of southern Germany remained Catholic. The pattern of state churches controlled to some extent by the secular government became normative for a large part of Protestantism. This new arrangement conformed to the rise of nationalism and contributed much to the fragmentation of modern Christian churches.

The establishment of a separate church meant modification of liturgy and other aspects of church life. Luther insisted on the importance of the sacraments but provided for their observance in the vernacular language. He made preaching (the word proclaimed) the focal point of the worship service. He could find only two sacraments—Baptism and Eucharist—to be scriptutally based (although he was inclined at times to retain confession and even to consider preaching as a sacrament). Accordingly, he reduced the seven traditional Roman Catholic sacraments to those two. Priests were urged to marry, and monasticism, no longer viewed as a higher form of Christian life, was rejected.

Lutheranism is today the predominant religious tradition of the Scandinavian countries. It has been incorporated into the Evangelisch Kirche of western Germany, and through immigration and missionary activity has spread through the world. It is one of the larger denominational traditions in America, separated into several different bodies reflecting, to some extent, their origins in separate European countries from which they were brought to America.

Reformed Traditions

By the sixteenth century, Switzerland was a loose confederation of small republican states enjoying self-rule. It was in Zurich that Ulrich Zwingli, a parish priest, began in 1522 to institute reforms similar to those of Luther. Zwingli was unyielding in his belief that the Scriptures alone were to be used as authority for Christians. This view immediately identified Zwingli with the Lutheran reform although the two were essentially unrelated. His modifications of liturgy and teachings were supported by the local city council. This political support solidified a break with Rome. In the next decade, other Swiss reformers, such as Martin Butzer and Guillaume Farel, arose. Several of the cantons (states) of Switzerland became Protestant. However, it was Geneva, under the leadership of John Calvin, that set the lasting pattern for Protestant communities which came to be known throughout Christendom as Reformed churches.

Calvin, a Frenchman who had fled France after defending Protestant reformers, brought to Protestantism an incisive mind that systematically formulated much of the Protestant position concerning doctrine and practice. As one who entered the Protestant community after its inception, Calvin generally agreed with its major tenets. He accepted Luther's "justification by faith" as the means by which humanity was to be related to God. Scripture, rather than the tradition of the church, was to be the ultimate authority. All of life was to be dedicated to God.

For Calvin, the universe was created to glorify God. The magnificence and wonder of God and His grace lie behind much of Calvin's emphasis on the centrality of God, His glory, and His power in Christian life. Calvin accepted the traditional concept of humanity's sinfulness and, as had Augustine in the early church, he taught that fallen humanity's self-centeredness made it impossible for persons to do any good by their own will or efforts. All good is to be credited to God. Fallen humanity is not free to choose good and evil, it can only choose evil. In this situation, God's gracious act of salvation comes at His discretion, to whom He wills. Humanity cannot will it or achieve it by works or even accept it when it is offered unless God makes it possible. Because all persons deserve condemnation, God's salvation of even a limited segment of humanity was seen by Calvin to be a joyous and wonderfully merciful act.

To Calvin it was a great comfort to know that God had elected at least some of humanity to salvation. This doctrine, commonly called "predestination" (see Chapter Seven), wherein some are chosen for salvation and others are not, became a hallmark of the Reformed communities. Calvin believed that the chief end of humanity is to glorify God, and he taught that humanity can best do this through clear obedience of God's will as delineated in Scripture. Since one can only trust in faith that he or she might be one of the elect, all are to live as if they are. Calvin spent much energy defining in a somewhat legal fashion what should constitute a Christian life. He based his ideas on the Scripture, emphasizing the Old Testament as a model for contemporary Christians far more than had Luther or Roman Catholicism.

Calvin also sought to institute what he considered the New Testament pattern of church and civil government in the city of Geneva. A consistory of laypersons and clergy ruled the church, which took upon itself the moral and spiritual supervision of the city. Failure to conform to the rule of the church brought excommunication. Territorial synods and presbyteries of laypersons and ministers connected individual congregations. Ministers were understood to be divinely called to their tasks but were required to receive the approval of the congregation. The civil government, divinely ordained as was the church, was to protect and promote the church and enforce its disciplines. Calvin succeeded in establishing close church-state relations, in which the church was very influential if not preeminent. Yet the pattern incorporated a congregational and republican model. Authority lay in the community (for church *and* state decisions), not in the rule or office of individuals. However, once officers were selected, they were to bring about reform in orderly ways.

Among the Reformed churches, patterns of worship were simplified. The sermon, as the proclaimed word, became the central focus. Extemporaneous prayer often replaced the formal prayers of the traditional Roman Catholic liturgy. An emphasis on teaching both in the home and in the church resulted in an ideal of highly educated laity and clergy. The insistence on a disciplined Christian life led to pietistic trends wherein vocational activity, recreation, and social life were to glorify God—one did not just attend to God in worship.

When England briefly returned to Catholicism under Queen Mary (1553-1558), Protestant leaders were exiled and some sought haven in Geneva, where they espoused Calvinistic theology. On their return to England, they were anxious to institute many of Calvin's modifications of church polity and practice. Much of the theology was in fact incorporated in Anglicanism, although the polity of Geneva was resisted. Modifications and changes of emphasis and interpretation, particularly in the doctrine of predestination, have occurred since Calvin's time, but basic elements of the Calvinistic reforms are still present in modern Reformed churches, such as the Presbyterian Church, the Church of Scotland, Dutch Reformed groups, and Congregationalists (now the United Church of Christ). Calvin's teachings have also been highly influential among English and American Baptists.

Anglicanism

The Anglicans were the third group representing a distinctive Christian tradition to arise during the Reformation. Although usually considered to be a part of the Protestant community, in fact, Anglicanism is a combination of ancient Catholic patterns of church polity and practice with some Protestant theology. Anglicanism draws its name from its historic roots in the Church of England, but modern churches in this tradition are spread worldwide, as a result of English colonial expansion. In America, this group is represented by the Protestant Episcopal—or simply the Episcopal—church.

The English break with the Church of Rome resulted from religious, political, social, and personal factors. Henry VIII, king of England and a contemporary of Luther and Calvin, headed a country that had long chafed under the political and economic power of the Holy Roman Empire as well as of the Roman church. The largest landholder in England, the Roman Church also had its own court system and generally was not as responsive or amenable to English interests as Englishmen thought it should be. Henry's rejection of the rule of the papacy had the large-scale support of his people, for they saw it as the freeing of England from foreign dominion.

The catalyst for the separation was Henry's desire to father a male heir for the English throne. Since his wife, Catherine, had not produced a male child, Henry sought the annulment of their marriage. When the Pope, under pressure from Holy Roman Emperor Charles V, who was Catherine's nephew, refused. Henry initiated actions which ultimately led to his appointment by Parliament as supreme head of the Church of England. He appointed as Archbishop of Canterbury and principal English ecclesiastical officer Thomas Cranmer. Cranmer then granted Henry his annulment. Henry's motivation was both political and personal. So far as the church was concerned, Henry appears to have had little idea that he was bringing major religious change. Under his reforms, episcopal order, liturgy, and practice were to continue in their traditional forms.

However, under the influence of Cranmer and those who followed him, an English Protestant theology rooted in the work of Wycliff, and influenced by Luther and Calvin, began to develop. Modifications of practice also appeared. Two groups emerged, those advocating the traditional Catholic theology and patterns of behavior, but not Roman control, and those seeking major Protestant modifications in theology, polity, and Christian life styles. This latter group, though divided amongst themselves, is most often referred to as Puritan for its wish to purify the church of its Romish patterns. The struggle between the two groups was intense throughout more than a century, yet the compromises imposed on the church during Queen Elizabeth's reign ultimately determined the character of the church. In essence it became a *via media* between traditional Catholicism and radical Protestantism. The Thirty-Nine Articles of Religion adopted under Elizabeth, although incorporating ancient doctrinal definitions, also reflected Protestant theological interests and assumptions. The Book of Common Prayer, also perfected under Elizabeth, incorporated with modifications the ancient rites of the Catholic church shorn of the elements most offensive to the Protestants (prayers for the dead, and so on). Clergy were required to accept the articles and to use the services of the Prayer Book in their churches. As a moderate church, the Church of England sought to identify itself with the ancient patristic period, the first four centuries of the Christian era, believing that it was reinstituting the true, original beliefs and practices of primitive Catholicism.

The Church of England reduced the sacraments to the two accepted by Protestants, but retained a stress on the efficacy of sacramental grace. Sermons were included but never became the central element in worship as they had in continental Protestant theology and practice. The parish system was kept intact, linking the appointment of parish priests and other church officials closely to political preferment. Priests were allowed to marry and monasticism was rejected.

As a state church, the Church of England has been subservient to the state but has largely influenced the ethical and moral principles of English society. In nations where church and state are separated, Anglican churches have usually combined episcopal forms of church organization with democratic participation of laymen in the governance of local congregations and the general assemblies of the church.

Other Protestant Groups

Much of modern Protestantism traces its history to the churches discussed above. Alongside these churches there have existed from the beginning a number of groups that have distinguished themselves by adhering to distinctive doctrines, attitudes, or practices, often supplemented by stringent moral teachings. Normally remaining comparatively small, some of these groups have grown, usually only when they have relaxed their restrictive life styles.

One of the earliest examples of this type of Protestant community began in Zwingli's church at Zurich. Some of his parishioners, led by their reading of the

Scripture, came to question whether there was scriptural justification for the practice of infant baptism. They came to the conclusion there was no warrant for such practice. Further, they came to believe that baptism should be accepted only by persons mature enough to choose consciously to be baptized. They proceeded to baptise each other. For that act, they came to be known as Anabaptists or Rebaptizers. Since infant baptism was for them wrong and of no effect they were in their own understanding properly baptized. The title of Baptists has followed this teaching and practice into the modern period. Soon the accepted mode of baptism among this group became immersion.

These groups and others that followed them, particularly in Holland, were also convinced that the state had no prerogative to determine the religious affiliation or beliefs of its citizens. This contrasted with most of the then-current Protestant thought, which had gained its own independence from Rome by depending on the support of local political units. Most Protestants insisted the state could and should decide which form of Christianity would be practiced in its territory. The Anabaptists essentially called for freedom of religion and separation of church and state. Holding this position, many Anabaptists had little alternative but to separate themselves from society, establishing a number of small independent societies rejecting allegiance to any state. These separated communities understood themselves to be establishing theocracies (states ruled by God). They established strict life styles, insisting on simple and unpretentious—spiritual—patterns. Both Protestants and Catholics persecuted them for threatening secular society and undermining the fabric of traditional political structure with its claim to divinely established authority.

Baptist groups that emerged in succeeding centuries accepted Anabaptist concepts of baptism and religious freedom, but frequently rejected the characteristic separation from society and refusal of political allegiance. Modern Mennonites, Amish, Brethren, and others have carried into modern times the idea of a separated society of Christians ruled by and structured on Biblical principles.

Anabaptists represent one type of sectarian group that separated itself from other Christian groups. By the middle of the seventeenth century there were many others. Each group felt itself to be the true embodiment of the faith. Out of the English Civil War (1640–1660), a struggle between Royalists (Anglicans) and Puritans, a number of such groups arose. One of the best known of these was the Quakers, or Friends. George Fox, distressed by the insincerity of nominal Christians and greatly troubled by their warring with one another, came to a religious experience which changed his concept of Christian expression. Fox taught that each person has a divine "inner light" which, if recognized, leads to spiritual truth—the revelation of Christ and the immediate awareness of his teachings. Truth therefore dwells within oneself. There is no need for church buildings, ministers, or traditional worship services. Sacraments are inward and spiritual, and therefore need no external representation. All men before God are equal, so there is no need to recognize class or cultural distinctions. Oaths are unnecessary because each Christian will by nature speak truthfully. Christians will neither go to war nor tolerate social injustice. Christian life empowered by the light will be characterized by good works accompanied by simplicity, purity, and truthfulness.

Fox's teachings gained a substantial following in the troubled times in which he lived, but also prompted persecution, because his movement rejected traditional religious and secular authority. Quaker meetings came to be occasions in which any person who felt led by the Spirit contributed to the service. Formal worship services were eliminated. Monthly meetings provided spiritual instruction, pastoral care throughout the community, and discipline of the members. William Penn brought Fox's teachings to America, establishing Quakerism in Pennsylvania, but allowing all groups to have religious freedom. Though small in numbers, Quakers have contributed ideas, leaders, and support to many causes, working on behalf of peace, race relations, human rights, and social justice.

The Anabaptists and Quakers represent sectarian movements that have spawned many differing groups since the inception of Protestantism. Proliferation of groups seeking change in cultural patterns, claiming particular spiritual inspiration or insight, or making a great variety of other claims has continued, especially in America. Most such groups are short-lived. The present diversification of Christian bodies is at least partly rooted in a characteristic Protestant conviction that each individual is capable of knowing spiritual truth and is personally responsible for expressing it—a conviction carried to extremes in Protestant sectarianism and its offshoots.

OFFSHOOTS: "DEVIATIONS AND HERETICS"

Schism and division in Christianity have most often been byproducts of particular emphases on traditional doctrines, polity or organization, or patterns of worship. A common group of basic beliefs has often been accepted, differences developing from specific nuances of interpretation, structure or liturgy.

Christianity has nevertheless witnessed a rise in the number of groups that reject orthodox understanding and practice, or sweepingly modify orthodox positions. Usually understanding themselves to be true, or more enlightened Christians, these groups have often been judged by Christians holding to traditional ways to be heretical. Heresy is, of course, a relative term—Protestants and Catholics branded each other heretics for several centuries until the more recent mutual recognition of their common kinship in Christ.

In the twelfth century, a group arose in lower Europe that strikingly exhibited some of the characteristic deviations from traditional Christianity. Known as the Cathari (or pure) in Italy and Spain, they went by the name Albigensian in France. They arose in a time when the clergy of the Catholic church were in a period of decadence, giving little moral and spiritual leadership to the people. Influenced by dualistic concepts that can be traced to the Manichaeism that attracted Augustine in the late Roman Empire, the Cathari taught that the universe contained two eternal powers, a good power represented by God and an evil power represented by Satan. The material world is the domain of the Devil where souls, which are basically good in nature, are imprisoned. Redemption comes in the freeing of souls from the dominion of the flesh. This is accomplished through repentance, a life of strict asceticism, and receiving "consolation." Those receiving consolation were the "pure," who lived strict ascetic, celibate lives of poverty and service. Recognizing that all cannot participate at this intense level, believers were allowed to live normal lives with the intent of seeking consolation before death. According to the Cathari, the role of Christ was to teach these truths to humanity. Reflecting their dualistic assumptions, they understood Christ to be a spiritual manifestation using a phantom body who did not suffer or die and thus was not resurrected. They rejected the sacraments as being forms of materialism. Their scriptures were the New Testament, spiritually interpreted, and the prophets of the Old Testament. They claimed that their teachings and practice constituted the only fully scriptural, true form of Christianity.

Extremely popular because of the moral examples set by the "Pure," the Cathari posed a real threat to Catholicism in portions of Italy, Spain, and southern France. The church responded with a crusade against them. Ultimately it instituted the Inquisition to eradicate the heresy. This campaign was so successful that by the fourteenth century the group no longer existed as an organized community.

Other divergent groups have periodically arisen throughout Christian history. From the earliest Christian centuries there have been those within the tradition who have rejected Trinitarian views of God's nature. In the second and third centuries, these persons were known as Monarchians (see Chapter Seven). They insisted on the unity, or *monarchy*, of God without recognizing an independent role in the Godhead of Christ and the Holy Spirit. Similar concerns arose during the Reformation. One of the best known anti-trinitarians of Reformation times was Michael Servetus, burned at the stake in Calvin's Geneva for his beliefs. Anti-trinitarians also found adherents in Poland and Hungary and became an organized movement in seventeenth-century England.

Modern forms of anti-trinitarianism have become known as Unitarianism. In America, the first recognized Unitarian community appeared at King's Chapel, Boston, in 1785. It became popular among traditional Congregationalists in the early nineteenth century and greatly influenced the Divinity School of Harvard University which until then had been firmly Calvinist. American Unitarianism tended to take a rationalistic view of the concept of God and was critical of traditional Christian formulations such as the doctrines of original sin and Calvinism's predestinarianism.

Modern American Unitarianism has become a broad-based religious community no longer officially committed to *any* official doctrinal definitions, Christian or otherwise. In fact, the Unitarian-Universalist Association encourages and even mandates its members to formulate personal creeds, or religious and moral convictions. Many contemporary Unitarians see religious truth as best expressed in commitment to social justice, to causes like those the Quakers have advocated.

A third pattern of divergence from traditional Christianity is represented by the Church of Jesus Christ of the Latter-day Saints. This American religious group arose in response to the teachings of Joseph Smith in the early nineteenth century. Smith, a native of upstate New York, claimed to have received a divine revelation from an Angel named Moroni. The revelation was the *Book of Mormon* (from this work the group takes its more common name, Mormon) engraved on gold plates, which Smith was divinely empowered to translate into English. The revelations given to Smith were many and elaborate. Principal among these were revelations about early American inhabitants who were descendents of refugees from the Tower of Babel. After great struggle in America, these people died, leaving their message in the *Book of Mormon*. According to its teachings, Jesus will return, gather the ten lost tribes of Israel in America and reign in a new Zion, or perfected world. Smith continued to receive revelations incorpoated into several books, the most important of which is *Doctrines and Covenants*. His revelations included the teaching that all persons ultimately will receive salvation and that believers will ultimately become gods. Among Mormons, the *Book of Mormon, Doctrines and Covenants*, and the Bible are considered to be scripture.

Smith, who was killed by a mob, was succeeded by Brigham Young. Young led a large segment of the group to Utah to escape the persecution they had experienced in the East and Midwest.

The Mormons, believing that there is a continual revelation through their leaders, developed close-knit communities. Family solidarity and responsibilities figured very prominently, and today Mormons have successfully attracted a large following throughout the world. By and large, they are socially and politically conservative, in spite of a now abandoned early practice of polygamy. Many of their beliefs distinguish them from orthodox forms of Christianity. The principal one of these is their claim to new and continual divine revelation to their leaders supplementing that given in ancient Palestine, recorded in the Bible, and interpreted by the doctrinal standards and creeds of the ancient church.

CHRISTIAN MYSTICISM

Religion, by its very nature, is concerned with aspects of life that transcend human limitations and comprehension, manifested in the spiritual dimension. One of these aspects involves the search for direct personal encounters with God. Such religious or spiritual encounters are understood in Christianity to be possible in a variety of forms, from the sense of *awe* or sacredness in the sacramental practices of the faithful to the sense of immediate union with God proclaimed by Christian mystics. Most Christian traditions have stressed personal knowledge of God, and therefore have known some aspects of mystical encounter. Eastern Christianity, with its more prominent spirituality, has throughout its history displayed high respect for the full mystical experience. In the West, where the practical and rational approaches to life have dominated, mysticism has been a more unusual phenomenon, but certainly it has been present in many of the variant branches of Western Christianity.

Mystical patterns are found in most religious communities. Christian mysticism is distinguished from other forms of mysticism in two significant ways. Because of its theistic orientation, Christian mysticism has normally rejected pantheistic concepts of the Divine. God and the universe are understood by Christianity to be distinct, so in Christian mysticism one is not discovering the Divine present in all reality including the material universe (the pantheistic concept) but rather is in contact with the Being that transcends all sense-perceived, discursively known reality, a reality distinct from His creation. Christian mystics, therefore, do not claim in their union with God to become God or to lose their human nature. While there is union of the wills, two distinct beings remain in the mystical experience. This concept distinguishes Christian mysticism from much religious mystical experience, including that of the Hindu and the Buddhist traditions.

Contrary to common assumptions, Christian mysticism has not been confined to the solitary saints seeking, through ascetic contemplation, individual union with God that distinguishes and separates them from the world. Mystics may and often do live quite active lives in the secular world. Mysticism is usually understood to follow a pattern in which the participant moves through purification from the self interests that tie one to the material world, to illumination in which one is certain in one's own life and being of God's love, and finally to a union of wills so that one's own being is immersed in the indwelling love of God. Union does not occur without discipline and dedication, but neither is it simply a personal achievement. It is a divine gift and carries with it fruits of humility, charity, and loving service often accompanied by suffering. St. Teresa of Avila, a sixteenth-century Spanish mystic, spent years in cloistered solitude moving through the mystical stages, yet the last portion of her life was spent organizing contemplative communities, teaching others about mysticism, and serving others. Christian mysticism is ordinarily expected to be displayed in a new life of service—the fruit of the experience.

A comprehensive catalogue of Christian mystics and their influence is beyond the scope of this account. Such a list would begin with Paul, the writer of the Gospel of John, St. Augustine, and St. Anthony. St. Francis, Meister Eckhart, and John Tauler offered a mystical response to the medieval involvement of the church in the materialistic grandeur of the age. One of the responses to the problems addressed by the Protestant Reformation was a renewal within Roman Catholicism of the mystical tradition. The Spanish mystics St. Teresa, St. John of the Cross, and St. Ignatius Loyola were active during this period. Jacob Boehme, George Fox, and William Law are examples of Protestant mystics in the sixteenth and seventeenth centuries. Modern spirituality has experienced a renewal of interest as humanity responds to the extremes of rationalism and secularism. This is supported by the tendency of modern psychology to give credence to the extrasensory, paranormal, and spiritual dimensions of life. Modern mystics influential in Christian life include Catholics Thomas Merton, Henri Nouwen, and Carlo Carretto; Protestants Rufus M. Jones, Evelyn Underhill, Muriel Lester, and Thomas Kelly; and Eastern Orthodox Christians Anthony Bloom and the anonymous author of *The Way of a Pilgrim*.

POPULAR RELIGION

Doctrine, organizational structure, and forms of worship do not merely separate differing Christian groups from each other. These elements often serve to create, strengthen, and transmit unity from community to community and from generation to generation. Perhaps even more important than these formal aspects of Christian tradition as sources of unity and meaning for groups and individuals have been the elements of popular religion. These are aspects of religious feeling and practice that sometimes go unnoticed in studies of religious history. Popular religion often provides a focus for family, congregational, and community-wide participation in religious groups and tradition.

Like most other religious traditions, Christianity observes a number of holidays commemorating events important to its history. For Christianity many of these holidays are based on Biblical or ecclesiastical happenings. Their observance may be prescribed in the liturgical calendars of the different Christian denominations. Christmas and Easter, commemorating the birth and resurrection of Jesus, respectively, probably are the two most widely celebrated of Christian holiday periods. Aspects of these holidays that may make the largest impact on participants frequently are those that have grown up spontaneously in popular tradition or even those that have been commercially promoted by secular interests. Santa Claus and the exchange of gifts and Christmas cards, going caroling, going to parties, perhaps an annual school Christmas pageant, or the community-sponsored performance of an oratorio like Handel's *Messiah* have come to symbolize Christmas for many individuals.

Various informally developed customs associated with the sacraments or with quasi-sacramental practices—marriages in Protestantism or wakes before funerals—may create bonds of unity and a sense of community among adherents. A Wednesday night church supper, regular participation at a church-sponsored bingo night, or the church's softball team may be a primary focus of religious identification and loyalty.

If one understands only the official theology and polity of a denomination, it is difficult to see which aspects of religious meaning are most alive to its adherents. In the Middle Ages in Europe, the importance of seeing and receiving benefit from various religious relics, alleged or genuine, became very great. Enough fragments of Christ's cross were supposed to have been in Europe to provide materials for several large buildings. These and a multitude of other relics, including branches from the burning bush associated with Moses' call, became objects of pilgrimage to many of the faithful. The crusades provided a rich body of fact and legend that appealed to popular imagination. Miracle and mystery plays, dramatizations of the Biblical stories by the guilds and crafts utilizing amateur talent, created comradeship. They were also eduational devices for whole towns and villages.

The revivals and camp meetings of frontier America were not only an important method of denominational recruitment but occasions for recreation, socializing, and finding marriage partners. Twentieth-century television evangelists make use of the most sophisticated methods of programming and public-relations techniques, copying the style, and at times employing the same performers, as those appearing on popular variety shows.

Stories of contemporary appearances of Christ, the Virgin Mary and other saints, often with special messages of encouragement for groups or individuals, have in most periods of Christian history generated ferver and devotion. During the past century reports of such appearances in Portugal (the Miracle of Fatima) and France (at Lourdes) have received acceptance and approval by the Roman Catholic hierarchy. Lourdes has become an important site of pilgrimage with many accounts of miraculous healings.

Apocalyptic speculations associated with signs of the end of the world or the transition from one spiritual age to another have also had large appeal. In the Middle Ages, the speculations of the Franciscan Joachim of Flora generated enthusiasm and scattered movements that became embroiled in conflict with the leadership of Catholicism. During the past two centuries, apocalyptic speculation has flourished among some Protestant groups and their offshoots. Only a few years ago, an American sect called the Children of God stimulated widespread reports that Jesus would return to the earth in 1975. There were many reports of preliminary appearances alleged to have already occurred. Reports of these appearances, usually second- or third-hand, were spread by word of mouth. At various times throughout Christian history, including the present, small or large groups have sold their possessions, abandoned secular occupations, and withdrawn to remote sites to await the visible return of Christ.

Often denominational leaders, sensitive to the moods, anxieties, and aspirations of the rank and file of their organizations and communities, have been able to make use of popular forms of cultural expression and symbols of cultural quest to give powerful new expression to the content of Christian faith. Some of the medieval Popes, as well as popular saints like Francis and Clare of Assisi, and, in our times, Thérèse of Lisieux, utilized forms of popular culture to revitalize Christian expression. Martin Luther and John and Charles Wesley also did this, especially as they developed new forms of Christian congregrational music and new forms of sermon and popular religious literature.

Sometimes Christian leaders are appalled at the forms that popular devotion and enthusiasm take, fearing the dangers of superstition and crude distortion that these can give to the content of Christian faith and life. Oftentimes, leaders are alarmed at the vast potential for exploitation of the gullible faithful by calculating charlatans. In contemporary America, there have been active magazine and radio campaigns to sell various guaranteed miraculous healing devices including prayer cloths, drops of water from the Jordan River, and "autographed pictures of Jesus Christ."

Despite the risk of superficiality and exploitation, popular forms of religious expression are probably indispensable keys to the understanding of what being an adherent to a particular denomination in a particular setting means. Popular religion indeed often tells us better than anything else what "being a Christian" means and has meant to the majority of Christians across the centuries.

CONTEMPORARY CHRISTIANITY IN EUROPE AND AMERICA: A CASE STUDY

Since the sixteenth century, humanity's understanding of itself and its world has vastly changed through modified pilosophical world views, expanded knowledge of the universe in its macrocosmic and microcosmic aspects, technological innovations that have modified physical existence, and new economic and political ideologies. Such change has demanded change in the structure and expression of Christianity. Basic theological issues and beliefs have continued to revolve around the purpose and role of humanity in relation to God and His will for the universe. Differing answers to these questions and modified structures in Christian groups have contributed greatly to the diversification of modern Christianity.

Influenced by these vast changes, medieval Christianity's monolithic synthesis of knowledge and life gave way to immense diversification in Christian thought, practice, and life styles. Although changes were slower in the East, the blending of religion and culture there has also changed. Russian Orthodoxy's continuing existence in frankly secular, atheistic society is a curious paradox of our time.

The present-day divisions among Christians in Europe are a direct consequence of the Reformation. Northern Europe, which was much more amenable to Protestantism, formulated its major church patterns in the century that followed the Reformation. Many of these still exist in the form of state churches based on the assumption that all citizens are members of the established church. Within these countries, however, religious freedom is normally accepted, so that an array of independent voluntary churches exists alongside state churches. The status of these groups may vary from country to country, but they are dependent on their members for support and evangelical enlistment. Proliferation of Christian groups in Europe has been slow since the seventeenth and eighteenth centuries—especially when compared to that characteristic of American Christianity.

European Protestant theologians led the critical literary study of Scriptures in the nineteenth and twentieth centuries wherein traditional concepts of the faith were examined using sociological, psychological, and historical tools (see Chapter Two). Their liberal theological stance gave a larger role to humanity and its capacities, and it contributed to the rise of modern Christian concerns for social, economic, and political justice. To conservatives, such inquiry often appeared to result in a questioning of basic Christian beliefs and the dilution of distinctive Christian moral and ethical standards.

Nineteenth- and twentieth-century Europe also experienced a revolution in the understanding of human life. Humanity came to be seen as self-sufficient and capable of solving the problems of life given time, discipline, and energy. This attitudinal change was accompanied by a process of secularization in which most of the social functions traditionally related to religion were assumed by the state or other social institutions. For many Europeans, this meant Christian thought and practice were reduced to a secondary, if not irrelevant, position. Individual participation in the outward forms of religion has fallen to an extremely low level. Culturally, much of the European ethical and moral pattern remains clearly based on Christian principles. Publicly, religion continues to be recognized as significant. Renewal of interest in religious issues has, nevertheless, been under way in recent years. Evangelical Christian groups and groups representing religions other than Christianity have found fertile fields in portions of Europe.

European Roman Catholics (mostly in southern Europe) responded to the Reformation by eliminating many of the abuses objected to by Protestants. However, in defending themselves against some of the innovations of the Protestants they tended to solidify the traditional teachings and patterns of the church. As a result, the authoritarian episcopal structure separating clergy and laity continued. Theological change was discouraged and the patterns of Christian life dependent on penance and the other sacraments remained in place. This conservative perspective unified the church, which retained a strong influence in the Southern European countries. Recently, however, it has experienced increasing disaffection in some strata of society, especially the working classes and intellectuals influenced by modern ideologies such as socialism or anarchism. The changes in European culture detailed above were slower in coming to southern Europe, but did bring forms of modern political and economic change. The Roman church continued to be the state church in most countries, and religious freedom came for many only in the twentieth century.

An essentially conservative perspective made it increasingly difficult for the Roman church to cope with the realities of modern society. Recognizing this, important nineteenth- and twentieth-century leaders, including Popes Leo XIII and Pius XI, called for greater social justice and addressed the needs of members of the working class uprooted by economic change and often barred from full participation in society. More recently, responding to the threat of nuclear war, the plight of the poor in the third world, and a need for greater Christian unity, Pope John XXIII called the Second Vatican Council in 1962. John not only invited the bishops of the Roman church but observers and representatives from other Christian communities. By this act he recognized the existence and relevance of other Christian groups—a fact Catholicism had been reluctant to acknowledge. The council took many steps to modify the Roman church. An expanded role was given to the bishops as counselors to the Pope. The church was defined as a "pilgrim church" in which both clergy *and* laity have significant roles. Liturgy was allowed in vernacular languages and modifications created new liturgical patterns. More conciliatory positions were pronounced relative to non-Christian religions and there emerged a new openness toward ecumenical involvement with other Christian bodies and individuals. Emphasis on scripture as a coordinate authority with tradition gave it a more central place in worship, private study, and devotion. Such changes in the tradition of the church brought modifications in attitude and practice that perhaps were unanticipated by the Council and caused some Catholics to think that the Pope and the Council had gone too far.

Nevertheless, they clearly made the church more responsive to the needs of modern culture. Also, John XXIII addressed two masterful and revolutionary papal letters—encyclicals—to Catholics and, in the case of the second letter, to all persons of good will throughout the world. *Mater et Magistra* (1961), one of the most electrifying documents to come under a Pope's signature, and the equally forceful *Pacem in Terris* (1963) called for worldwide efforts to eliminate human need, achieve social justice, and reverse the threat of war and possible nuclear destruction. Such efforts on behalf of peace, justice, and global understanding have been continued by Pope John's successors, Paul VI and John Paul II.

Developments in European thought and practice have until recent years anticipated changes taking place in America. Christian thought has followed the lead of European theologians through much of American history. However, the new setting of Christianity provided a different social climate for its practice. Differences between American and European Christianity have been present from the earliest colonial period. The state churches that existed in the Colonial period gradually ceased to exist after the principle of separation of church and state was incorporated into the fabric of America life. Largely Protestant in its early history, American Christianity epitomized the diversity of thought, structure, and practice that evolved during the Reformation. In America, the spirit of individualism and the sense of progressive change nurtured a climate where new Christian denominations continually arose to meet personal, social, and theological needs. Such patterns continue to be a part of the American scene. Although the majority of Christians are found in the ten to fifteen largest denominations, 1980 figures showed at least 250 denominations with more than one or two congregations. If all of the single-congregation churches were added to these figures, several hundred other denominations would be added to these numbers.

America has been broadly affected by the same intellectual and cultural changes that have wrought the modern transformation of Europe. American responses have sometimes paralleled those of Europe, but in the area of religion, the differences are obvious. Because religious groups in America are voluntary and aggressively recruit members, American church participation has continued to be substantial. Over sixty-eight percent of adult Americans claim some church affiliation. Public practice of religion remains relatively high despite slackening interest in recent decades. America's mainline denominations are large enough to include within themselves persons of many theological persuasions and practices. As a result, it has sometimes been said that conservatives of one denomination may be closer to conservatives of another denomination than to liberals of their own denomination. The same may be said of liberals. Large denominations tend to include persons of very diverse theological positions and many social and cultural backgrounds. Mainline denominations tend to offer pluralistic ministries to meet the needs of various groups. Smaller denominations are often more unified in theological and social positions and enforce stricter discipline on their members. They may reach elements of society who feel neglected by mainline groups.

While the changing intellectual and theological climate of the nineteenth and twentieth centuries was welcomed by many, especially in America, it was also resisted by conservatives in mainline denominations and among many adherents of smaller religious groups. These persons held to their views of Biblical infallibility and rejected the optimistic views concerning human abilities taught by liberalism. Such attitudes were incorporated in various movements such as that revolving around the Moody Bible Institute in Chicago. *The Fundamentals*, a twelve volume publication published privately from 1909-1915, stated the case against the innovations in religious teachings. The Five Fundamentals supported by this movement were: the verbal inerrancy of Scripture, the deity of Jesus, the virgin birth, substitutionary atonement, and the physical resurrection and bodily return of Christ. While probably not everyone in the movement agreed entirely with the tenets stated in *The Fundamentals*, together they constituted a strong element of resistance to the changes in the churches to accommodate new ideas and trends within the society.

Emphases among conservatives have changed since the beginning of the century, but the general sentiment has remained strong. Often known now by the broad title Evangelicals and incorporating a greater variety of interests than traditional fundamentalists, the movement has experienced substantial expansion in recent years. Seminaries representing the interests of the movement have become recognized and are generously supported. Radio and television evangelists have created a whole new phenomenon of electronic ministries cutting across traditional denominational lines with a conservative Bible-centered message. Many have also sought to influence political and moral issues in the nation. Through support of scholarships and endowments, attempts have been made to influence the academic theological community, the traditional stronghold of liberal theological innovations. The liberal-conservative polarity, always present in American religion, does not appear to have lessened, though its forms continue to change.

Although Roman Catholicism entered America with the Spanish missionaries and was one of the earliest American religious groups, its strength came with nineteenth-century European migration into the country. In America, Catholicism served as a conservative force. It gave many immigrants a feeling of unity and continuity with their origins. In its new cultural setting, however, American Catholicism became progressive, calling for change and modernization within the church. Though questioned by some conservatively oriented Catholics, Vatican II and its modifications have been welcomed by many Americans as a step toward making the church relevant to the times.

QUESTIONS

1. From the information contained in the chapter how would you account for both the unity and diversity present in modern Christianity?

2. Compare and contrast the principal characteristics of eastern Orthodoxy with those of western Catholicism.

3. Roman emphases in thought and life tended to be practical and often cast in legal modes. What were the consequences of these emphases on the development of western theology and practice?

4. What did Martin Luther mean by the "priesthood of all believers?" How did that belief contrast with traditional Roman Catholic concepts of the priesthood?

5. What were the major branches of the Protestant Reformation? How did they contrast with each other?

6. What were the characteristics of the Anabaptists that separated them from their fellow Protesants? How were they viewed by other Protestants and Roman Catholics?

7. On the basis of which concepts of authority did the Quakers reject traditional patterns of Christian worship?

8. On what bases are religious groups usually labeled as deviations from the norm within Christian tradition? List and comment on several of these groups.

9. How is Christian mysticism distinguished from mystical motifs and patterns in other religions?

10. In what ways does the modern setting of Christianity contribute to its diversity? Is this a threat to Christianity or one of its strengths? Explain.

FURTHER READING

ABBOTT, WALTER, ed., *The Documents of Vatican II.* New York: Herder and Herder, 1966.

AUCLAIR, MARCELLE, *Teresa of Avila,* trans. Kathleen Pond. New York: Doubleday and Co., 1959.

BAINTON, ROLAND H., *Here I Stand: A Life of Martin Luther.* Nashville, Tenn.: Abingdon Press, 1960.

BOEHMER, HEINRICH, *Road to Reformation.* Philadelphia, Penn.: Muhlenberg Press, 1946.

BRAITHWAITE, W. C., *The Beginnings of Quakerism.* Cambridge, Mass.: Cambridge University Press, 1961.

BROMILY, G. W., *Zwingli and Bullinger,* Philadelphia, Penn.: The Westminster Press, 1953.

BURNS, E. M., *The Counter Reformation.* Princeton, N.J.: Princeton University Press, 1964.

CANNON, W. R., *History of Christianity in the Middle Ages.* New York: Abingdon Press, 1960.

CHADWICK, OWEN, *The Popes and the European Revolution,* Oxford: Clarendon Press, 1980.

CLEBSCH, WILLIAM A., *England's Earliest Protestants.* New Haven, Conn.: Yale University Press, 1964.

CORBETT, JAMES, *The Papacy: A Brief History.* Princeton, N.J.: Van Nostrand Co. Inc., 1966.

DICKENS, A. C. *The English Reformation.* New York: Schocken Books, Inc., 1964.

DÖRRIES, HERMANN, *Constantine the Great.* New York: Harper and Row, Publishers, 1972.

FURLONG, MONICA, *Merton: A Biography.* San Francisco, Calif.: Harper and Row, Inc., 1980.

FOX, GEORGE, *Journal of George Fox.* Cambridge, England: Cambridge University, 1952.

HALLER, WILLIAM, *The Rise of Puritanism.* New York: Columbia University Press, 1938.

HANSEN, KLAUS J., *Mormonism and the American Experience.* Chicago, Ill.: University of Chicago Press, 1981.

KNOWLES, DAVID, *The Nature of Mysticism.* New York: Hawthorn Books, 1966.

_____. *Christian Monasticism.* New York: McGraw-Hill Book Company, 1969.

_____. *The Middle Ages.* New York: McGraw-Hill Book Company, 1968.

LITTELL, FRANKLIN, *The Anabaptist View of the Church.* Boston, Mass.: Star King Press, 1958.

_____. *The Origins of Sectarian Protestantism.* New York: The Macmillan Company, 1968.

MCNEILL, J. T., *The History and Character of Calvinism.* New York: Oxford University Press, 1954.

MEYERDORFF, JEAN, *The Orthodox Church.* trans. John Chapin. Nashville, Tenn.: Pantheon Books, 1962.

MODULE, JACQUES, *The Albigensian Crusade: An Historical Essay.* trans. Barbara Ware. New York: Fordham University Press, 1967.

NOUWEN, HENRI, *Thomas Merton, Contemplative Critic.* San Francisco, Calif.: Harper and Row, Inc., 1980.

OUTLER, ALBERT, *John Wesley,* New York: Oxford University Press, 1964.

SCHMEMANN, ALEXANDER, *The Historical Road of Eastern Orthodoxy,* trans. Lydia W. Kesich. New York: Holt, Rinehart, and Winston, 1963.

SYKES, NORMAN, *The English Religious Tradition.* London: SCM Press, 1953.

UNDERHILL, EVELYN, *Mysticism,* New York: E. P. Dutton and Co. Inc., 1930.

WARE, TIMOTHY, *The Orthodox Church.* Baltimore, Md.: Penguin Books, 1951.

WARNER, H. J., *The Albigensian Heresy.* New York: Russell and Russell, 1967.

WILLIAMS, GEORGE, *The Radical Reformation.* Philadelphia, Penn.: The Westminster Press, 1962.

WORKMAN, H. B., *The Evolution of the Monastic Ideal.* London: Epworth Press, 1927.

chapter six
FAITH
AND KNOWLEDGE

MONOTHEISTIC FAITH
AND THE KNOWLEDGE OF GOD

Behavioral scientists who study religion as a factor in individual and group behavior frequently warn against overemphaisizing the belief or cognitive side of religion. Although most religious traditions do involve beliefs—for instance beliefs about the nature of God or the gods, and about the origins of the natural universe and the relation of humans to it and the Divine—the belief-claims of a religion may be relatively unimportant in comparison to other aspects of the religion. The way of life it sanctions (moral code) or the cultic and ritual celebrations that make it a focus of group and individual identity are equally important. In a novel that gives a popular but well-informed and accurate fictional portrayal of a Jewish rabbi who uses the methods of Talmudic interpretation to solve crimes, Harry Kemelman has Rabbi David Small say this about the belief side of Judaism:

> One immediate difference between Judaism and many other religions is that we're not bound by an official creed. With us, it's largely an accident of birth. If you're born a Jew, you're a Jew at least until you convert to some other religion. An atheist who was born a Jew is therefore a Jew.[1]

[1] Harry Kemelman, *Tuesday the Rabbi Saw Red* (New York: E. P. Dutton, Inc., 1975), p. 50. Used by permission of the publisher.

Kemelman's character stresses not only that holding specific beliefs is not the criterion of one's being a Jew, though certainly it would be possible to speak about the characteristic belief-claims, or credal content, of Judaism. He emphasizes that, from the point of view of many Jews, living according to the religion's moral and ritual code is a matter of much greater importance than is affirming characteristic Jewish beliefs.

Similar considerations may hold for many Christian groups. However, throughout the history of Christianity and for many Christian groups and denominations, there has been a greater concern about defining and justifying religious beliefs than has been characteristic of most (or perhaps of any) of the other major religious traditions of the world. Characteristically, Christians—especially the leaders of most Christian groups—have held that it is important to know what one is supposed, as a Christian, to believe. Indeed, for many groups it has been held that all adult Christians should understand, if not be able to justify, the basic Christian beliefs.

There are several reasons for the emphasis among Christians on defining, understanding, and justifying Christian beliefs.

1. The early conflict between Christians and Jews (discussed in Chapter Three) concerning the correct interpretation of the Jewish Scriptures caused Christians to seek and emphasize methods for the precise definition and interpretation of scriptural teachings.

2. Christianity arose and spread throughout the non-Jewish parts of the Roman Empire during a period in which many philosophical schools flourished. Some of these schools (Stoicism and Epicureanism, for instance) made dogmatic claims about the truth of their teachings.

Although early Christian teachers and writers found much to admire in the moral code of Stoicism, they rejected what they thought of as its crudely materialistic concept of God. The Stoics thought of God as the divine element fire, from which successive universes emerge and to which they return. Stoics believed mature humans were able to grasp the intelligible order of things and the rational moral law that should govern human conduct, because human reason is a spark of the divine reason, or logos. The Stoics emphasized a life founded on acceptance of the divine rationality, dedicated to doing one's duty in all circumstances. They advocated a life of virtuous self-control.

Christians found little to admire in Epicurean philosophy. Epicurus, a Greek philosopher of the fourth century B.C.E., accepted the theory of Democritus that all reality, including the human mind or soul, and even the gods, is composed of atoms. Thus humans and gods were held to be mortal. Epicureanism was a secular approach to life that sought to deliver humanity from religious superstition, including belief in or fear of an afterlife.

Other philosophical schools advocated positions of *scepticism*, holding that nothing can be known with certainty. Thus, the need to combat both the dogmatism of philosophical schools that seemed to teach doctrines contrary to the major themes of Christianity and sceptical positions that denied that Christians or others could arrive at a sure grasp of truth contributed to the Christian emphasis on precise definition and justification of belief.

3. In order to justify not merely their religious beliefs and practices but their very legal right to exist as a religious movement within the Roman Empire, Christians also appealed to philosophical arguments and the teachings of Greek and Roman philosophers to oppose the polytheistic beliefs of popular Roman, Greek, and Asiatic religious cults of the day. As early as the sixth century B.C.E., Xenophanes and other Greek philosophers had ridiculed the anthropomorphic polytheism of Greek civic and cultic religion. Later, Socrates, Plato, and Aristotle condemned popular views of the gods that made them only glorified humans, with human vices magnified (*e.g.*, vindictiveness, spite, jealousy, and sexual promiscuity). Christian preachers and writers used the arguments of Greek philosophical thinkers to support monotheism and to argue for the credibility of Christian claims.

Among the earliest Christian apologetic writings—writings that attempted to give a reasoned defense and justification of the Christian religion—are treatises addressed to the Roman Emperors Antoninus Pius and Marcus Aurelius (the famed Stoic philosopher) by Justin Martyr, a second-century Christian Platonist. The complex of philosophical doctrines, methods, and attitudes known as Platonism seemed to many of the earliest Christian thinkers to be most congenial to the spirit of Christianity. Justin (ca. 100-165 C.E.), before his conversion to Christianity, was a Platonic philosopher. As a young man, he sought philosophic enlightenment from various schools. Stoic materialism repelled him, as did Pythagorean insistence on the study of mathematics as a necessary condition of philosophical insight. An Aristotelian philosopher impressed him as interested only in the fees he could collect. However, among the Platonists Justin believed that he found true wisdom.

By Justin's time, Platonism had gone through a varied and complex history. Though Plato (ca. 428-348 B.C.E.) believed that ultimate philosophical insight must be born in the process of dialogue and inquiry and cannot be adequately expressed in writing, certain Platonic doctrines formed the basis of the inquiries of his immediate successors in Athens at the Academy, a research center that Plato had founded and directed. Among these doctrines were (1) that reality is ultimately spiritual rather than material; (2) that the material realm is in a state of constant flux, making our knowledge of it at best uncertain; (3) that the true realities are eternal, unchanging forms or patterns, which material realities at best imitate or mirror or in which they participate; (4) that our minds (reason) can know these forms through intellectual insight or intuition if we rise above attention to sense experience and the distractions of bodily appetite and concentrate on seeking a vision of the ideal, spiritual, and eternal; and (5) that since our minds or souls possess the capacity to rise from the material to the spiritual, we are in fact immortal and in some sense, at least potentially, divine.

Platonism evolved through a phase of intense interest in abstract, mathematical analysis of philosophical truth into a phase of philosophical scepticism emphasizing the uncertainties of the material realm, and the worthlessness of sense experience as a source of knowledge. In fact, for several centuries, in marked contrast to Plato's optimism about the power of the mind to grasp eternal truth, the Platonic school, opposing Stoic dogmatism, was one of the major sources of sceptical philosophy. However, by Justin's time there had been a revival of a non-sceptical form of Platonism. This revival resulted in the so-called Middle Platonism, which was especially strong during the secondary century C.E. Middle Platonism was characterized by an emphasis on the reality of the spiritual and the need to cultivate the soul by virtuous life, religious piety, and philosophical inquiry. An emphasis on the Divine or Supreme Reality, God as holy, transcendent, far removed from the material world but approachable through religious reverence, moral self-discipline and philosophical quest, made Middle Platonism congenial to Christianity with its roots in a Jewish monotheism that also emphasized the transcendent remoteness but nearness to human life of the Creator. After his conversion to Christianity, Justin continued to profess this philosophy and possibly should be thought of as one of the important second century Middle Platonists. (See Chapter Three for discussion of Justin's understanding of scripture.)

4. Later controversies, either between Christians and non-Christians—for instance, Muslims of the early Middle Ages who used Greek doctrines and methods of analysis to interpret and state Islamic beliefs—or controversies among Christian groups reinforced and contributed to the Christian tendency to emphasize correct definition, understanding, and interpretation of belief. Many Christian groups have moved closer to each other in their willingness to find agreement in patterns of belief during the past few decades. In earlier centuries some of these groups mutually *defined* their positions *against* each other. Catholic belief was defined *against* Lutheran or Anglican belief, Methodist (Arminian) *against* Presbyterian or Baptist (Calvinist).

5. Finally, the rise of modern Western scientific theorizing and procedures emphasizing precision and experimental verification has not only presented challenges to Christian belief and raised questions about the compatibility of religious belief with the results, methods, and attitudes—the thought-style—of science, but has contributed to new fashions of thought. The sharp emphasis on objectivity, precision, and verifiability in science has given rise to dichotomies affecting the interpretation of religion that, if they existed at all in earlier societies, were not felt nearly as sharply as they have been in Western societies since the seventeenth century. For instance, the meaning of any religious belief, since the rise of scientific thought, must be assessed by asking whether it is meant literally or symbolically, whether it claims metaphysical, historical, or mythical truth or significance, whether it is to be interpreted in the same way that a specific or factual claim might be treated or in some other way, perhaps in some special religious way.

All of these factors, then, have contributed to the emphasis within varying Chrisitan groups and traditions on the importance of the belief or credal aspect of Christianity—not just the importance of holding certain beliefs, but the importance of being able to define, understand, and justify them. Still, though, Christianity, like Judaism and Middle Platonism, has emphasized God's ultimate transcendence of all finite realities. Thus, one of the major questions for Christian belief has been: How is it possible, or is it possible, for limited, finite human minds to know and understand the infinite, transcendent God? To what extent are human reason and language necessary or useful or adequate in helping us to know God or to understand and communicate religious truth?

DISCLOSURE AND FAITHFULNESS

It is frequently noted that in contrast to theistic Greek philosophers like Plato and Aristotle, the authors whose writings are found in the Jewish Scriptures did not develop rational proofs for the existence of God or rational analyses of the divine nature. Aristotle, for instance, *proves* the necessity of God's existence in order to explain how and why the physical universe is kept in motion. By rational analysis, he shows that God must be an eternal, unchanging reality, perfectly actual (*i.e.*, without imperfection, incompleteness, or potential for change) whose nature it is to *think* what is eternal and intelligible (*i.e.*, God eternally thinks His own consciousness). Aristotle's manner of thinking and writing is foreign in tone and substance to the Jewish Scriptures. In them, one finds historical narratives in which the authors hold that God has acted and revealed himself; writings that praise God for His goodness, power, wisdom, and faithfulness as revealed both in His acts and in the natural world which He has created; and a legal and moral code governing human interaction held to be directly revealed by God.

In the Jewish Scriptures, there are frequent assertions that God has revealed Himself to specific human beings and groups before they knew Him, almost always before they knew Him fully. The account in the first few chapters of the Book of Exodus of the freeing of the Hebrew tribes from Egyptian slavery is a good example of the Hebrew attitude. Moses, who is pictured as having fled from Egypt because he has killed an Egyptian taskmaster while trying to rescue a Hebrew from mistreatment, finds refuge with Midianite tribesmen. One day while tending flocks in the vicinity of a holy mountain, he receives a divine summons. The summons is in the form of a bush that is burning without being consumed. Moses, approaching the bush, hears a voice that identifies itself as the God of the fathers of the enslaved Israelites—Abraham, Isaac, and Jacob—and Moses is commanded by the voice to return to Egypt and bring a message to the Israelites that their God—whom they seem to have forgotten—will lead them from Egypt and give them a land of their own. Moses is fearful both that the Israelites will not know who the God of their fathers is and that the Egyptian ruler will not recognize this God's authority or power, but God promises to put his seal on Moses' authority by *signs*. God will reveal His power and Moses' role as His spokesman through mighty acts. There follows an account several chapters long of the contest between the Egyptian pharaoh's stubborn will and the power of God as manifested in the successively more impressive and frightening displays of His power, the culmination of which is the safe passage of the Israelites through the Sea of Reeds (Red Sea) as the sea opens for them, only to close on the pharaoh's army, drowning the Egyptians, once the Isralites are safe (Exodus 1-15).

For the Jewish Scriptures, the major problem is not *how* to arrive at knowledge of God through the use of reason. Rather, it is how to respond fittingly and appropriately to God's self-disclosure. Pharaoh did not, indeed could not, respond appropriately to God because his heart was hardened. The appropriate response would have been reverence, willingness to act in accordance with God's will, faithfulness in doing this, and gratitude for God's self-disclosure and His faithfulness in carrying out His revealed purposes. Not only in the early period of Israel's history but throughout the prophetic period, extending into the time of postexilic Judaism, it was expected that God would frequently disclose Himself through specially chosen agents—prophets called to speak for God, priestly figures or seers, people who in special circumstances bore the divine word, and performers of signs that could leave no doubt about the presence and will of God.

However, another avenue beyond that of such special revelations of God's reality and will increasingly came to be emphasized in Jewish belief. Especially writings in the Jewish Wisdom tradition (Proverbs, Job, Ecclesiastes), the hymns and sacred poetry of Israel (Psalms), and the writings of some of the prophets (*e.g.*, Isaiah 40-55) stress that reflection on natural processes and the experiences of daily life will result in knowledge of God's nature and His will. According to these writings, the natural order reveals its Creator—a powerful God who is just, wise, and faithful to those who are faithful to Him.

The Twenty-ninth Psalm is a hymn of praise that sees God's dynamic power revealed in the storm. In fact, the Psalms are full of images drawn from the natural realm, evidencing the conviction that God had revealed Himself in and through His creations not only as a God of power and wisdom but as one of supreme kindness, compassion, and faithfulness (Psalms 23; 42). The preservation of the natural order itself—the orderliness of nature, as manifested in the starry heavens and the progress from night to day and from season to season (Psalm 19)—also reveals the Supreme Creator to be careful, caring, and consistent. Many of the Psalms stress God's self-revelation in specific and special historical circumstances of the past (Psalms 44, 77). Frequently these are coupled with prayers to God that He reveal His power by delivering His people in present, difficult circumstances and the faith that He will do so.

One note that emerges in later Jewish prophetic, liturgical and wisdom literature is the emphasis on the transcendent holiness and power of God and the corresponding finitude of human life. The insight into God's transcendence—His power and holiness—is proclaimed as arising through reflection on the intrinsic limitations of finite existence, its transitoriness and fragility, its mortality. This theme is present in Psalms 49 and 90. It is present also, in ways that contrast with each other, in the Books of Job and Ecclesiastes. Job, who had complained about God's justice or lack of it, since, he, a righteous man, had experienced terrible and undeserved sufferings, is granted a vision of the transcendent glory of God. Humbled, Job withdraws his complaints and gratefully worships the supremely wise and powerful Creator. Though holy and transcendent, God draws close to those who seek Him persistently. The author of Ecclesiastes attempts to instill humility and wisdom by showing the intrinsic limitations of human life. In Ecclesiastes, God seems very remote from humans. Nevertheless, through reflection, humans gain insight from Him into their lives and the nature of the world they inhabit.

Some of the Proverbs and many of the intertestamental literature of Judaism stress the divine wisdom as the means by which the world has been created and is sustained. It is a reality by which those who respond *wisely* (with insight and faithful obedience) can govern their lives. This leads to a very striking *personification* of God's wisdom. That is, God's Wisdom is treated as if it were a personal being in itself, as in Proverbs 8:

Does not wisdom call,
does not understanding raise her voice?
On the heights beside the way,
in the paths she takes her stand;
beside the gates in front of the town,
at the entrance of the portals she cries aloud:
"To you, O men, I call,
and my cry is to the sons of men.
O simple ones, learn prudence;
O foolish men, pay attention.
Hear, for I will speak noble things,
and from my lips will come what is right;
for my mouth will utter truth;
wickedness is an abomination to my lips.
All the words of my mouth are righteous;
there is nothing twisted or crooked in them.
They are all straight to him who understands
and right to those who find knowledge.
Take my instruction instead of silver,
and knowledge rather than choice gold;
for wisdom is better than jewels,
and all that you may desire cannot compare with her.
I, wisdom, dwell in prudence,
and I find knowledge and discretion.
The fear of the Lord is hatred of evil.
Pride and arrogance and the way of evil
and perverted speech I hate.
I have counsel and sound wisdom,
I have insight, I have strength.
By me kings reign,
and rulers decree what is just;
by me princes rule,
and nobles govern the earth.

I love those who love me,
　and those who seek me diligently find me.
Riches and honor are with me,
　enduring wealth and prosperity.
My fruit is better than gold, even fine gold,
　and my yield than choice silver.
I walk in the way of righteousness,
　in the paths of justice,
endowing with wealth those who love me,
　and filling their treasuries.

The Lord created me at the beginning of his work,
　the first of his acts of old.
Ages ago I was set up,
　at the first, before the beginning of the earth.
When there were no depths I was brought forth,
　when there were no springs abounding with water.
Before the mountains had been shaped,
　before the hills, I was brought forth;
before he had made the earth with its fields,
　or the first of the dust of the world.
When he established the heavens, I was there,
　when he drew a circle on the face of the deep,
when he made firm the skies above,
　when he established the fountains of the deep,
when he assigned to the sea its limit,
　so that the waters might not transgress his command,
when he marked out the foundations of the earth,
　then I was beside him, like a master workman;
and I was daily his delight,
　rejoicing before him always,
rejoicing in his inhabited world
　and delighting in the sons of men.

And now, my sons, listen to me:
　happy are those who keep my ways.
Hear instruction and be wise,
　and do not neglect it.
Happy is the man who listens to me,
　watching daily at my gates,
　waiting beside my doors.
For he who finds me finds life
　and obtains favor from the Lord;
but he who misses me injures himself;
　all who hate me love death.

Personification of God's Wisdom and stress on it as the source and governor of the created world is present in the intertestamental writings—*The Wisdom of Jesus the Son of Sirach* and the *Wisdom of Solomon* (Ecclesiasticus). During this period, many of the commentators on the Jewish Scriptures began to stress that God had revealed Himself by means of the two sorts of sources mentioned above. First, they saw instances of special revelation in significant historical events and specially called persons. They also saw a more general or universal revelation present in the created universe, to be discerned in the orderly processes of nature and the cause and effect laws that can be discerned in human interaction (for instance, that the evil-doer will ultimately come to grief, that fools and wicked persons will cause their own undoing, but that the righteous will find strength and ultimate prosperity through their faithfulness and honesty). It came to be emphasized that the culmination of both these forms of revelation is to be found in the Torah or Pentateuch, the first five books of the Jewish Scriptures. The Torah was given through God's special revelation to Moses. It includes, contains, and in some senses is, the special revelation of God's will. It is the code of conduct whose adoption is the appropriate response by God's people to His mighty acts of salvation, the bond of His covenant with Israel. Yet increasingly, the Torah (more than the Law but including it) came to be described as the embodiment of God's Wisdom itself, the concentrated essence of the wisdom through which the world was created and is sustained. Thus, a bridge was built between the two forms of revelation, special (that given in unique circumstances to specially chosen persons) and general (that available to the insightful and obedient discernment of humanity generally). In the Torah, they are seen to be one and the same.

Thus, the problem of the knowledge of God as interpreted in Judaism does not concern reason's ability to reach beyond itself as it has so frequently in later Western thought. Rather it is practical in nature. Knowing God is a problem because of human blindness, the refusal to discern what is obvious about the way humans should respond to God—with grateful obedience—and to their fellow humans—with justice, kindness, and compassion. The wise person is the one who is not willfully blind but whose humility and willingness to obey allow discernment of God's law, either as specially given or at work everywhere. Wisdom leading to obedient response culminates in knowledge not only of God's law but in reverent devotion to the lawgiver.

FAITH, REASON, AND REVELATION

The concept of two major sources of knowledge of God, which in reality are one, has frequently been the starting point for Christian thinkers. As we have seen, the two sources or kinds of knowledge of God came to be described as general and special revelation. In Christianity as in Judaism, the concept of a general revelation available to all humans reflecting rationally on their experience is based on the belief that God creates and sustains the natural universe by means of His Wisdom, Power, and Goodness. Thus, the effects and, for some thinkers, the presence of God's Wisdom, Power and Goodness can be discerned in the structure, order, and flow of natural events.

Paul, in his letter to the Romans, held that non-Jews who worshipped false gods (idols) and behaved immorally were blameworthy even though they had not received the special revelation from God that Jews had received.

> For what can be known about God is plain to them, because God has shown it to them. Ever since the creation of the world his invisible nature, namely, his eternal power and deity, have been clearly perceived in the things that have been made. So they are without excuse. . . .
>
> **(ROMANS 1:19-20)**

The concepts of general and special revelation are usually *connected* in Christian thought by showing that the same divine wisdom that is responsible for creating and sustaining the natural realm is also discernible in the special providential acts of God in human history. Thus, the spirit of God inspires and empowers prophetic leaders like Moses, Samuel, Elijah, Isaiah, and John the Baptist to carry out his purposes. In their words and actions, God's wisdom, power, and goodness are apparent. God speaks and acts through them.

The author of the Gospel of John gave the most influential of all Christian formulations of this belief. In the prologue, he affirmed that the wisdom of God that is the source of the entire world was and is also present in the decisive event of God's special revelation, namely, the person and work of Jesus. Thus, for John's Gospel and most subsequent Christian thought, Jesus is more than a prophet inspired and empowered by God, more even than the expected Messiah of Judaism. Jesus is a human being who also is a unique self-disclosure (revelation) of God, one in whose person and work God is fully present:

> In the beginning was the Word and the Word was with God, and the Word was God. He was in the beginning with God; all things were made through him, and without him was not anything made that was made. In him was life, and the life was the light of men. . . . And the Word became flesh and dwelt among us, full of grace and truth; we have beheld his glory, glory as of the only Son from the Father.
>
> **(JOHN 1:1-4; 14)**

The term *word* used in John's Gospel is a translation of the Greek *logos*, which had been used to refer to the divine reason, or law, governing the natural order as early as the sixth century B.C.E. by the philosopher Heraclitus. Later logos was used by the Stoics to mean the divine reason. It had been adopted by Jewish thinkers in explaining and interpreting the Jewish concept of the wisdom of God.

The belief that the wisdom of God at work in the whole created realm is uniquely present in the person of Jesus is explicity expressed in several places in the New Testament, including the Gospel and First Epistle of John, Colossians (1:15-20), Hebrews (2:10), and the Gospel of Matthew.[2]

[2] See M. Jack Suggs, *Wisdom, Christology and Law in Matthew's Gospel* (Cambridge, Mass.: Harvard University Press, 1970).

Because of the connection of special and general revelation—because both ultimately are God's direct or indirect disclosure of Himself—some Christian thinkers have stressed general revelation as providing a very important preparation for special revelation. Such thinkers have reasoned in this way: It is because *some* knowledge of God is available to us from reasoned reflection on our experience generally that we are able to recognize special disclosures of God's will or of Himself. Even if special revelation goes much farther than the generally available knowledge that we may arrive at about God through reason, if we did not have at least some concept of God, however dim, incomplete, or inadequate, we would not be able to recognize special events or instances of God's self-disclosure. We would not be able to tell the difference between true and false claims to special revelation. Unless we understood, however dimly, *who* God is (in the sense of the passage from Paul's letter to the Romans) the very idea of a message from God would not occur to us, and the ability to recognize or distinguish true messages from God, or messages from the true God, would be nonexistent. According to Paul, because people had failed to pay attention to what they had been given the power to know about the true God they became worshippers of false gods.

Justin Martyr has been mentioned as one who found the concepts of Platonic philosophy helpful to his understanding and reception of the Christian message. Justin believed this even though after his conversion to Christianity he criticized some aspects of Platonic philosophy and the philosophical approach to truth apart from Christian revelation.

In general, there have been at least four ways in which Christian thinkers have found the use of reason (related to general revelation) to be of possible value in leading one to the acceptance or better understanding of Christian truth. Some thinkers have advocated or utilized more than one of these uses of reason to help persons reach religious knowledge.

Belief in Reason

Some, though not many, Christian thinkers have argued that reason by itself is adequate to the discovery of religious truth. In the twelfth century, at the beginning of economic and cultural revitalization of Europe, there was a tremendous burst of enthusiasm on the part of some Christian philosophers for the use of methods of logical analysis and proof to explain and establish Christian doctrines, like the doctrine of the Trinity, that most have thought of as being far beyond the power of human reason to comprehend. The twelfth-century attempt to use reason as a universally adequate source or criterion of religious truth produced a crisis and was perceived by some Christians as a threat to the integrity of Christian doctrine and the authority of the church.[3] Peter Abélard, perhaps the greatest philosopher and theologian of the early twelfth century, did not go to the extreme of holding that all Christian truth can be established by reason, but his enthusiasm for the use

---

[3]M. D. Chenu, O. P., *Nature, Man and Society in the Twelfth Century* (Chicago and London: The University of Chicago Press, 1968). See especially the first chapter.

of logical analysis to explicate Christian doctrine led some of his opponents, including the famous mystic St. Bernard of Clairvaux, to charge that Abélard went too far in trying to discover by reason what can only be given by (special) revelation and received and held by faith.

In the eighteenth century, Christian thinkers known as deists (discussed in Chapter Four) wanted to rid Christian teachings of all appeal to the miraculous and supernatural in order to bring harmony between the Christian approach to truth and that of the new (Newtonian) science. The deists were willing to make rational reflection on experience the sole source and criterion of religious truth. A deistic thinker like Thomas Jefferson could argue, for instance, that the message of Jesus was not a supernaturally given special revelation. Rather, it was the purest and most sublime moral philosophy of human history. The eighteenth-century German philosopher Immanuel Kant argued in his *Religion Within the Limits of Reason Alone* for belief in God and a purification of the concept of God based on the knowledge of morality that is universally available to rational beings.

Reason Depending on Revelation

The belief that a major part of Christian belief can be arrived at by ration reflection (general revelation) has not been a majority opinion among Christians. Many have believed that rational knowledge leading to insight into the nature of eternal (necessary) truth, the self (or soul), and God may serve a vital function in preparing for the reception and assisting in the understanding of what Christianity teaches about God and our relation to Him. St. Augustine (354-430 C.E.), perhaps the most powerful post-New Testament influence on later Western Christianity, like Justin, found in Platonic philosophy an important preparation for understanding and accepting the Christian message. As a child and young man, Augustine had been exposed to Christian teaching largely through the influence of his mother. For a time he dismissed Christianity, becoming an adherent of a religion, Manichaeism, that was one of Christianity's contemporary rivals. Later, becoming disillusioned with Manichaean answers to his religious doubts and moral problems, Augustine began to study Platonic philosophy, most effectively represented in Augustine's time by the Neoplatonic school deriving from Plotinus (205-270 C.E.). As a result of the study of Platonic thought, many of Augustine's religious questions were answered and many of his objections to Christian belief were removed. Particularly, he was impressed with the Neoplatonic treatment of God and the soul as nonmaterial, spiritual realities, and with its teaching of evil as being *not* a reality in itself coeternal with God (as Manichaeism taught) but as the absence of good, as a falling or turning from God.

Plato had taught that all knowledge of true reality, of eternal truths (like the truths of mathematics or the nature of plant and animal species) is innate within the soul (or mind). Thus, one should cultivate or "go into" one's soul to find truth, turning from distractions of sense experience and the realm of material objects. Augustine did not accept the concept of innate knowledge. Instead, he made a subtle modification of Plato's theory of how we acquire knowledge. All true knowledge (*e.g.*, such as the discovery of truths of mathematics) depends on an illumination of the mind by God—ultimately by that "Light which is the Light of men" mentioned in John's Gospel. Thus, even in ordinary knowing we are dependent on a kind of revelation to the mind from and of God. So for Augustine, even general revelation is not something simply put into the world that the mind appropriates. It is an event in which there is active communication by God to the actively receptive human mind. Such revelation *does* prepare the mind to receive specially revealed, saving truths, for it can bring the mind (or soul) to knowledge of its own spiritual nature and of its need for a right relation to God. It can bring the individual to recognition that one can find fulfillment only in knowing and loving God. It also can show the mind (or soul or self) that it is helpless in establishing this relation apart from God's grace. Thus, awareness of how the mind is illumined, even in ordinary knowing, can bring the mind to knowledge of the nature of God as a spiritual being. But this sort of knowing must be completed by illumination concerning the special acts of God's self-disclosure. Augustine remarked that he found much about God *the logos*—the Word or Wisdom of God—in Platonic philosophy, but did not learn from philosophy that "the Word became flesh and dwelt among us." Augustine learned about God's love of and saving power toward lost humankind only through the church's proclamation and the Christian scriptures attesting to the saving event of Jesus Christ.

A later Christian thinker, Anselm of Canterbury (1033-1109), sometimes called the father of scholasticism, was also influenced by the Platonic tradition. Anselm was convinced that we have the ablity to arrive by rational reflection at a true concept of God base on our own innate awareness of the contrast between our finitude and that which is not finite (God). We thus are aware that God, if He exists, must be the perfect, all-powerful, all-wise, absolutely good being. A perfect being must be free of all limitations. It cannot be dependent on any other being. It follows from this, Anselm believed, that one cannot, without contradiction, think of God as not existing, since the concept of a being that might not exist is not the concept of a perfect being. This line of argument is sometimes called the ontological proof of God's existence.

In a sense, for both Augustine and Anselm *faith* precedes understanding and reasoning about God. In this sense, faith is a sort of deep-level inner awareness of our need for and dependence on God. We may try to suppress this awareness. But reasoning may bring to full clarity what the sense of our finitude means and thus prepare the way for a faith that is an explicit commitment to the God proclaimed in the Christian message. Naturally, this second level, or explicit, faith, will involve various *beliefs* about God, but it continues and brings to self-awareness faith of the first level, faith as awareness of our dependence on God.

Reason Supporting Revelation

Still other Christian thinkers have understood human reason to be capable of bringing humans to *inferential* knowledge of God derived from reasoning about the physical universe. (Anselm, Augustine, and many Christian Platonists accepted this use of reason in addition to reason oriented to the inner realities of the soul.) Christian Platonism, as modified by creative thinkers like Augustine, Anselm, and the Franciscan Bonaventure (1221-1274) was the major philosophical influence on Christian thought from its beginnings until the thirteenth century. At that point, under the influence of such thinkers as Albert the Great (1193?-1280) and Thomas Aquinas (1225-1274), the philosophy of Aristotle became dominant.

Aristotle, who had been a student, colleague, and friend of Plato, had much in common with him. One of the greatest differences between Platonic and Aristotelian approaches is the theory of knowledge, of how we acquire and validate truth. Aristotle was an empiricist. Empiricism is the belief that all human knowledge is derived from sensation. Thus, instead of believing that we use reason to clarify and discover truths innate within the mind (as Plato had taught), Aristotle believed we arrive at truth by extracting information (generalizing) from memory-images that originally come to us by way of the five senses.

Partly because of his acceptance of Aristotle's empiricist theory of knowledge, Aquinas drew a sharper line between general and special revelation than the Christian Platonists did. This resulted in his drawing a rather sharp line between the subject matter of rationally acquired knowledge (philosophy and what we would call natural science) and knowledge with principles and content derived from special revelation (theology). For Aquinas, the human mind is adapted to knowledge of material objects derived from sense experience. Humans are not and will not be able to know spiritual entities, the soul or God, fully and directly—intuitively— in the present life. We can, however, through rational reflection on sense experience, arrive at certain knowledge *about* God and the soul. We can know with demonstrative certainty that God exists and that our souls are immortal. We do not have an innate concept of God and God's existence is not immediately self-evident to us (as Anselm's ontological proof assumed). But we can know God through His effects. We can infer the existence of God as the supreme, necessary Cause of the contingent (and therefore created) world of nature. Otherwise we would not be able to understand our experience *of* nature.

Aquinas believed that five ways, or lines, of reasoning lead to knowledge of the existence of God and to an understanding of some of his attributes. These lines of reasoning, usually called cosmological proofs of God's existence, begin with facts of our experience of the physical universe and end with the necessity of concluding that God is their ultimate cause. They concern the existence of motion, causal processes, contingent being, degrees of value and purposive processes in nonrational nature.

Aquinas and Aristotle believed that the natural order disclosed by rational reflection on sensory experience is characterized by purpose and values. This is certainly true of human life. Human life has ends or goals associated with our natural capacities and tendencies. Through reflection on *human* experience, we can arrive at the content of the *moral* law. Aquinas agreed with the Greek and Roman Stoics in holding a "natural law," or "law of nature," approach to morality. Humans can, through right reasoning concerning natural capacities and needs, arrive at a sound understanding of their rights and duties. He was convinced that all of the Ten Commandments given in the Jewish Scripture (Exodus 20:1-17; Deuteronomy 5:6-21), with the exception of the commandment concerning Sabbath observance, can be discovered by reason. (Some Christians have regarded the Ten Commandments as a foundation not only of Jewish but of Christian morality, indeed as a set of basic moral principles valid for all humanity.)

Why, then, is there need for special revelation? According to Aquinas, it is twofold. Although there is available to humankind natural knowledge concerning God and morality that *might* serve as a basis for understanding and reception of further special revelation and that *might* be used to guide humans in their social interaction, this (general) revelation may not be effective. Not everyone will possess the time, intelligence, or means to arrive at natural knowledge of God or morality. Also, human beings are fallen, sinful, and not naturally good as originally they were created to be. They are inclined to disobey the moral law and to be partial and self-interested in interpreting it. Therefore, God has in various ways provided in special revelatory events much that could have been and that sometimes has been discovered through reasoning.

The other aspect of specially revealed truth recognized by Aquinas concerns those aspects of God and ourselves that transcend our limited power of knowing by rational reflection on sense experience, but that are related to our need for salvation. These truths cannot be discovered by the use of reason alone, since the human mind in the present life can know material objects directly, but cannot know God in His essence. We cannot even know directly that our minds (or souls) possess an eternal destiny. Nevertheless, certain truths related to God's essential nature—the doctrine of the Trinity, for instance—and His saving activity—the Incarnation—have been revealed because they bear on our salvation. Much that we need to know for our spiritual welfare about the church, the sacraments and the Christian life is of this nature. Such truth is not irrational but transcends the capacity of human reason.

Thus, for Aquinas, general and special revelation should work together. General revelation can prepare our minds for understanding and accepting special revelation. Special revelation can reinforce or make us intially aware of the truths of general revelation. By and large, the truths of general revelation will first be acquired as special revelation, taught by the church and accepted and held by faith as the Christian participates in the sacramental life of the church and is obedient to its authority. If acquired through ratonal reflection, they are no longer held by faith.[4] Here it should be noted that for Aquinas *faith* means the intellectual acceptance of a belief not conclusively demonstrated by rational means, held on the basis of the church's authority. Faith is made possible by God's grace. This use can be contrasted with the concept of faith held by Augustine and Anselm, where the term

---

[4] See the discussion in Aquinas, *De Veritate,* 14, 9; Also Grederick Copleston, S. J., *A History of Philosophy,* Volume 2, Part II (Westminster, Maryland: The Newman Press, 1950), Chapter Thirty-Two.

signified an innate, not necessarily explicit or reflectively held, orientation of the self as a spiritual being to its Creator.

Reason Questioning Itself

A fourth way in which reason has been seen as preparation for the reception of the Christian message involves use of reason to show its own inability to discover truth. During the fourteenth century, many Christian thinkers drew an even sharper line between what can be known by natural reason and what is given in special revelation than Aquinas had done. These thinkers were called nominalists. Nominalism is the philosophical view that only individual things exist. There are no general truths or common natures, or essences, of things among the basic components of reality. General truths are only artificially fabricated grouping devices that the mind uses to deal with collections of individual things in a convenient way. Thus we use the concept *dog* to deal with a large number of individuals, similar in important ways, that are really unique.

The term that contrasts with *nominalist* is *realist*. Realists, of which there have been a great many kinds in philosophical history, believe that general concepts such as *dog* or *human nature* are discovered and not invented. If our concept of *dog* is correct, it corresponds to something objective that dogs have in common. It is this common element, or essence, that *causes* all dogs to resemble each other. For nominalists, dogs simply have been found to resemble each other in various ways. That is why we use the term *dog* to describe them, not because some essence *belongs* to them all in common. For the realist, to know the concept of a thing or species gives us deep and accurate knowledge about it. For the nominalist, a concept is simply a summary of what has been observed in the past. This may not continue to hold in the future. Nominalism tends to go with empiricism. However, Aristotle and Aquinas were empiricists *and* realists, though realists of a different kind than Plato was. If you hear someone say something like: "It is contrary to human nature for a mother to want to give up her baby for adoption," you are probably hearing someone who is a philosophical realist, whether consciously so or not. A nominalist would be more likely to say, "Eighty-one percent of all mothers interviewed say that they would not want to give up their baby for adoption." For the realist, the essence or common nature may simply exist somehow above or apart from the things that manifest it (Plato). It may be a formative power or structure within the particular things that share it (Aristotle). It may be an *idea* in the mind of God in accordance with which He has created the particular things that belong to common species (Aquinas). For nominalists it is none of these.

The nominalists were more radical empiricists than Aristotle and Aquinas. For them the generalizations about experience that we arrive at through rational reflection do not disclose the *real* nature of things. Thus, rational reflection on the mind's contents cannot give certainty. It cannot give us certainty even about the realm of material objects disclosed in sensory experience, much less lead to conclusive proofs of the existence of God, the nature of the self or soul, or the contents of morality. Morality cannot be derived from rational reflection on our capacities and needs. Rather it depends on the arbitrary commandments of God.

Possibly the greatest of the medieval nominalists was William of Ockham (1280?-1349). As a Christian theologian, Ockham may be said to have placed even greater stress on special revelation than most of his predecessors had, since he limited the capacity of human reason to arrive at truth. Thus the truths about God and morality that Christianity teaches are to be held by faith (in the sense understood by Aquinas) and acquired through God's grace as one participates in the sacramental life of the Church. The sacraments, as channels of God's grace, enable the Christian subjectively to have faith in beliefs that are objectively valid, though not rationally provable, because they are proclaimed by the church.

Like the nominalists, the German philosopher Kant (1724-1804) attempted, as he said, to limit the claims of reason to make room for faith. In his *Critique of Pure Reason*, Kant argued that metaphysical and religious beliefs cannot be proved or disproved by theoretical, or scientific, reason, since it is by its nature limited to dealing with questions that can be formulated in terms of observational and experimental procedures and confirmed or rejected accordingly. Kant *did* believe that reason in its moral use is adequate as a basis and criterion of religious belief.

More radical had been the seventeenth-century mathematician and scientist Blaise Pascal (1623-1663) who in a brilliant work left unfinished at the time of his death, but later published as *Les Pensées*, argued from the finitude of human reason to the need for volitional (willed) commitment to God and a life of faith. In something of the same spirit, the nineteenth-century Danish thinker, Søren Kierkegaard (1813-1855), was convinced that reason is simply not adequate to answer the fundamental questions of life. In a series of highly ingenious writings, Kierkegaard attempted to awaken "the individual" in his readers to the impotence of scientific, philosophical, and socially defined "objective truth" in dealing with questions about the meaning of one's life. Awakened, "the individual" may be prepared to hear the plain Christian message in sermon and Scripture and respond with a leap of faith, a decision to commit one's whole life to the God who became incarnate at an arbitrary place on earth in an aribitrary period of human history.

This fourth use of reason—to show reason's own limits in the hope that this will lead to recognition of the need for the appropriation of (special) revelation by faith—often leads to positions that are highly critical of the use of reason at all as preparation for religious belief or as a source of knowledge about God. Generally, thinkers who reject the use of reason entirely stress the vastness of the contrast between God and finite human reason. They find nothing in common between naturally acquired and specially revealed truth. The rejection of reason has never been a majority position among Christian thinkers, but has had important representatives. Tertullian, a second-century Christian whose theories concerning the doctrine of the Trinity had permanent influence on Latin (Western) Christianity, held that philosophical reasoning is of no value in preparing the mind to understand or accept Christian truth. About some Christian beliefs, such as that in the Resurrection, Tertullian wrote, "I believe it *because* it is absurd," meaning that the transcendence of rationally-based expectations is one criterion of truth about God.

Martin Luther ridiculed attempts of the Christian scholastic theologians to use philosophical reasoning in the interpretation and defense of Christian beliefs. Luther referred to reason as "an evil beast" and "the devil's whore."

Karl Barth (1886-1968), perhaps the most influential of all twentieth-century Protestant theologians, also stressed the discontinuity between what can be known by human reason and the revealed truths of Christianity. The nominalists had emphasized the inability of reason to know *anything* with certainty. Thus, natural knowledge cannot provide a starting point for or support of belief concerning God. Barth agreed, saying that God is "Wholly Other" than we are and than the whole realm of what our finite understanding can grasp. Barth also stressed the sinful-ness—self-centeredness and selfish distortion—to which all human reasoning is subject. This brings us back to the quotation from Paul's Letter to the Romans with which this section began. Paul stressed the ability of humans to know God through evidences of His created world. But in the same passage he spoke of an ever-increas-ing corruption of humanity resulting from human refusal to recognize the true God. Barth, pursuing the theme of the lost capacity of fallen humanity to know God, argued against his former theological collaborator, Emil Bruner. Brunner insisted that even though the corruption of human reason through sin makes it impossible for humans to know God apart from God's special self-revelation, there is a point of contact in human awareness of finitude and need between God's revelation and human reception of it. Barth denied this. There is no connecting link between humans and God, and no basis in human capacities or sense of finitude for knowing God, until God himself in His self-disclosure in Jesus Christ creates the connecting link and gives fallen humans the ability to receive knowledge of God and of their need of Him.

Mystics

In contrast to the four ways of understanding reason as preparatory to appropriation of revelation, *and* in contrast to the stress of Christians like Tertul-lian, Luther, and Barth on holding to Christian truth by simple faith, Christian mystics have stressed the possibility of direct, personal experiential communion with God—which is genuine knowledge *of*, not *about*, God (See Chapter Five). This mystical communion is passively received, given by grace, and not achieved, though it may be prepared for by moral self-discipline, asceticism, and prayer. Mysticism has some affinity with the Platonic use of reason, since it stresses withdrawing one's attention from the world known in sensory experience and "going into" the soul. In fact, many of the great Christian mystics have held to the Platonic philosophy, though others, like Aquinas, have not. Many mystics argue that such an experience *does* constitute knowledge of God. The question of whether this is a general human capacity possessed by all or a special gift of God's grace to some Christians may be answered differently. As we have seen, Aquinas and the majority of mystical writers within the Catholic tradition have held that it is a specially conferred grace, not a possibility, source, or criterion in human nature generally—certainly not in fallen human nature—of the knowledge of God. Many Protestant thinkers, from Luther and Calvin forward to Barth, have been suspicious of mysticism and the claims of mystical theologians. Others, like the Quakers, have recognized the possibilities of mystical experience by emphasizing the presence of the inner light or the Christ within as an aspect of human nature generally and thus potentially as a source of knowledge of God. On the basis of such belief, Rufus M. Jones, a distinguished American Quaker, led a team of Friends to Germany to appeal to Adolf Hitler on behalf of Jews who were being persecuted prior to World War II, hoping that Hitler would respond to "the Christ within" and change his course of action.

CONFLICTS INVOLVING SCIENCE AND CHRISTIAN BELIEF

This chapter has described efforts by Christian thinkers to deal with the question of how one legitimately can claim to have arrived at knowledge about God. Christians have, as we have seen, attempted to answer this question since the very beginnings of the Christian movement. The question, however, assumed special importance with the rise and triumphs of modern science. Certain aspects of the encounter between the new science and the various branches of Christianity have produced the belief that the methods and results of scientific inquiry contain distinct threats to commonly held Christian beliefs.

One of the most significant early instances is the case of Galileo Galilei (1564-1642). Recent scholarship has shown that the conflict between Galileo and the Inquisition is not as clear-cut an example of the repression of scientific truth by religious authorities as has sometimes been imagined. Galileo, in attempting to establish the truth of the Copernican theory that the sun is at the center of the planetary system and that the earth is one of the planets that revolves about it, had explicitly raised fundamental questions about correct methods of interpreting the Scriptures. Since he was not a theologian, Church officials felt that Galileo was trespassing on their territory. Also, the church had ruled that the Copernican theory could be taught only as a hypothesis, not as established truth. Some theologians and ecclesiastical officials were reluctant to accept Copernican astronomy, because it was generally held in medieval times that the Bible teaches that the earth is at the center of the planetary system and that the sun moves around it. Also, Aristotelian philosophy, which held to an earth-centered model, had been successfully integrated into Christian doctrine by such thinkers as Aquinas and John Duns Scotus and their interpreters.

Not all theologians and religious officials opposed the Copernican theory. Urban VIII, prior to becoming Pope, took great interest in the new astronomy and urged Galileo to write about it, cautioning him only to treat Copernicanism not as established truth and to be certain to give a number of "convincing" arguments to support the accepted Ptolemaic (earth-centered) model of the universe. In *Dialogue on the Great World Systems* Galileo pretended to do this, but actually put the Pope's convincing arguments into the mouth of the dull-witted, tradition-bound Simplicio, thus seeming to ridicule them. The Pope was angry and withdrew his support from Galileo, insisting that he be disciplined.

Apparently a number of other personal and institutional feuds had some bearing on the Inquisition's judgment requiring Galileo to recant his astronomical views and placing restrictions on his future activities. Some scholars have even debated whether falsified evidence—a forged memorandum to the effect that Galileo had earlier been forbidden even to write on Copernicanism—was introduced against him.[5]

However that may be, Galileo *had not* presented in his works and *did not have* decisive evident to support the Copernican over the Plotemaic system. This was accomplished a generation later by Sir Isaac Newton (1642-1727), who drew on the work of Galileo's contemporary Johann Kepler (1571-1630) (whose work Galileo had apparently overlooked or undervalued). Galileo, one of the greatest experimental and theoretical scientists of all time, has frequently been portrayed as a scientific martyr to repressive religious authority. He was not exactly that, though what the Inquisiton did in this instance may have hindered scientific progress in parts of Europe. It did bring discredit to some Christian institutions and their leaders.

The New Science, after receiving its Newtonian form, was largely welcomed by European Christians as providing powerful support for belief in an all-wise, all-powerful God who had created the universe in accordance with the simple yet beautiful laws of nature that Newton had discovered. Deists used Newtonian science as a platform for purging Christian belief of what they considered the fanciful tangle of traditional theological dogma held both by Catholics and by Orthodox Protestants. Many Christians, like Joseph Butler (1692-1752), a bishop of the Church of England, argued that the new Science was comptabile with traditional belief. Butler, especially in his famous *Analogy of Religion*, attacked Deism and defended traditional orthodoxy. In contrast, David Hume (1711-1776), a sceptic, made a devastating attack on the "rational religion" of deism and also ridiculed traditional or orthodox Christian belief, trying to show that the new psychology with its radically empiricist theory of knowledge left no room for rational belief in religion *or* in science. According to Hume, there are good subjective (essentially instinctive) grounds for accepting scientific results but not religious beliefs, which he believed to be the result of credulity and superstition, producing intolerance and fanaticism in those who hold them.

Probably of longer-lasting significance for relations between science and Christianity than either the Copernican or the deist controversies was the conflict in England involving Darwinism. Prior to 1859, when Darwin published *The Origin*

---

[5] For the entire Galileo controversy as well as this point one should consult the works by Langford, de Santillana and Raven included in the bibliography of the present chapter.

of Species, there had been some shocks to the then generally accepted belief that the Book of Genesis teaches that Divine creation of the universe happened in six days about 6000 years ago. Geological evidence indicated that the earth was much older than this and that geological changes have occurred gradually over long periods of time. Darwin's work presented evidence indicating that plant and animal species were not distinct creations that appeared all at once 6000 years ago, but have evolved over a much longer period of time in accordance with the principle of natural selection. One very controversial part of Darwin's theory held that the human species was not specially created, but has evolved like other species from earlier and simpler forms of life.

Darwinism, thought to be in conflict with a literal interpretation of the book of Genesis, was also thought to seriously question the accepted religious belief that natural processes and human history are divinely created and guided. However, Darwin's evolutionary theories were soon being championed by representatives of the churches who argued that there is no fundamental problem if one holds the belief that God created and sustains the universe, but in doing so uses the methods, including the law of natural selection, discovered by science. Influential leaders in the Church of England, like Charles Kingsley (1819-1875), pointed out that even in the ancient church and pre-Christian Rabbinic Judaism the creation accounts in Genesis were not necessarily taken literally and that Christian thinkers like Augustine had suggested accounts of the creation process not entirely unlike later evolutionary ones.

Perhaps what has usually been perceived by most Christians as the greatest potential threat of the new scientific attitudes is the increasingly successful attempt by scientists to explain natural phenomena as purely mechanical, purposeless processes. Freudian and behavioristic schools of psychology, sociobiology, and recent inquiries into brain functioning have seemed perhaps even more threatening than Darwinism, since they have either speculated about or actually created models of human behavior that apparently reduce the human to the interplay of purely natural, random, ultimately chemical and physical, processes.[6]

It has frequently been argued that in a mechanistic (deterministic or statistically random) universe, the person—with every significant concept of human freedom, responsibility, value, or dignity—disappears. The philosopher Kant, one of the first to formulate a philosophy of the new science, argued that it is necessary and legitimate for science to attempt to explain all natural phenomena in terms of mechanical principles, but that a deeper, less abstract level of our experience reveals the realm of morality—of pesons, personal freedom, and God. Such scientifically trained religious thinkers as different as the Catholic scientist-priest Pierre Teilhard de Chardin, the Anglican theologian C. E. Raven, and the British mathematician and philosopher A. N. Whitehead have argued that ultimately scientific under-

---

[6]One recent, highly controversial but ingenious argument by a distinguished contemporary biologist for the view that science discloses a universe entirely without purpose and none of whose parts requires the categories of purpose or value for their understanding is Jacques Monod, *Chance & Necessity* (New York: Alfred A. Knopf, Inc., 1971).

standing will suggest—and cannot do without—the category of *purpose* or *value* for its comprehensive interpretation of our experience of nature.

Science has not been without its critics. Some conservative Christians even now argue that a scientific theory like Darwinism, which is *only* a theory, should not be taught as fact and that the competing theory of the six-thousand year-ago Creation derived from a literal interpretation of Genesis should be given equal time in public-school science courses. Critics of *this* and other "scientific creationist" positions argue that the term theory in science does not entail lack of confirmation and is not used in *this* way to contrast with the term fact. Instead, a scientific theory is a system of laws and principles used to organize, explain, and predict a potentially unlimited number of facts within a a well-defined field of investigation subject to observational and experimental tests. This suggests that it is not accurate to refer to religious beliefs as scientific theories, since what people ordinarily call religious beliefs to not function in this way. They cannot be given limited-frame precision and cannot be tested by using experimental or observational methods. This has been expressed by some writers when they have said that religious beliefs and scientific theories belong to different logical levels or to logically different fields of our language.

A few years ago it was not uncommon to hear it said that scientific statements deal with the *what* (the factual) and religious statements with the *why* (the value) dimensions of our experience. In light of recent studies of the roles of theorizing and experimental testing as they affect acceptance or rejection of scientific theories, this distinction is too simple. J. Bronowski, Thomas Kuhn, and other interpreters of contemporary science have shown that the results of scientific inquiry themselves are embedded in and presuppose a value framework. Facts themselves are not absolutes, they are relative to the theoretical frameworks used for establishing and interpreting them. As Kenneth E. Boulding observed:

> Even at the level of simple or supposedly simple sense perception we are increasingly discovering that the message which comes through the senses is itself mediated through a value system. We do not perceive our sense data raw; they are mediated through a highly learned process of interpretation and acceptance.... What this means is that ... there are no such things as "facts." There are only messages filtered through a changeable value system.[7]

This need not mean that scientific inquiry becomes subjective or arbitrary, though some critics, like Paul Feyerabend, may have suggested as much. In some ways the new understanding of what goes on in scientific theorizing and experimentation has brought scientific thought closer to the moral and religious dimensions of life. But for many thinkers this has served to indicate that great care must be used both *not* to reduce one type of thinking—scientific or religious—to the other and *not* to draw the conclusion that either invalidates or can replace the other.

[7] Kenneth E. Boulding, *The Image* (Ann Arbor: The University of Michigan Press, 1966), p. 14.

RELIGIOUS LANGUAGE: THE PROBLEM
OF TALKING ABOUT GOD

Much current inquiry into the question of religious truth (or religious knowledge) has focused on the logic of religious language. The twentieth-century philosopher Wittgenstein (1889-1951) cautioned philosophers against looking for an overall theory of the "nature" or "meaning" of language. Rather, he pointed out that there are many different language activities that humans engage in and many different language uses. Context—what Wittgenstein referred to as "language game"—becomes all-important.

Thus, it may be a fundamental mistake to try to find common standards of meaning and verifiability for scientific and religious statements. This has led many philosophers to explore certain *noncognitive* uses of religious language in which the speaker does not and perhaps does not *intend* to convey information. Rather, noncognitive use of language expresses feeling, makes a commitment, helps to cement the bonds of solidarity of a group, or does any other of innumerable possible things about which it would be ridiculous to suppose that questions of truth or falsity arise, as they would if the language use were assumed to have cognitive content (*i.e.*, to claim to convey information). As has often been pointed out, when a minister says the words in a marriage ceremony, "I now pronounce you united in holy matrimony," or in a baptismal service, "I baptize you in the Name of the Father, Son, and Holy Ghost," no one would think that the purpose of the minister's expressions is to give information. Rather, the minister is using language performatively, to accomplish something. Still, the position asserted by some that *all* religious language is noncognitive seems extreme and would not be accepted by most religious persons.

Some present noncognitivist theories of religious language remind one of the view of the seventeenth-century British philosopher Thomas Hobbes (1588-1679). Hobbes held that since God is completely beyond our understanding—even the word *infinite* he held to have no meaning for us—when we speak of God we are not saying anything at all, we are merely expressing feelings and attitudes of reverence. We are praising God rather than characterizing or describing Him. In his own time, Hobbes was suspected of being an atheist, but his view has connections both with some of the most recent and some of the oldest Christian understandings about the use of language concerning God.

The so-called negative way of speaking of God, elaborated by Christian mystical writers (greatly influenced by an unknown author long thought to be Paul's convert Dionysius the Areopagite, now usually called pseudo-Dionysius) consists in successively *denying all* attributes to God. For instance, one denies that God is a material object, since material objects are limited by space and time. Ultimately, one denies *every* distinct possible characteristic as applying to God since even calling God *wise, good* or *powerful* limits Him by suggesting the way these concepts apply to finite entities. At the end of the negative way, *all* limitations have been removed from our concept of God. Since this may seem to leave the concept totally empty, many Christian thinkers, though admitting the value of the way of negation, have insisted it should be followed by a positive or affirmative way.

This is possible, according to Thomas Aquinas, because though none of our terms designating finite characteristics apply to God univocally (with the *same* sense that they have when applied to finite things) they can be used, with caution, *analogically.* Since God is the source of all that exists then there must be in Him as their ground or source something (not necessarily something distinct from His entire essence) that corresponds or is analogous to the positive qualities of finite things. Thus there is an analogy between God's Wisdom and human wisdom. So we can legitimately affirm that God is wise, making it clear that God's wisdom is a kind of superwisdom that is not literally or univocally like human wisdom. Some terms would never be applied to God. We would never say that God is evil or that God is foolish or deceitful.

The concept of analogy is not without its difficulties. Some of the greatest Christian thinkers have declined to use the term, preferring the terms *symbol* and *symbolic* to those of *analogy* and *analogous.* Thus the twentieth-century Protestant theologican Paul Tillich (1886-1965) asserted that there is *one* literally true statement we can make about God, namely that God is being-itself (or the power of being of everything that exists). Everything else that we can say about God is a symbolic (presumably nonliteral or metaphorical) statement. For Karl Barth the method of analogy could be used not as a part of our natural reasoning ability, but only on the basis of insights given to faith. Thus, Barth spoke of the Analogy of Faith in contrast to Aquinas' Analogy of Being.

As noted earlier, some thinkers have suggested that there are different levels of discourse—scientific, axiological (*i.e.,* dealing with norms, duties, and values), and metaphysical or religious. At each level the use of terms like *literal, well-defined, precise, verified, acceptable,* and *meaningful* might differ significantly from their uses at the other levels. If some kind of connection between the different levels could be shown, the result might be a usefully modified version of Kantian philosophy, one perhaps resembling the views of the more empiricist-oriented American thinker C. S. Peirce (1839-1914). If no connection should be found between the different levels of language use, then we might be left with some version of the Wittgenstein language games approach to the different areas of human discourse. Each area—religion, science, morality—might be seen to have its own rules, its own standards of what is acceptable and what is not, with no need or possibility of being related to other language fields.

In the twentieth century, then, the need of religiously committed persons to understand the ways language is used in science and to the ways in which philosophers analyze language is evident. But it is equally evident that users of religious language have contributions to make to scientific and philosophical inquiries into language and the possibilities of its meaningful uses.

AUTHORITY

Much that has been said in this chapter derives from and leads back to a question that has deeply divided Christians, the question of religious authority. Who—what person, persons, group; or what—words, records, institutions, experiences—is/are entitled, according to Christian belief, to settle either ultimately or provisionally the question of what is true or false in the area of Christian belief and practice?

The ultimate Christian response to this question has usually been: God. God is the ultimate source of religious authority. The extended discussion of the concepts of general and special revelation earlier in the chapter is an attempt to explain how many Christians have tried to show *how* God discloses Himself, makes knowledge about or of Himself available to human groups or individuals. But further attempts at operationalizing this Christian understanding of authority have produced great diversity. Certainly the Scriptures of the Old and New Testaments have been accepted as authoritative by the great majority of Christians. Both Eastern Orthodox and Western Catholic branches of Christianity have emphasized the authority of tradition along with, and indeed to some extent as including, that of the Scriptures. For both, the Scriptures are an inspired crystalization of already existing prophetic (Old Testament) and apostolic (New Testament) traditions. The Scriptures themselves are subject to interpretation in the light of earlier and continuing tradition. For both Eastern Orthodoxy and Western Catholicism, the role of the bishops becomes all-important in interpreting Scripture and tradition. For the Orthodox, the seven Ecumenical Councils have a decisive position, and in theory the ultimate interpreter of Christian truth would be such ecumenical councils.

For Roman Catholics, the teaching office of the church, expressed either in what has been a universally accepted and proclaimed part of Catholic tradition, or in what the bishops proclaim in ecumenical councils, or what the Pope proclaims when speaking *ex cathedra* functions in theory to define religious truth authoritatively.

Protestants like Luther and Calvin made Scripture *alone* the source of authoritative interpretation in areas of doctrine and practice. Both argued that interpreters of Scripture should be well-prepared scholars. However, correct interpretations ultimately depended on the illumination of the mind and heart of the Bible scholar by the Holy Spirit. But the Protestant answer that the criterion of religious truth is the Bible as illuminated by the Holy Spirit led to meta-questions concerning criteria of Spirit-illumined Bible interpretation.

Most Protestant groups, including those originating during the Reformation Period, have adopted credal statements (often including one or more of the historic creeds originating in the ancient and medieval church). They have seen these statements as based on Scripture but also as giving direction to its correct interpretation. They have utilized catechisms for the same purpose. Catechisms are summaries of Christian doctrine in a standard question-and-answer format. They are thus suitable for memorization and have been widely used by Catholics and Protestants for teaching children and young people basic Christian beliefs. As mentioned above, in some Protestant groups they have served as authoritative credal statements. The shorter and longer catechisms compiled by Martin Luther may be taken as authoritative statements of Lutheran theology, in Luther's understanding derived from the Bible but also providing keys and criteria for its interpretation. The same is true of catechisms originating among Reformed groups, such as the (Presbyterian) Westminster Shorter Catechism. The Church of England adopted thirty-nine authoritative articles of religion.

Among American Methodists a catechism, containing such questions and answers as the following, was available for use:

> Section I.   1. (Q) What is Christianity?
>
> (A) Christianity is the religion of God's redeeming love, manifested in the incarnate life, the atoning death, and the glorious resurrection of Jesus Christ, the Founder of the Kingdom of God.
>
> 2. (Q) Who is Jesus Christ?
>
> (A) The Son of God and the Son of Mary; very God and very man; and the only Mediator between God and man.[8]

Apparently the Methodist catechism was not used widely for educational purposes and certainly not as an authoritative standard of doctrine or criterion of scriptural interpretation. However, American Methodists do not lack doctrinal standards and criteria. They have twenty-five articles of religion (representing an adaptation made by John Wesley from the Church of England's thirty-nine); some additional articles that emerged in different Wesleyan offshoot groups; some general rules relating to conduct drawn up by Wesley for Methodist societies within the Church of England; and John Wesley's Standard Sermons, his Explanatory Notes on the New Testament and the hymns composed by his brother Charles. The most recent doctrinal statement of America's United Methodist Church seems to make the whole body of credal and doctrinal statements of the various Christian traditions relevant for making contemporary theological decisions. This example perhaps illustrates as well as can be done the extent, variety, and flexibility of what doctrinal standards can mean for some Christians.

Other Protestant groups have repudiated credal statements. Influenced by the empiricist psychology of John Locke, and his assumption that the Bible approached without theological preconceptions will yield an overall consistent body of teaching, the Disciples of Christ have long asserted "no creed but Christ." The Churches of Christ, which are historically related to the Disciples, and some Baptist groups

---

[8]*The Standard Catechism* (New York and Nashville, Tenn.: The Methodist Book Concern, 1929).

have also resisted acknowledging any doctrinal statements or standards except the Christian Scriptures.

Even from the human scholarly point of view, the question of what are the correct methods of Biblical interpretation to find the intended meaning of the human author, or the intended message of the God who is believed to have inspired the human author, have been difficult to answer. Early Biblical scholars, like the celebrated Origen (185-255 C.E.) argued for different levels of meaning—including literal and various symbolic levels—within the Biblical text. Origen argued for faithfulness to the intention of the text but felt both that the text sometimes demands symbolic interpretation and almost always has levels of depth and richness of meaning. Protestants by and large argued for *only* the literal level, but held that even the literal meaning of a text may take highly symbolic forms (as in Genesis where God is described as walking in the Garden of Eden). The rise of critical-historical approaches to the study of scripture in the eighteenth and nineteenth centuries (see Chapters Two and Four) helped, but also further complicated, attempts at interpretation, leading to the recent fundamentalist/liberal split over the question of how one should approach Scripture. This latter-day controversy is perhaps a further instance of the impact of science on religion, since most Biblical scholars had become convinced that they must use the same methods and possess the same objectivity when studying the Bible as scientific historians use in their studies of the past.

Some Protestants have appealed to various kinds of subjective experience—from the inner light of the Quakers to charismatic revelations received by contemporary Pentecostals—as authoritative.

Contemporary Christians show few signs of giving up on the effort to deal with the issues that this chapter has presented. Some hold that answers are implicit within traditionally oriented positions (*e.g.*, the Thomistic, Augustinian, Anselmian, Kantian, and so on) though these may be in need of much clarification and reconstruction. Others feel that radically new approaches are needed and imminent.

QUESTIONS

1. What did Christian thinkers of the first few centuries admire in Platonic philosophy?

2. What are the major differences in the approach to knowledge about God taken by a great philosopher like Aristotle and by the authors of the Jewish scriptures?

3. What do the terms *general* and *special* revelation mean as they are used in the present chapter? Explain the importance attached by Jewish and Christian thinkers to general revelation as a preparation for and criterion of special revelation.

4. Explain—compare and contrast—the four ways in which Christian thinkers have found the use of reason as being of possible value in relation to revealed truth (special revelation).

5. Explain the reasons given by Tertullian, Luther, and Barth for rejecting the use of reason as a basis or preparation for the acceptance or understanding of revealed truth (special revelation).

6. What effect did Aquinas' empiricist theory of knowledge have on his views about what we can come to know about God through the use of natural reasoning?

7. Compare Aquinas' cosmological approach to the knowledge of God with the ontological approach of Anselm.

8. What would be the consequence of holding a completely noncognitivist view of religious language? Do most religious persons think that at least some of their religious "beliefs" contain claims to being *true* and are therefore cognitive? Discuss and explain.

9. Explain the way of negation and the positive or affirmative way of speaking about God. What is the purpose of each? How does Aquinas' concept of analogy apply to them?

10. In what ways have catechisms and credal statements been important to some Protestants because of Protestant emphasis on authority of the Bible?

FURTHER READING

AUGUSTINE, *Confessions*. (Available in many translations and editions).
_____. "On the Teacher" in *Augustine: Earlier Writings*, Trans. J. H. S. Burleigh, Vol. VI LCC. Philadelphia, Penn.: The Westminster Press, 1953.
BARRETT, CYRIL (ed.), *Wittgenstein: Lectures & Conversations on Aesthetics, Psychology, and Religious Belief.* Berkeley and Los Angeles, Calif.: University of California Press, 1972.
BARTH, KARL, *The Knowledge of God and the Service of God According to the Teaching of the Reformation.* London: Hodder and Stoughton, 1938.
BLACKSTONE, WILLIAM T., *The Problem of Religious Knowledge.* Englewood Cliffs, N.J.: Prentice-Hall, Inc., 1963.
BOURKE, VERNON J., (ed.), *The Pocket Aquinas.* New York: Washington Square Press, Inc., 1960.
BRONOWSKI, J., *Science and Human Values.* New York: Harper & Row, 1965.
BUTLER, JOSEPH, *The Analogy of Religion.* (Available in many editions.)
COPLESTON, F. C., *Aquinas.* Baltimore, Md.: Penguin Books, Inc., 1955.
DILLENBERGER, JOHN, *Protestant Thought & Natural Science.* Nashville, Tenn. and New York: Abingdon Press, 1960.
DUPRÉ, LOUIS, *A Dubious Heritage: Studies in the Philosophy of Religion after Kant.* New York: Paulist Press, 1977.
FERRÉ, FREDERICK, *Basic Modern Philosophy of Religion.* New York: Scribner's, 1967.
FEYERABEND, PAUL, *Against Method.* London: Verso, 1978.
GILKEY, LANGDON, *Naming the Whirlwind: The Renewal of God Language.* Indianapolis, Ind., and New York: Bobbs-Merrill, 1969.
HARTSHORNE, CHARLES, *Anselm's Discovery.* LaSalle, Ill.: Open Court, 1965.
_____. *A Natural Theology for Our Time,* LaSalle, Ill.: Open Court, 1967.
HEIM, KARL, *Christian Faith and Natural Science.* New York: Harper & Brothers, 1953.

HICK, JOHN H., *Philosophy of Religion* (2nd Ed.). Englewood Cliffs, N.J.: Prentice-Hall, Inc., 1973.

HUME, DAVID, *An Enquiry Concerning Human Understanding.* (Available in many editions.)

KIERKEGAARD, SØREN, *On Authority and Revelation.* Princeton, N.J.: Princeton University Press, 1955.

KUHN, THOMAS S., *The Structure of Scientific Revolutions,* Second Edition, enlarged. Chicago, Ill.: The University of Chicago Press, 1970.

LANGFORD, JEROME J., *Galileo, Science, and the Church* (revised ed.). Ann Arbor, Mich.: The University of Michigan Press, 1971.

LONERGAN, BERNARD J. F., S. J., *Philosophy of God, and Theology.* Philadelphia, Penn.: The Westminster Press, 1973.

MASCALL, E. L., *Existence and Analogy.* Hamden, Conn.: Archon Books, 1967.

NEIBUHR, H. RICHARD, *The Meaning of Revelation.* New York: The Macmillian Company, 1941.

RAVEN, CHARLES E., *Science, Religion, and the Future.* Cambridge, Mass.: Cambridge University Press, 1943.

SANTILLANA, GIORGIO DE, *The Crime of Galileo.* Chicago, Ill.: University of Chicago Press, 1955.

SMITH, JOHN E., *The Analogy of Experience.* New York: Harper & Row, 1973.

____. *Reason and God.* New Haven, Conn. and London: The Yale University Press, 1961.

TEILHARD DE CHARDIN, PIERRE, *Man's Place in Nature.* New York: Harper & Row, 1966.

WHITEHEAD, A. N., *Science and the Modern World.* New York: The Macmillan Company, 1925.

chapter seven
CHRISTIAN BELIEFS

Chapters Three, Four, and Five emphasize some of the great variety and diversity of attitudes, organizational structures, and liturgical patterns that have characterized the Christian religion throughout its nearly 2,000 years. In the present chapter an attempt is made to characterize the unity of Christian belief. This is not an easy undertaking. Variety and diversity have been and are as much a feature of Christian belief as they are of liturgical and organizational practice. In the pages that follow there will be mention of differences of position or emphasis concerning major facets of Christian belief. These will, however, be kept to a minimum. Thus the reader should be aware that perhaps all of the statements below could be qualified. Also, differences will be found even among articles of faith that most representatives of "mainline" streams (Eastern Orthodox, Catholic, and Protestant) of Christianity substantially agree on. Others both within and beyond these groups, differ in various ways. The same might be said about any of the major world religions— Islam, Buddhism, Hinduism. Despite these differences, it is at times valuable to attempt some characterization of what Kenneth Boulding has called "the Image," that is, some characterization of the way the world, reality, and truth appear to adherents of the religion. Thus, in the present chapter we are interested in seeing how the world, reality, and truth appear to an ideal representative or modal adherent of the Christian faith.

GOD

For *polytheistic* religions there are many gods, and the gods belong to the universe of other beings, including humans and animals. The gods are usually more powerful and more mysterious than other beings. They may even be called immortal, though usually there are stories concerning the origin or birth of various gods. Some gods may even die. Their lives and activities are much like those of humans—they fall in love, become angry with one another, show good will or enmity to humankind. The gods of traditional Japanese religions, the Holy People of North American Indian lore, and the Olympians of classical Greek mythology and cult are examples of this-world gods who are individuals with relatively well-defined personal characteristics within the larger totality of things.

In *pantheistic* religions and philosophies, on the other hand, as in some forms of Hinduism and Chinese Taoism, the Divine is not ultimately individual or personal at all. The Hindu Brahman is a being without *any* characteristics. It is the *one* reality "without a second," without anything else beside it. Brahman is beyond or beneath what we take to be the realities of our experience (which are *not* realities but illusions, unreal or imaginary shadows that derive from and conceal the only true reality). Even the gods of Hindu myth and cultic devotion—the compassionate Vishnu, the dynamic Shiva, the implacable Kali—are only appearances, images, shadows of the one Brahman.

For *deistic* forms of theism—for example, the Islamic religion and Christian deism—there is an eternal God who created the universe, but stands radically above and frequently apart from His creation. In such religions, God is conceived as having only perfect attributes and none of the more human (or anthropomorphic) qualities that the polytheistic deities possess.

In Judaism and Christianity God is conceived of in a strikingly different way from any of these other traditions. God is conceived of, as is Allah of Islam, as being the eternal Creator who transcends His creation. Like the Gods of Islam or Christian Deism, the God of Judaism and Christianity possesses only positive attributes in his perfection. He is also conceived of as abeing active within the world. He has created (the God of Islamic tradition is also conceived of in this way). Finally, however, He is held to have made Himself fully present, to have revealed Himself, in a decisive sense, completely and perfectly at some point in the created realm. For Judaism, God has embodied his wisdom in the Torah.[1] Christians speak of God as having become incarnate in the world in a human life, in a man named Jesus who

---

[1] Whether Judaism should be described as incarnational in outlook may be subject to debate. Certainly it is not the intent of the authors to impose an incarnational view like that of Christianity onto Judaism. However, the analogy of the Torah as in some very important sense containing—with inexhaustible depth and richness—or *being* an embodiment of God's wisdom seems importantly analogous to Christianity's understanding of the incarnation of the divine wisdom in the man Jesus. A reviewer of *Exploring Christianity* suggests that the same point should be made concerning Islam's concept of the self-revelation of Allah in the *Qur'an*.

lived in first-century Palestine. Christians also believe that after the actual historical period during which Jesus lived in Palestine, having been raised from the dead, he continued and continues to manifest the Divine Presence, to *be* God Incarnate. They believe that after the resurrection of Jesus, God's immanent activity in the world, which had in Jewish tradition been referred to as the activity of the Spirit of God, began to be manifested in new ways within the lives of followers of Jesus. It was also manifested by means of the practices, procedures, and traditions of the community—the Christian church—which had come into being to be an extension of the presence and work of the Incarnate God. Thus, of all the major Christian doctrines, that of the Incarnation seems central to the uniqueness of the Christian proclamation. In other religious traditions, for instance, Hinduism and Greek mythology, gods frequently take on, for a time, human form. What Christians have affirmed about the Incarnation of God in Jesus Christ involves a radically different kind of claim.

Some contemporary Christians might quarrel with much of the preceding. This is discussed more fully in Chapter Nine. Throughout Christian history some Christians have disagreed about such statements, but what it describes has been believed and affirmed by the majority of mainstream Christians for many centuries.

Christians, then, typically, believe in one God, who both transcends the universe that He has created and who sustains it, is immanent in it, who became and remains incarnate in a series of specific events, and who by having taken on human nature as the man Jesus belongs to it.

In the early centuries of Christian history there was much controversy about the attempt to interpret what God must be like if all of the things said of Him above are true. What has come to be called the Doctrine of the Trinity emerged during the first 400 years of Christian history as attempts were made to define the limits of what can and should be said about God if His oneness, transcendence, immanence, and incarnateness are to be related without misrepresenting or neglecting any of the four. According to orthodox Christian doctrine, God is in essence and nature one, but within His oneness there are three real aspects or persons. The Greek and Latin terms that were translated by the English term *person* as used in the ancient doctrinal formulations do *not* suggest three separate beings. Our word *aspects*, or even *dimensions*, possibly conveys more of what was meant than our present use of the term persons. The three aspects (or "persons") within the one eternal God were called God the Father, God the Son, and God the Holy Spirit. In orthodox theology, God the Father is associated with that eternal and uncreated source of potency and power, the root of all being. God the Son (or Word or Logos) is associated with the eternal tendency within God to express Himself, to create. God the Spirit is associated with the eternal connectedness between these two, the relationship between God as uncreated power and God as creative actuality. Traditionally the attributes of power, wisdom, and love are associated with the three persons of the Trinity, though it is quickly pointed out that these attributes are not separable. That is, God the Father is not just powerful but wise and loving as well; God the Son is not just wise but loving and powerful as well.

Two points about the orthodox concept of the Trinity are important to emphasize. First, orthodox theology insists that the distinctions between Father, Son, and Spirit are the *only* real distinctions within God. We may suggest other distinctions, as between His justice and His love, but in fact, His justice *is* His love and vice versa. All His attributes are inseparable. Second, orthodox theologians (*e.g.*, Augustine) insisted that, looked at from the outside, it would be impossible to say anything we ascribe to God (*e.g.*, creation or redemption) was done by *one* person of the Trinity. God the Trinity always acts as one. The whole of God the Trinity creates, redeems, and so on. To speak of different persons of the Trinity is in effect to emphasize different aspects or dimensions of God's action and Being.

Both in the ancient church and in modern times some Christians have strenuously objected to what came to be the accepted or orthodox doctrine of the Trinity. Some rejected it outright as a form of polytheism. In modern times the suspicion of an overt or concealed polytheism within trinitarianism was one of the concerns of seventeenth-, eighteenth-, and nineteenth-century Unitarians. Some Unitarians thought of Jesus as being a specially God-inspired man but were unwilling to say that God Himself, as the Second Person of the Trinity, the Divine Logos, or Son of God, had become incarnate in Jesus. In other words, they were willing to call Jesus *a* (or *the*) Son of God, but were not willing to say that the eternal God, that is, God the Eternal Son, or Word, had become and remained incarnate in Jesus.

Others throughout Christian history have *affirmed* a Trinitarian theology that was judged inadequate by adherents of the prevailing or orthodox point of view. Although there are numerous examples of such positions, two major Trinitarian views are worthy of special mention. These approaches are sometimes characterized as being either *tritheistic* or *modalistic*. Sometimes they overlap, though they conflict in an important way.

A *tritheistic* approach to the Trinity treats the different *aspects* of God as three separate or substantially distinct individuals. One such school of thought was Arianism. According to Arianism, named for its advocate Arius (250-336 C.E.), Jesus Christ was the first of created beings, a divine being created by, but in some sense distinct from, God. Jesus became an intermediary between the eternal God and the rest of His creation. Arianism was condemned as heretical by the Council of Nicea in 325 C.E. The phrase in the Nicene Creed, asserting that God the Son "was begotten not made" is a specific repudiation of Arius's views. However, Arianism continued for some time to be a significant rival to the orthodox concept of the relation of God the Father to the Son of God. Today's Jehovah's Witnesses hold a view of the relation of God the Father to Jesus Christ not unlike that of Arianism. (In a truly tritheistic view the Holy Spirit would be a third divine being, distinct from Father and Son. The center of Trinitarian controversy seems to have been the relation of the First to the Second Person of the Trinity; consequently, the heresies were frequently ditheistic rather than tritheistic.)

The dominant ideas of most tritheistic or ditheistic positons are developed as *Monarchianism*—seeing God the Father as the Supreme God above the other aspects of the divine nature. The others are conceived of as separate individuals dependent on the Father, who is not dependent on them. Also, *Subordinationism*—subordinating the Son to the Father and (perhaps) the Spirit to the Son and Father. Sabellianism (condemned by the Council of Constantinople in 381 C.E.) was a view that can be characterized as Monarchian and Subordinationist. In some ways Sabellianism also exemplifies modalism, the other major type of Trinitarian heresy.

The second major family of heretical positions concerning the Trinity was *modalism*. There were many forms of modalism. For each of the three aspects of God were seen as not being real distinctions *within* God. For one form of modalism, of which there were several varieties, there are three successive ways in which God manifests himself in human history. There is the epoch of God the Father, the Creator, and Lawgiver—God as described in the Old Testament. Then there is the Age of the Son, God the Redeemer—the period of redemptive activity of Jesus Christ described in the Gospels. Finally, there is the Age of the Spirit, either inaugurated at Pentecost or at some later point in church history—or just about to be initiated. This is an age in which increasingly the presence and gifts of God are, or will be, made available to believers.

The other major form of modalism was exhibited in the belief that in Himself God does *not* contain three distinct dimensions or aspects of being, but that the three persons of the Trinity are only concepts by means of which we humans apprehend the various ways in which God appears to us. These varieties of modalism say, then, that the doctrine of the Trinity describes God as He appears to us, or as we think of him, not as He is in Himself.

Against both of these positions, the orthodox understanding of God as Trinity insisted that there are three real and genuine aspects, functions, or dimensions of the true God, mutually interrelated and each always present to the others and involved in all that God does. Thus, God was held by orthodox Christians to be capable of, and to have, genuine community within unity, so that to say that God glorifies or loves Himself does not speak either of fragmentation or of massive egotism. We will see later that this way of speaking about God had very great significance for the way in which Christians answered questions concerning who Jesus is and how Jesus, the man from Nazareth, was and is related to God.

As noted in Chapter Six, there always has been much discussion about the adequacy or appropriateness of using finite, or human, language attributes to characterize God. One related issue has recently generated much discussion and some controversy. This is the traditionally accepted use of masculine pronouns to refer to God. It cannot be denied that traditional Hebrew thought about God often seems highly partriarchal. But feminine and female aspects were also ascribed to God in Hebrew thought and in the Jewish scriptures. For example, the wisdom of God frequently was spoken of as being feminine (see Chapter Six). Christian scripture, Christian theological thought, and popular Christian religious language have almost overwhelmingly characterized God, whether in reference to the one

Divine Being, or to the three persons of the Trinity, in masculine terms. However, Christian theological thought about God at its most literal has affirmed that (1) God is neither male nor female; (2) God is the source of maleness and femaleness in the created world; (3) God can appropriately be characterized symbolically as being both male and female; and (4) God transcends the distinctions between male and female, masculinity and femininity. How best to speak of God from Christian points of view is one of the major issues of our time (see Chapters Six and Nine). There is some tendency now to attempt to guard against sexist practices by speaking of God always as having both male and female characteristics, using both or neither forms of the pronoun. Alternatively, there seem to be tendencies to drop sexual language entirely when speaking of God.

To sum up: Christians believe in a God who is one and eternal, whose goodness and being are perfect and inexhaustible, the source and creator of all that exists. According to Christians, God's goodness and being *are* inexhaustible. Therefore, humans are not capable of complete or adequate definition, description, or comprehension of them. Nevertheless, adequate evidence of God's nature, His inexhaustible and eternal power, wisdom and love, is present both in the world He has created (Romans 1:19-21) and in His disclosure of Himself in the life, death and resurrection of Jesus Christ (John 1:18). All that has ever existed or that will exist has its source in and is dependent on God. Yet not any or all of what has existed or will exist can exhaust God's being or power. All that has existed or will exist is made through God's wisdom, yet God's wisdom infinitely transcends all finite reality. God's very nature—the meaning and motive of His power and wisdom—is love (I John 4:8). This love is without limit (Hosea 11:9).

THE CREATED WORLD

For Hinduism, the natural universe is an illusion. For a religion like the Manichaeism that St. Augustine embraced before becoming a Christian, the material world, the realm of natural process, is evil, a prison in which the spiritual part of the human soul is imprisoned, longing to be released to the pure spiritual realm beyond the physical universe. In contrast, Christians believe that God has created the universe from His power, through His wisdom, by and for His love (Genesis 1:2-2:3; Proverbs 8:1, 22-31; John 1:1-5). The created world is therefore good (Genesis 1:31), made to achieve and manifest natural perfection in accordance with the potentialities of its created nature. Thus the created universe and all things in it were created in order to share in and manifest God's goodness, and His love, power, and wisdom. One of the classical confessional statements of Reformed Christianity, the *Westminster Shorter Catechism*, in answer to the question: "What is man's chief end?" replies "Man's chief end is to glorify God and to enjoy Him forever." In an analogical sense, traditional Christianity has affirmed that this answer might be extended to characterize the purpose and destiny of each thing and of the totality of created things.

EVIL

The Christian affirmation of the goodness of the created world has been the occasion of profound questioning about the origin and purpose of evil in the created world. For religions like Hinduism and Buddhism, evil is ultimately unreal. In Manichaeism and Zoroastrianism, evil was explained as the result of the activity of a power or principle independent of and antagonistic to the good god. For Christianity, nothing exists that is not in some sense created by or dependent on God. This is expressed in the statement that according to Christianity, God creates *ex nihilo* (from nothing). Also, Christianity affirms that the contrast between good and evil and the existence of evil are not illusory as Hinduism affirms and are not, as Buddhism teaches, simply the manifestation of our own imperfect way of looking at things. Rather, evil is a distorted and tragic actualization of good natural capacities and spiritual powers within the universe that God has created. These, as created by God, were and are good and were intended to be used to bring about further good. As misused to produce a distorted goodness, these natural capacities have themselves become distorted and evil.

The existence of evil has been one of the largest stumbling blocks to Christian belief. Two of the most vocal twentieth-century critics of the Christian theistic position, the philosophers Bertrand Russell and Antony Flew, though criticizing all of the traditional arguments given by Christians for believing in God, found the existence of evil the most telling objection to Christian claims that a good, wise, powerful, and loving God created the universe we inhabit. Flew challenged Christians to witness the agonized death from cancer of the throat of a small child while continuing to affirm the reality or goodness of God.

Traditionally, at least two kinds of evil have been identified as requiring explanation if the Christian concept of the goodness of God and His creation is to be maintained, *natural* and *moral* evil. Natural evil refers to calamities and occasions of suffering that befall people and other sentient beings. To many observers or participants, such injury and pain seem disproportionate to any possible good that could result from the events involving them, and the events cannot be explained as resulting from the intentions of intelligent finite beings. Natural evils include such things as earthquakes, tornadoes, and diseases that cannot be prevented. Why would God have created a universe in which such things happen? If He is all powerful He presumably could have created a world in which they would not occur. *Moral evil* refers to evil that is deliberately done by or results from the actions of rational creatures. These include crimes, acts of aggression, and acts of injustice or unkindness that cause suffering in their victims. Why would God endow rational beings with the possibility of having evil intentions, of doing evil actions, of harming themselves and others if God presumably could have created a world in which everyone would always, freely or under compulsion, choose to do good?

A traditional Christian answer to the question of the existence of natural evil has been that the whole created universe and not just its human part has been involved in a catastrophe of cosmic significance, namely the fall from created good-ness known as sin. Paul, in his Letter to the Romans (8:19-23), asserts that the whole creation is longing for its deliverance from bondage to the futility which has befallen it. So even the answer to the question of natural evil would depend on the answers that Christians give to questions about moral evil.

A more recent answer given by, among others, Christian process philosophers and theologians,[2] does not necessarily make sin, or a corruption of nature, the cause of natural evil. In the freedom of the natural order, natural evil is not con-trolled or willed by God, they assert. The process position maintains genuine free-dom at every level of the finite world, though rational and conscious creatures are capable of exercising freedom deliberately and more consistently than those that do not possess conscious rationality. The difference is one of degree. A character in a novel by Aldous Huxley once suggested that rattlesnakes represent a species that long ago went wrong by choosing (however unconsciously) to become pred-ators and to meet the dangers of their environment by secreting and injecting venom. This view would seem to exemplify the process position, giving one form of natural evil at least a partly moral dimension. However, such things as tornadoes would not be examples of moral evil. On the process view, however, they would not result from God's will or God's intention, but simply from the interaction of natural events.

Sin

Traditionally, Christianity has affirmed that humankind was originally good and endowed with the freedom, as a part of its created goodness, to choose be-tween good and evil in achieving self-actualization. Choosing good would lead to genuine fulfillment for the human self and humankind. Choosing evil would lead to negation, frustration, and suffering. A critic like Antony Flew has asked why being able to choose what is evil and destructive should be part of a created good-ness. The Christian response generally has been that the highest forms of value and fulfillment are to be found in the actualization of individual personality or charac-ter and of interpersonal relations involving and expressing love and community. Such actualization entails learning to prefer and affirm the good when there is a genuine possibility that it will not be chosen, and learning to put the welfare of others and of the group ahead of limited selfish interests. Christians have argued: if the highest good an individual can attain is to become a person who freely gives love to God and to fellow human beings, this good can become actual only in

---

[2]Process philosophy and process theology are terms frequently used to describe the views of thinkers influenced by concepts of the British philosopher Whitehead (1861-1947) and of his American interpreter Charles Hartshorne. God is basic to Whitehead's thought, having both eternal and temporal aspects. According to Whitehead, God always is active to bring about the highest possible realization of value in any given situation but finite realities down to the lowest levels of existence (*e.g.*, subatomic particles) possess genuine degrees of freedom. Thus God influences but does not totally determine or control events.

genuine choice. Thus, a being who would be good "automatically" would not be good at all. Also, unless persons are vulnerable to injury, pain, and suffering as possible consequences of choice, choice would have no meaning. Everything would be equally good. Thus the *necessity* that natural evil be possible seems implied in the possibility of moral evil, and the *necessity* that moral evil be possible seems implied in the possibility of good.

In the Genesis story of the fall of Adam and Eve (Genesis 2-3) Adam and Eve were given a large degree of free choice about what they *might* do, but were told by God what they *should not* do—they were told not to eat the fruit of one of the trees in the garden they inhabited. Nevertheless, they were not compelled not to eat this fruit—they were not compelled to obey God. In choosing to disobey, they forfeited their original innocence.

It has been mentioned in Chapter Six that some Christians have interpreted the narratives of the first few chapters of Genesis literally as describing the events that took place with the creation of the universe, including the parents or ancestors of the human race. Other Christians have understood the stories of creation and fall to be mythical and symbolic, but nevertheless to reveal important spiritual truths.

Within the ancient church, interpreters like Origen, St. Augustine, and others treated these stories as containing a large number of symbolic elements. In the modern period, a number of Christians who have understood the Genesis account of Adam and Eve not as literally or historically true have found it of decisive importance in revealing the nature and reality of sinfulness as a common human condition. According to this understanding, sin—original sin—is an attitude shared by humans that manifests itself in destructive acts, frequently even in acts that appear to be constructive but are not, since their motivation is distorted by sinful selfishness. In interpreting the Genesis story as an account of original sin, the twentieth-century Protestant theologian Reinhold Niebuhr argued that the story does not really intend to tell us about the origin of sin, but about its presence and pervasive power in all humans. Niebuhr was particularly impressed with the human tendency to do apparently unselfish and altruistic deeds which really manifest individual or group selfishness. Thus for Niebuhr, Adam and Eve, rather than being historical individuals, are symbols representing all humanity.

According to traditional Christian concepts of original sin, whether or not the Genesis story is interpreted literally, human beings have lost the power to choose good, even though humanity retains moral freedom. External actions and conscious attitudes have been corrupted by a deep preconscious or unconscious selfishness. Original freedom is understood by Christians to mean that humans are created in God's image (Genesis 1:26-30). But original freedom involves the power of humans to separate themselves from God, the source of their lives (and of all life), to separate themselves from their own creative, fulfilling possibilities and from right relation to themselves and other created beings. Christians by and large have affirmed that there was (is) no need for human beings to misuse their freedom and alienate themselves from God, self, other humans and other finite beings. But *exactly this* has happened. The state of separation, of self-destructive estrangement is real. One aspect of the meaning of original sin is the claim that once this estrangement has taken place—once sin has entered human history—there is no way that humankind can recover its lost health, wholeness, or innocence by its own efforts. Based on literal readings of parts of the Genesis account, some of the early church fathers (including Augustine) characterized sin as biologically inherited from Adam and Eve. Some recent Christian thinkers, influenced by contemporary developmental psychologists like Sullivan, Erikson, Fairbairn, or Winnicott, have spoken of the spread of an original attitude of anxiety or mistrust from parent to child by a kind of psychological contagion. Thus, whether the Genesis account is interpreted as literal or as symbolic, Christians who affirm the reality of original sin see humanity's fallen state as something with contagious power that has affected all humanity since the beginning of human history.

A number of controversial points emerged in Christian theological debates related to the concepts of the fall and original sin. Two will be mentioned here. First, if God foreknew humankind would fall did this mean that humans were never really free? Nothing that is not in some sense already determined can be foreknown. Some Christians, called predestinarians (including Augustine), argued that a thing can be foreknown without foreknowledge being its cause. They also argued that sin by fallen humans involves freedom, though fallen humans are not free not to sin. In sinning, humans do what they will. Therefore, they are responsible, even though they could not will to do otherwise. Thus, for Augustine and other predestinarians like Luther and Calvin, God's foreknowledge did not predetermine human sin, but in some sense sin was predetermined or predestined by another aspect of God, His will. Yet though they are predestined to sin, humans nevertheless sin freely, since they follow their own wills in sinning.

Some Christian thinkers, especially contemporary process thinkers, have insisted (in contrast to predestinarian thought) on a radical dimension of freedom in the created world possessed not just by humans but by other finite beings. Thus, for them God does not entirely foreknow the future, much less predetermine it. This, such thinkers have argued, is the only way to affirm a future in which *genuine* freedom can operate.

The majority of Christian thinkers, however, do not accept the extreme predestinarian view of Augustine and the early Protestants. They also do not accept the limited God of process theology. Instead, they have affirmed three beliefs. First, God foreknows the future, but since God's relation to time is not like ours, His foreknowledge does not *determine* future events. Rather all of our time is eternally present to God. Second, God's providential will does have a determinative effect on what we call future events. This does not nullify but takes account of and makes use of human freedom. Third, all humanity suffers from fallenness and is thus incapable by its own efforts of arriving at goodness. Nevertheless, because of their freedom, humans are responsible for their sinful condition and for their misuse of freedom, which in its fallen state is used to nullify itself.

A second major controversy related to the doctrine of original sin concerns Pelagianism, a view espoused by the British monk Pelagius and opposed by St.

Augustine. Pelagius taught that Christ merely assists humans to exercise their innate capacity of free choice, a capacity never fully lost. Thus, each human is capable of exercising freedom to obey or disobey God's commandments.

Augustine opposed this view. Though Christ has made it possible for the guilt of original sin to be removed by baptism (or in exceptional cases in other ways) humans are still subject to sin's power, and the final removal of the power of original sin is the culmination, rather than the precondition, of the Christian life. According to Augustine and many of the founders and heroic figures of Christian monasticism who influenced him, the Christian life is a pilgrimage largely undertaken to overcome the residue of original sin within the Christian. It is through God's grace at every step of this pilgrimage that the process of transformation will be brought to its completion. Augustine coupled his view of the effects of original sin with a rigid predestinarianism, according to which it is completely God's grace that determines who will and who will not be brought to salvation.

Western Catholic Christianity condemned Pelagianism but did not entirely agree with Augustine. Thomas Aquinas and Western Catholicism generally made room for genuine human cooperation with God's grace, though that cooperation is made possible through grace. Early Lutherans and Calvinists tended to follow Augustine's predestinationism, admitting that predestination and salvation are mysteries of God's grace that humans cannot entirely grasp. Most recent Protestants have moved to a position indistinguishable from that of Catholicism. Indeed, it is sometimes taken to be an essential part of the Christian understanding of human nature to insist on a degree of genuine freedom in moral choice in contrast to the determinist views of many secular psychological movements.

The Devil and the Demonic

The New Testament speaks of demonic powers or beings to whom, before the coming and work of Christ, the world had fallen prey. It refers to Beelzebul, or Satan, presumably the lord of the powers of evil. To many Jews and to the Christian author of the New Testament Book of Revelation, the Roman Empire was not merely an evil human organization, it was a supreme manifestation and tool of the demonic kingdom.

Such thought was characteristic of first-century Judaism, though not of the Judaism of earlier Old Testament periods. There is an intelligent being called Satan in the Old Testament Book of Job. *This* Satan is not demonic or evil, but is one of God's servants. Beliefs about the demonic held in Judaism apparently were largely a result of contact with Babylonian and Persian (Iranian) religious thought. By the time of Jesus, such beliefs were widespread. However, the New Testament writers tend to presuppose rather than to expound such beliefs.

Many recent Christians have seen Satan and the other demonic beings as *symbolic personifications* of the evil encountered in human life. But others reject such beliefs as myths that explain away human responsibility for the evil that is perpetrated in human interaction ("The devil made me do it"). Others have seen demonic figures as valuable symbolic expressions of trans-human causes and consequences of alienation from God, as natural powers perverted or distorted from creative roles they might have played, as symbolic representation of real though not individual forces or events. Some have found them to be valuable symbolic expressions of the power that evil assumes in corporate human life (as in Nazism or Communism) or in impersonal human organizations (like economic or political institutions) that can oppress people. Thus, the symbols would be valuable corrections of the belief that only *individual* humans can do evil.

Probably the great majority of Christians, however, have understood the devil to refer, literally, to spiritual beings, independent of humanity, that originally were good but through misuse of freedom are now corrupt and destructive. These corrupt beings have been seen not as wholly responsible for the corruption of human goodness, but as contributors to it. The demonic powers have been seen as parasitical on both God's goodness and human freedom.

Christian theological thought that accepts the demonic's literal truth would caution against taking the *human* ways of picturing these forces—the devil and demons—as being accurate representations. Orthodox theologians who take the concept of the devil literally caution that to depict the devil anthropomorphically with sublime grandeur, as in Milton's *Paradise Lost*, or crudely, as in comic strips, is as misleading as the anthropomorphic depictions of God (however valid from an artistic pont of view) in Michaelangelo's or William Blake's visual representations of the Divine as a handsome, elderly man. Karl Barth has written *a propos* of the petition in the prayer that Jesus taught his disciples (see Luke 11:2-4 and Matthew 6:9-13), "Deliver us from the Evil One:"

> In the sixth petition of the Lord's prayer we are not concerned with . . . minor temptations, which are . . . relative and bearable. . . . It is rather a question of the infinite menace of the nothingness that is opposed to God himself. . . . Our Reformers, Luther as well as Calvin, were acquainted not only with the small temptations but also with the great one. They knew it was with the Devil that they had to deal. For him they had no respect, since he is not respectable. But they knew that he exists. . . . We perceive and feel his power. To tell the truth, it is only a pseudo power. It is not a real power. The terrible thing about it is that it acts, although this action is unreal.[3]

Thus, even Christians who believe that the devil and the demonic are to be taken as literal concepts warn against taking *too literally* the images and representations humans have used to depict them. They would warn that if evil is truly a disintegrative force, then, rather than being the suave and sophisticated playboy of film and fiction, the devil is simply a boiling ocean of discontent.

This view of the demonic powers, whether taken as literal or symbolic, is entirely consonant with Augustine's understanding, which has largely been accepted by Christian tradition, of evil as not a positive force or power but as absence of, or distance from, the Good (God). Sin is a spiritual being's turning from the true object

---

[3] Karl Barth, *Prayer According to the Catechisms of the Reformation* (Philadelphia, Penn.: The Westminster Press, 1952), pp. 72-74.

of its love (God) to a false or (relatively) unreal object. Thus Augustine's view explains both natural and moral evil. Christians making use of the concept of the demonic, either as literal or as symbolic, would also point to the claim, as Mark's Gospel shows clearly but elliptically at its beginning, that the powers of evil have in principle and in fact been broken by the redemptive activity of God in Jesus Christ (Mark 1:12-15). Mark's Gospel also suggests in a later passage that with the coming of the Messiah and the advent of the Kingdom of God, humans do not need to be concerned about the powers of evil external to them as sources of danger. They are to be concerned about the possibilities of evil within their own hearts. This is where the Messiah is to wage his ultimate battle and where his followers must wage theirs (Mark 9:9-13).[4]

The Forms of Estrangement

According to Christian belief, then, freedom is an aspect of the destiny of created spiritual beings. This is part of what it means to say that they are created through God's wisdom and for His love: They share His nature and reflect His creative freedom. But with freedom, created beings possess the power to turn against their created goodness. They have the power to separate themselves from the source of all life, to separate themselves from their creative possibilities and from right (fulfilling, good) relationships to other created beings. God creates free beings. There was and is not need that created beings use their freedom to alienate themselves from God, from self, from other finite beings. Yet Christians believe that freedom actually is, has been, and was misused (I Corinthians 15:21-22; Genesis 3:1-7; 4:3-7; Romans 1: 18-32, 5:12-14; James 1:13-15). Christians believe that self-destructive alienation from God, self, and neighbor actually has entered the world, and that, having entered the world, it spreads by a kind of contagion to finite beings before they are able consciously to take precautions against it. Thus, Christians believe that all human beings, when they come to mature self-awareness (Romans 7:15; Luke 15:17), find that they are cut off from God, from right relation to themselves, their fellow humans, and the whole created universe, by a self-rejecting/self-affirming attitude that denies God, neighbor, and self.

Christians have identified two major forms of this self-destructive attitude called sin: willfullness and self-indulgence. Willfulness is the insistence on having one's way even if it means self-destruction. Self-indulgence is self-pity as the results of one's willfulness. Christians believe that all conscious finite beings, when they come to genuine self-awareness, find themselves lost in wrong relation to God and created reality, cut off from geniune life, and, because of willfull and self-pitying attitudes, helpless to find true life (Romans 7:21-24).

---

[4]This is, admittedly, a difficult and obscure passage. The interpretation given here rests on the argument that this passage, contrasting God's external protection of Elijah of Old Testament days from the power of his external evil enemies with the complete vulnerability of John the Baptist and the Christ to the power of *their* external enemies, interprets Jesus' entire ministry at midpoint, connecting the beginning and end points—namely, his victory over the demons in Chapter I and his struggle with and victory over temptations in Gethsemane, leading to his sacrificial death.

REDEMPTION AND RECONCILIATION

Christians believe the ultimate answer to the existence of evil, in either its natural or moral form, is to be found in the redemptive activity of God in Jesus Christ. Traditionally, Christians have affirmed that God acts, will act, and once did act in Jesus Christ from the same love, the same wisdom, and the same power manifested in the creation of the world to redeem it and reconcile it to itself and to Him. In the life, death, and resurrection of a human being called Jesus who lived in Palestine in the first century C.E., the fullness of the uncreated wisdom of God—vitalized and made effective by His love and power—entered the history of His created world. (John 1:1-5; 9-18; Hebrews 1:1-5; Colossians 1:11-20; Philippians 2:5-10; I Corinthians 1:22-25).

Traditionally, this belief has been referred to as the doctrine of the Incarnation. In the life, death, and resurrection of Jesus, God took (takes) the willful alienation and suffering of the created world into Himself and overcomes it. By doing this He made (makes) it possible for all who will receive His gift of life through faith and repentance to rise from the death of self-destructive alienation to a new life of right relation to God, self, and neighbor.

The name of the Christian doctrine concerning the event of redemption and reconciliation is Atonement. There has never been a definitive statement about the Atonement. Some Christians, like St. Anselm of Canterbury, have spoken of the sacrifice of Jesus on the cross as substitutionary. It was satisfaction for the guilt that humankind incurred before the righteous God, a satisfaction provided by God Himself since humanity was (is) incapable of paying it. Others, particularly in the ancient church, have emphasized that in the Atonement God achieves a victory over the powers of evil to which humankind has become subject, thus providing the way by which the captives are set free. Others, like Abélard and St. Augustine, emphasized the subjective effect on humankind, whose attitudes of willful and self-indulgent selfishness are (were) broken when they see (saw) the sacrificial love of the innocent God-Man given for them on the cross. This concept of Atonement is sometimes called the moral influence or exemplary theory.

It has not been necessary for Christians to choose among these theories, though to many contemporary Christians the satisfaction theory of Anselm seems excessively legalistic, dependent on medieval theories of penal justice and on the medieval hierarchy of relations between nobility, commoners, and serfs. In the past, the moral influence theory has been criticized as being overly subjective. However, Christian thinkers have seen some validity in treating the views as metaphors and utilizing all of them, and others, to characterize the central affirmation that God in Jesus reconciles the world to Himself.

Related to the Christian understanding of Incarnation and Atonement were many controversies about the person of Christ. These involved the question of how Jesus is related to God. This issue has been touched on in discussion of the doctrine of the Trinity. Here, it must be said that probably the most tangled of all theological controversies in the ancient church concerned the nature of the personal identity or being of Jesus Christ.

In some offshoots of Jewish Christianity, Jesus was viewed as a man who, because of his righteousness, was named or designated Messiah and Son of God (usually at his baptism). This view of the relation of the human Jesus to the divine Christ (or word) is usually called adoptionism. It was held by at least one segment of a Jewish Christian group called Ebionites. Their view was described and criticized by the Alexandrian Christian, Origen, and others in the ancient church. The Ebionites emphasized the human nature of Jesus, namely his having achieved righteousness, as being that which made him able to bring salvation to humanity.

More common were positions emphasizing the divine nature in contrast to the human. The earliest Christian orthodoxy seems to have held God had in some sense united with or taken on human nature by becoming incarnate. Because of this, human nature, without being annulled, was granted the power to triumph over the temptations we experience and conquer the evils we are subject to. Thus, human salvation was accomplished and became possible for all humans to receive. Some forms of a widespread movement or family of movements called gnosticism presented variations of, or deviations from, this emphasis.

According to gnosticism, the Christ came in apparent human form to teach the qualified (spiritual) among humanity the way to salvation. Presumably, not all forms of gnosticism, which was strong in the second and third centuries C.E., were Christian. For those that were, the Christ plays the role of the Divine Enlightener, the Teacher. Already referred to in the New Testament—the Gospel and Epistles of John and certain of Paul's letters seem in part directed against gnostic emphases— Christian forms of gnosticism denied the reality or importance of the humanity of Jesus.

For some gnostics, the human Jesus was only a phantom or an illusion made use of by the Divine Spirit-Christ who had come to teach the way of escape from the bondage of material existence. For other gnostics, the Christ was only temporarily united with the human Jesus, departing before the crucifixion. Gnosticism resembles and partly overlaps with Docetic forms of Christianity, which held that to accomplish human salvation, the Christ only *seemed* to become human and suffer and die on the cross. Also, the second-century movement known as Marcionism, begun by Marcion, resembles gnosticism in seeing the God of the Old Testament as a harsh or even evil being, not the God who sends the Christ into the world to free imprisoned humanity. For Christian forms of gnosticism and Docetism *only* those humans who are spiritual (in contrast to the majority of humans) will respond to the spiritual Christ who comes disguised as a man.

Throughout Christian history, many later Christologies (teachings or doctrines about Christ) emphasized the divine at the expense of the human in the person of Jesus Christ. Some of these are discussed in other chapters. For the Monophysites, Jesus Christ was essentially divine in nature (see Chapter Three). In Jesus Christ there was a human body with a divine soul or spirit. Nestorius (d. 451 C.E.) and the Nestorians affirmed both divine and human natures in Jesus Christ but drew a sharp line separating the two natures. Thus for Nestorius, the divine logos did not suffer and die, the man Jesus did.

What was at issue in all the controversies was the question of how the Atonement could take place unless in some unique and legitimate sense in Jesus Christ there is both full and complete humanity and unique and full self-revelation of God. The position that became known as orthodox, championed by Athanasius (ca. 298-373 C.E.) and by many others, insisted that there must be both and that both natures must be full and complete. On this basis, Nestorianism, Monophysitism, and a host of other positions were condemned. Several of the Ecumenical Councils dealt with the Christological conflict. The first Nicene Council's trinitarian formula was related to it. But the formula adopted by the Council of Chalcedon in 451 C.E. probably had the most permanent and decisive influence, though it was rejected by the Monophysites and contested by others for a long time. What Chalcedon affirmed is that

> We all with one accord teach men to acknowledge one and the same Son, our Lord Jesus Christ, at once complete in Godhead and complete in manhood, truly God and truly man, consisting also of a reasonable soul and body, of one substance with us as regards his manhood; like us in all respects, apart from sin; as regards his Godhead, begotten of the Father before the Ages, but yet as regards his manhood begotten, for us men and for our salvation, of Mary the Virgin, the God-bearer; one and the same Christ, Son, Lord, Only-begotten, recognized in two natures, without confusion, without change, without division, without separation; the distinction of natures being in no way annulled by the union, but rather the characteristics of each nature being preserved and coming together to form one person and subsistence, not as part or separated into two persons, but one and the same Son and Only-begotten God the Word, Lord Jesus Christ. . . .[5]

In recent centuries both traditional—conservative or orthodox—and revisionary, or liberal, forms of Christianity have usually affirmed a unique divine and human reality in the one Jesus Christ. Liberal Christians have sometimes charged that more conservative theologians, while paying lip service to the full humanity of Jesus, have tended to let the humanity be swallowed up in the divinity in a kind of modern docetism or gnosticism. To conservatives, liberals often have seemed to emphasize humanity at the expense of deity. Schleiermacher (1768-1834), often called the father of Protestant liberalism in Germany, emphasized the deity of Jesus Christ. But like early adoptionism, he also made Jesus' humanity, namely his perfect consciousness of God (his sense of absolute dependence, trust, and obedience), the basis of His role as redeemer.

Earlier discussions of Christology, soteriology (the doctrine of salvation) and the Atonement focused on the person and work of Christ. With the rise of the historical caution resulting from the work of Schweitzer and the form critics (see Chapter Two) concerning our ability to discover either a connected account of Jesus' work or a key to his personal attitudes (*e.g.*, such as what his consciousness or self-understanding was) some later Christian thinkers shifted from the person and work

[5] Quoted in Henry Bettenson (ed.), *Documents of the Christian Church* (New York & London: Oxford University Press, 1943, pp. 72-73.

of Jesus to what God has accomplished in the *event* of Jesus Christ. The theologian and biblical scholar Rudolf Bultmann spoke of God's action in Jesus as the ultimate event in which we encounter the possibility of salvation or new life. This possibility comes to us as a demand and opportunity for faith, by which Bultmann meant openness to the future. The openness of faith means that we meet our neighbor with the neighborly love that the Gospels show to be both what God demands and what the event of salvation in Jesus Christ makes possible.

Frequently contested, often a source of puzzle and paradox in attempts to talk about who Jesus Christ is and how it is that Christians believe God has acted in him to bring salvation to the world, the Council of Chalecedon's formula, nevertheless, became the major way by which later Christian thinking about Jesus found much of its inspiration and its self-imposed limits.

THE WORK OF THE SPIRIT

The beginning of and growth in Christian life for individuals and the continuing life of the Christian community as a whole have always been associated in Christian thought with the work of the third person of the Trinity, the Holy Ghost or Holy Spirit. As already noted, the Spirit as well as the Son is associated with the work of creation. In Jewish Scripture and tradition the Spirit is the bearer of messages and of power to designated individuals and groups. In the New Testament, the Spirit is at times referred to as the Spirit of Jesus (or of the Lord). The spirit is given to his apostles as the source of new life. It is the implanting of Christ in individual believers (Galatians 2:20).

Although there were controversies in the ancient church concerning the work of the Spirit and its relation to the other two persons of the Trinity, by and large these were overshadowed by the controversies concerning the relation of the first and second persons to each other and of the second person of the Trinity (the Word or Christ) to human nature in Jesus.

One of the most significant of the controversies involving the relation of the Spirit to the Father and the Son contributed to the rupture between Eastern Orthodox and Western Catholic branches of Christianity. (Chapters Three and Five emphasize geographical, cultural and political sources of the gradual stages leading to the final rupture in 1054 C.E.) As early as the fifth century in some areas of the western Church the word *filioque* (and from the son) had been added to the phrase in the Nicene Creed saying that the Spirit proceeds from the Father. By the ninth century, *filioque* was used throughout the West. The Eastern Church responded indignantly, partly because, according to its beliefs, such a change could not be made without the approval of an Ecumenical Council involving *all* the bishops of the church, Eastern and Western. The outcome was mutual excommunication of Western and Eastern leaders, Pope and Patriarch. Since that time, Eastern theologians have defended the belief that the Spirit proceeds *from* the Father, whereas

Western theologians, Protestant[6] as well as Catholic, have tended to argue that the assertion that the Spirit proceeds from both Father and Son captures the Trinitarian position more fully, expressing the community and dynamic sense of God's three-in-oneness and mutuality while fully avoiding tritheism.

COMMUNITY

Christians affirm that God's revelation of His wisdom, love, and power, His reconciling gift of Himself, was given to specific, actual human beings. The names of many of them are recorded in the pages of the New Testament: Peter, Mary, James, John, Andrew, Philip, Paul. Many others are named (see the gospels and I Corinthians 15).

Christians believe that after his burial, Jesus was raised from the dead by the power of God, and actually appeared to many of these people. Jesus' resurrection and the future gift of God's love, the power and wisdom that come through the Holy Spirit (Acts 2:1-21; I Corinthians 12:12-13), made them into a community. As a result of what they told others about God's self-disclosure in Jesus, many others became part of this community. The community, the church of Jesus Christ, still exists. Needless to say, it exists in many forms or denominations that have had difficulty recognizing the legitimacy of each other. The members of this community (of these groups) are still proclaiming what they believe to be the good news of God's self-revelation, of the salvation that He brings in Jesus Christ. They affirm that wherever the message is proclaimed, other human beings are being called by the Holy Spirit into the community of redemption and reconciliation. Christians believe that God's reconciliation has actually happened; it is a present possibility for all who will receive the good news of it. They believe that God is still at work bringing His purposes to fulfillment and completion.

In the New Testament the term saint (having the connotation of one who is set apart or holy) is used by Christians to refer to each other. Later the term came to designate Christians of the early and later periods whose lives manifested outstanding holiness. In Western Catholicism and Eastern Orthodoxy, in contrast to most branches of Protestantism, there have flourished many traditions about the saints. A practice of religious devotion, or veneration, directed toward the saints has also flourished. Within Roman Catholicism there are official channels and procedures by means of which deceased Christians may be recognized as saints. The conferral of this status and title is called canonization. It is believed that devotion to the saints can enhance one's spiritual growth and be a source of aid in one's life.

The veneration of Mary, the mother of Jesus, has been of special importance,

---

[6]Karl Barth, for instance, strenuously argued for the *filioque* concept in his massive work *Church Dogmatics.*

with some differences of emphasis, for both Eastern Orthodoxy and Roman Catholicism. The Gospels of Luke and Matthew, which give accounts of the birth of Jesus, refer to Mary as the virgin mother of the Savior. Traditionally, both Eastern Orthodoxy and Western Catholicism have venerated her as "the mother of God." Since very early days of Christian history, Mary has been venerated as the virgin Mother of Jesus. Roman Catholicism has argued that she remained throughout her life a virgin, whereas Protestants, traditionally accepting the virgin birth of Jesus, have argued that the Gospels support the view that after his birth she lived a normal married life with her husband, bearing the children referred to in the Gospels as Jesus' brothers and sisters. In Western Catholicism in the nineteenth century, Mary's immaculate conception (her conception and birth in a sinless state, free of the guilt and power of original sin) was proclaimed as official dogma. In the twentieth century Pope Pius XII proclaimed as dogma her bodily ascension into heaven at the culmination of her earthly life.

Protestants have tended to exalt the saints, including the virgin Mary, but not to advocate direct acts of devotion toward them. Typically, Protestants have seen the dogmas concerning Mary, and to some extent Catholic devotion to her, as obstacles in the way of Christian unity.

SACRAMENTS

Christians have almost universally affirmed the importance of the corporate life of the Christian community in worship. The sacraments have been of central importance in worship for most Christian groups. Differences in the number of sacraments recognized (seven for Eastern Orthodoxy and Roman Catholicism, two for most Protestant groups, none for the Society of Friends) are discussed in Chapter Five. Here it is important to note that although most Christians see the sacraments as being means of obtaining grace (and spiritual growth) for partakers of them, there have been widely varying interpretations of their nature. Roman Catholics, Eastern Orthodox worshipers, and some Protestants (Lutherans and some in the Anglican tradition) hold that in the sacraments God's grace is objectively present, and to such a degree that they have used the term *real presence* to signify its objectivity. Thus, for Roman Catholic belief, during the celebration of Mass (or the Lord's Supper) the bread and wine literally become the body and blood of Christ.

Martin Luther stressed the real presence of God in the sacraments to the extent that he was not able to agree with Calvin and other Reformation theologians who stressed the spiritual rather than physical presence of God in the sacraments. Some Protestants in the Reformed tradition do not go as far as Calvin in stressing even spiritual presence, but see the sacrament of the Lord's Supper as a *memorial* or commemoration of Christ's sacrificial death. Baptists tend to avoid use of the word sacrament, speaking of baptism and the Lord's Supper as *ordinances* instead. For Roman Catholics, the mass is in an important sense a reenactment, a re-offering of Christ for the sins of the world. Most Protestants avoid the idea of reenactment but see the sacrament as more than a memorial. Though some Protestants use the term "means of grace" to describe the sacraments, others reject the term as being too close to the Catholic view.

Different views about the significance of ordination to the priesthood or Christian ministry, whether ordination is regarded as a sacrament or not, affect ways in which Christians of different backgrounds have been able to interact with each other. Those Christians accepting the concept of an objective succession of authority and spiritual endowment from the apostles, transmitted by ordination, have frequently been unable to accept the validity of ministerial ordination and orders in groups that do not belong to this line of succession. They have also frequently not been able to accept the validity—apart from certain exceptional cases— of sacraments administered by such ministers. There is a typically objective concept of the priesthood held by Eastern Orthodox, Roman Catholics, and some Protestants according to which ordination indelibly confers the status of priest on one who has received it. In contrast, there is an extreme Protestant concept of Christian ministry according to which the minister is and remains a layperson, perhaps with special educational or personal qualifications, who has been designated either permanently or temporarily to exercise the ministerial office. Most Protestants hold concepts of ordination and of the ministry that fall between these two types.

The sacraments involve physical events and physical acts or elements. The ceremonial acts involved are understood by Roman Catholics as the material or matter of the sacrament. Its form (and that which gives the ceremony efficacious power to be a channel of grace) depends on the use of the appropriate (definitive) words of institution by one who is entitled to use them.

Many Protestants have defined *sacrament* as "a visible sign of an inward and spiritual grace." One frequently cited Protestant definition or criterion of the true church is "where the Word is rightly preached and the sacraments duly administered."

With all their differences concerning number, mode, and efficacy, Christians believe that the sacraments were instituted by Christ and that participation in them is an important part of Christian life and growth for the individual Christian and the body of Christian believers.

SCRIPTURE

The earliest communication of the message about Jesus was in spoken language. Jesus' teachings, accounts of what he had said and done, and the story of his death and resurrection, were passed on by the original members of his community. As time passed, written accounts of this teaching, and of these traditions began to be made. Letters were written from leaders of the community—from Paul, John, James, and Jude—to groups within the community. Other writings based on the spoken words of and about Jesus that had been handed down by members of the original community, "gospels," also began to appear. These told the story, the good news, of what God had done, of what He was still doing, and of what He intended to do in and through Jesus Christ and His Spirit. As these began to be circulated, they were used in worship and in instruction among groups of the followers of Jesus. Christians soon began to regard some of these writings—which we now call the New Testament—as inspired Scripture, as a record of the events in which God had revealed Himself. (In Chapter Six some account is given of different attitudes of Christians toward interpretation of Scripture. See also Chapter Two.)

During the second century C.E., a Christian named Marcion argued that Christians should reject the Jewish scriptures. He produced a "canon" of Christian Scripture containing his abridged version of Luke's Gospel and of some of Paul's letters. Some scholars believe that in reaction to Marcion, the trend toward an orthodox listing or canon of Christian Scripture began. From the second century on there was near agreement by orthodox Christians as to what writings the Christian Scriptures should contain, though there was no unanimity for several centuries.

Christians believe that the record of events given in the Scriptures contains God's revelation of Himself, since it allows people of all times to participate in the original events of His self-revelation. That is, Christians believe that the written record can, with the help of God's Holy Spirit, become revelation now. Christians also regard the Jewish Scriptures, which most Christians call the Old Testament, as inspired, as part of God's self-revelation, since the events of His self-revelation in Christ grow out of the events recorded there, are prepared for and foreshadowed by them. These writings, the Old and New Testaments, are regarded by Christians as a gift of God, through His Holy Spirit, to His church and to the world. (See Appendix One and Two for further explanation of Biblical writings.)

THE CHRISTIAN LIFE

Christians traditionally have believed that when one enters the Christian community—whether as a baptized infant or as an adult convert—one embarks on a pilgrimage or way of life that ideally involves disciplined growth toward a likeness to Christ. Traditionally, Christian life (based on concepts and terms used in Paul's letter to the Romans and on the Gospel and First Epistle of John) has had three stages. First, justification and regeneration, in which one is reborn and freed of the guilt of original sin, with the likeness or nature of Christ planted as a seed within. The second stage is sanctification, which is ordinarily understood to be a process. This is seen as a pilgrimage in which God's grace and one's own self-discipline and devotion nurture the seed of the Christ-nature until it grows to maturity. Lastly, Beatitude, Blessedness, or Entire Sanctification is seen as both the culmination of the Christian pilgrimage and its goal. Most Christian groups teach that it is usually achieved after the present life with entrance into the state of eternal blessedness called Heaven.

In New Testament times, growth into saintliness was proclaimed as normative for all Christians. When Christianity became the official religion of the Roman

Empire, distinctions began to be made between two classes of Christians, those called to pursue the pilgrimage toward sanctification with intense, complete and concentrated commitment (largely those who had entered the monastic life) and Christians who attempted to avoid major sin but probably could not achieve sanctification in this life. These would anticipate a period of purgatorial discipline in the next life as preface to entry into the blessedness of knowing and loving God as He is.[7]

With the Reformation, the concept of Purgatory was rejected by Protestants along with the concept of a higher monastic life aimed at sanctification and a lower secular life aimed at avoidance of sin. Some recent critics of Protestant practice, including some Protestant self-critics, have argued that with the Protestant idea of sanctification's again becoming normative for all Christians, by and large it was equated with moral rectitude or even with conformity to society's codes of ethical virtue.

At present, within both Catholicism and Protestantism, there seems to be a re-emphasis on "spiritual formation"—on growth in the Christian life. This includes renewed emphasis on self-discipline, prayer, and meditation as aspects of the Christian life. However, emphasis on personal spiritual growth need not conflict with the concept of ministering to one's neighbors (*i.e.*, to those in need whoever or wherever they may be). Christian mystics like St. Francis of Assisi, St. Francis of Sales, St. John of the Cross, and the Quakers taught that the duty to serve one's neighbor must frequently take precedence over concentration on personal spiritual growth, though in theory the two should not conflict. Concern for the neighbor should be intensified by spiritual growth.

Christians believe that through Jesus Christ and the Holy Spirit, created beings can be restored and perfected in genuine life. Beings possessing self-awareness, human beings ("made in the Image of God"), acquire through Christ the possibility of a life of consciousness of God's copresence with them, of life in and with God. Christians call this possibility of continuous consciousness of God's reality and presence with them prayer. Prayer is both the openness of humans to God and God's openness to them. In prayer, God gives Himself, His power, wisdom, and love to his creatures. Augustine expressed this well in the opening part of his famous *Confessions*, which is itself a sustained and extended work of prayer and meditation. "Lord, Thou hast made us for Thyself, and our hearts are restless till they rest in Thee" (Confessions 1, i).

FULFILLMENT: THE NEW AGE

We have seen in Chapters One and Two that for many within first-century Judaism, the expected kingdom of God was to take place on this earth, perhaps greatly perfected or transformed. Jesus' descriptions of the coming Kingdom do not seem

---

[7]The concept of purgatory was discussed in theological works of such early Christian writers as Origen and Cyprian. It became an increasingly important part of western Catholic belief.

to have been very specific about what it would be like. In fact, his major stress was on the availability of the Kingdom *now* as a spiritual possession of those for whom God's will had become the decisive reality of their lives. The earliest Christians apparently expected an imminent return to earth by Jesus with an inauguration of God's kingdom in its fullness. This expectation characterized both Jewish and gentile Christians.

As Christianity became almost entirely gentile and began to take root as a major institution of the Roman Empire, the concept of the coming of God's Kingdom as a cosmic event involving a renewed or restored earth was postponed indefinitely into the future. Even the term Kingdom of God—so important in the teachings of Jesus—came increasingly to have only a minor or secondary role in Christian proclamation.

What became of increasing concern to many Christians was the destiny of the individual soul after the present life. Hebrew religion had not emphasized the immortality of the soul, a concept belonging to Greek Platonism, the mystery religions, and gnosticism, but the raising to new life by God of the whole person— the resurrection of the body. Medieval Christianity tended to accept the immortality of the soul, which at death would go to blessedness (Heaven), misery (Hell), or discipline (purgatory) but which ultimately at the Last Judgment would be reunited with its transformed body for salvation or for eternal punishment. Recently, Catholic theologians have reexamined the concept of purgatory, a doctrine usually rejected by Protestants.

The majority of Christians no doubt believe in, and the majority of Christian denominations have affirmed, a continuation of individual life beyond this life. Only a small number of Christians have rejected belief in this continuation of "subjective" life as opposed to believing only in "objective immortality" (continued influence). The Christian Scriptures are extremely reticent in their descriptions of the future life (see, however, Paul's letters, especially I Corinthians 15). Popular religion has elaborated greatly on the nature of Heaven and the future life. The religion of the American frontier spoke of a beautiful city with mansions of ivory and streets of gold. Serious theologians, in line with Paul's teaching about the progression of stages of the Christian life, have emphasized the spiritual nature of the new life and emphasized that it is probably better not to interpret it as a continuation of the present life but as its transformation and perfection.

Popular religion has also elaborated on the Christian concept of Hell as eternal punishment. Hell has also been given striking treatment in works of literature (Dante's *Divine Comedy*) and visual art. Some Christian groups, the Universalists, for instance, have rejected the idea of eternal punishment as incompatible with God's love, mercy, and compassion. The Christian scriptures rarely speak of Hell or eternal punishment. Indeed the concept of eternality associated with it is inferential. When the Scriptures do speak of a time or place or event of judgment involving condemnation and punishment the language is highly metaphorical. The word often associated with Hell in Jesus' usage referred to a canyon or pit outside the city of Jerusalem which figured in some Jewish apocalyptic literature. Hell was originally, as the contemporary novelist Anthony Burgess has noted, "a rubbish dump outside Jerusalem."[8]

Many contemporary Christian denominations are as reticent as the scriptures, or more so, about eternal punishment. However, it should be said that a consensus found in Christian theological tradition emphasizes that the concept of Hell can be interpreted as affirming God's mercy. If popular images of Hell as a place of physical torture are excluded, the concept is seen to refer to a condition of voluntary or self-chosen absence from God. Thus, the concept of Hell refers to God's granting the individual freedom to use the gift of freedom self-destructively, in ways that alienate the individual from God, self, and others. The end result of such a use of freedom would be suicidal. The concept of Hell can be seen as a way of affirming that God allows freedom to be carried to such a limit but still affirms and minimally preserves the individual from absolute self-destruction. One might say that the doctrine of Hell signifies that God chooses to preserve even those who ultimately would negate themselves and Him. The term eternal *punishment* is therefore perhaps inappropriate.

Although the continued, or transformed, life of the individual has been an important theme of Christian belief, it has not been thought of as merely an individual concern. That is, the Christian concept of salvation is not individualistic but communal, ultimately involving the whole created universe.

In recent times, Christians have reemphasized the communitarian aspects of the kingdom. Some adventist sects have revived expectations of the imminent physical return of Christ to the earth. Other Christians have internalized the concepts of the Second Coming, the Last Judgment and the kingdom, seeing them as giving symbolic expression to the importance of each moment of life as lived in God's presence. Some Christians, like the theologians of the social Gospel, have seen the kingdom of God as an actual norm to be translated into the structures and processes of present society. During the first years of the twentieth century, Walter Rauschenbusch proclaimed that the family, and the educational, religious, and political institutions of our society were largely Christianized. All that remained was to bring the spheres of economics (through socialism) and of international relations (through effective world government) in line with the already Christianized parts of the social order, thus fulfilling the ideals of the Kingdom of God. Others, like Reinhold Niebuhr, stressed the ideal of the Kingdom as an important instrument of judgment that can bring us to repentance, humility, and action aimed at establishing relative justice, an ultimate goal or norm that is always coming but never is.

Christians affirm that in Jesus Christ God has established the rule of His love over the universe. He has overcome the evil and alienation that reject His Love. In many ways this rule, the reign of His love, remains hidden. Christians affirm that it is known in principle to those who are members of His community, but most

---

[8]Anthony Burgess, *The Clockwork Testament or Enderby's End* (New York: Alfred A. Knopf, Inc., 1976), p. 4.

Christians have confessed that very often even members of His own community are not as conscious of God's power and wisdom triumphing in love as they could and should be.

To much of the world outside His community, the power and wisdom of His love, its rule and reality, seen unrealistic and unrealizable. But, Christians believe, these will not always be hidden. In Scripture, sermon, and theological work they affirm that God even now is bringing His purposes to fulfillment. In almost every Christian service of worship they proclaim that He is even now carrying His work to final perfection, to that point in time or beyond time when 'the kingdoms of this world" will become "the Kingdom of our Lord, and of His Christ" (Revelation 11:15), to a point in time or beyond when He *shall* reign forever.

Since the earliest days of the Christian community, His followers have believed and asserted that they are living in "the last days" (I John 2:18). For the most part, Christians do not believe this conviction should lead to complacency or arrogant self-assurance on their part. Rather, it is a ground of humility and repentance and a motive for serious efforts to let their lives be dedicated to God's Will, whether this means taking the message to others in missionary and evangelistic efforts or working for peace and justice in contemporary society. Christians continue to assert that God is faithful to His Promises (II Peter 3:3-4, 8-10; II Corinthians 1:19-20) and that the new age has already begun, that the new life in Christ and His spirit is a present reality (II Corinthians 5:17; Luke 17:20-21; Revelation 3:20) whose fulfillment is assured. They see this assurance as more than a word of judgment on the world; they see it as a promise and a demand.

QUESTIONS

1. Compare and contrast the Christian concept of God with those of polytheistic, pantheistic, and deistic religious traditions.

2. How does orthodox Christian Trinitarianism differ from and resemble the views that the present book calls tritheistic and modalistic?

3. Discuss what is meant by natural and moral forms of evil and explain why thinkers like Russell and Flew find the existence of evil a problem for Christian belief.

4. What do Christians understand by the term "original sin?" Explain the relation of this concept to the Biblical story of Adam and Eve.

5. List and interpret (explain) the different symbolic concepts of the demonic mentioned in the present chapter.

6. In what way did the Council of Chalcedon's way of speaking of the divine and human natures of Jesus contrast with other ways (*e.g.*, Ebionite, gnostic, Monophysite, Nestorian)? What does the present chapter intend when it speaks of Chalcedon's statement as setting "self-imposed limits" for later Christian attempts to express beliefs about Jesus?

7. Compare and contrast Roman Catholic and Protestant beliefs and practice concerning the sacraments and veneration of the saints and the Virgin Mary.

8. Why did Marcion want to reject the Jewish scriptures (Old Testament) as canonical for Christians? Why did orthodox Christianity insist on including it?

9. Describe what sanctification means, or has meant, in Christian tradition.

10. Often prayer is thought of as a way in which humans make known their requests to God. Why do you think the Christian concept of prayer is explained in a very different way in the present chapter?

11. Describe how the concept of fulfillment—including beliefs in coming of the kingdom, the Second Coming of Christ, and the Last Judgment—has been interpreted with different emphases during Christian history.

FURTHER READING

AULÉN, GUSTAF, *Christus Victor: An Historical Study of the Three Main Types of the Idea of the Atonement.* London: S. P. C. K., 1970.

BARTH, KARL, *Church Dogmatics,* Volume I, Part 1. New York: Scribner's, 1936.

BETTENSON, HENRY (ed.), *Documents of the Christian Church.* New York & London: Oxford Univeristy Press, 1947.

BLOOM, ANTHONY, *God and Man.* New York: Paulist Press, 1971.

BONHOEFFER, DIETRICH, *Creation and Fall; Temptation: Two Biblical Studies.* London: SCM Press Ltd., 1959.

BOSLOOPER, THOMAS, *The Virgin Birth.* Philadelphia, Penn.: The Westminster Press, 1962.

CARRETTO, CARLO, *The God Who Comes.* Maryknoll, N.Y.: Orbis Books, 1974.

CONGAR, YVES, *Tradition and Traditions.* New York: The Macmillan Company, 1967.

FLEW, ANTONY, *God and Philosophy.* London: Hutchinson & Co., Ltd., 1966.

FORSYTH, P. T., *The Person and Place of Jesus Christ.* Grand Rapids, Mich.: William B. Berdmans Publishing Company, n.d.

KALLAS, JAMES G., *Jesus and the Power of Satan.* Philadelphia, Penn.: The Westminster Press, 1968.

KNOX, JOHN, *Jesus: Lord and Christ.* New York: Harper & Brothers, 1958.

KUNG, HANS, *On Being A Christian.* Garden City, N.Y.: Doubleday & Company, Inc., 1976.

LEWIS, C. S., *The Great Divorce.* New York: Macmillan Publishing Co., Inc., 1946.

____. *The Screwtape Letters* and *Screwtape Proposes a Toast,* New York: Macmillan Publishing Co., Inc., 1961.

MELLERT, ROBERT BOROS, *What Is Process Theology?* New York: Paulist Press, 1976.

NIEBUHR, REINHOLD, *The Nature and Destiny of Man.* New York: Scribner's, 1953.

PAGELS, ELAINE, *The Gnostic Gospels.* New York: Random House, 1979.

PANNENBERG, WOLFHART, *Jesus—God and Man.* Philadelphia, Penn.: The Westminster Press, 1968.

____. *Theology and the Kingdom of God.* Philadelphia, Penn.: The Westminster Press, 1969.

RAHNER, KARL, *The Trinity*. New York: Herder and Herder, 1970.

RAUSCHENBUSCH, WALTER, *Christianizing the Social Order*. New York: The Macmillan Co., 1912.

RAVEN, CHARLES E., *The Creator Spirit*. Cambridge, Mass.: Harvard University Press, 1927.

RUSSELL, BERTRAND, *Why I Am Not a Christian*. New York: Simon and Schuster Inc., 1957.

SEEBURG, REINHOLD, *Text-Book of the History of Doctrines*. Grand Rapids, Mich.: Baker Book House, 1956.

chapter eight
RENEWERS AND REFORMERS: REPRESENTATIVE PATTERNS

The changes that inevitably come in any community of believers are often responses to social, political, and intellectual modifications in the cultural setting of a religion. However, change just as often is effected through the direct influence and leadership of particular persons and movements. The introduction of new ideas, interpretations, practices, as well as the modification of traditional patterns, brings reform or renewal. In Christianity, the use of the term Reformation to designate a historical event in the sixteenth century has occasionally meant the limitation of the concept of reform to that specific event. Reform takes place, however, throughout Christian history. It has many patterns, some reflecting drastic change and others occurring imperceptibly. It is the intent of this chapter to investigate representative patterns of reform as they have been present in Christianity.

Reform and renewal often bring with them tension and conflict. This is a natural response since change introduces unfamiliar and often emotion-laden ideas and practices. Resistance on the part of those who wish to conserve the tradition often leads to clashes with liberal or progressive persons who wish to expand horizons and reappropriate the truth by making it relevant to changing conditions. Persons representing either of these positions understand their own opinions to be the proper means of continuing and estabishing true religion. Much of the conflict between Christian believers throughout history can be traced to differences about the ideas and practices initiated by reformers. Yet, renewal and some-

Mother Teresa. Photo used by permission of Religious News Service.

times reform is not always disturbing, for it may occur in a manner that does not threaten but supplements current thought and practice. In these cases, it is usually only slowly perceived and appropriated by the larger community of Christians. Examples of many types of renewal and reform will be found in the following discussion.

THE APOSTLE PAUL

It may appear strange to some for the Apostle Paul to be listed among the renewers and reformers of Christianity, yet it was his work and thought more than that of others in his time that molded much of subsequent Christianity. His successful evangelization of large portions of the Greco-Roman world opened Christianity to a worldwide mission unfettered by its origin as a Jewish sect.

Paul, born in Tarsus of Asia Minor, was a Jew of the Diaspora and a Roman citizen. Receiving training as a Rabbi, he was studying in Jerusalem when he came into contact with Christianity. A Pharisee by training and inclination, he perceived Christianity as a threat to the traditional teachings of Judaism. Under the authority of the Sanhedrin, he persecuted Christians and was on his way to Damascus to seek them out when he had a vision that he understood to be an appearance of the resurrected Jesus. Converted by this experience to believe in Christ, he spent some years in preparation before becoming a Christian missionary to Asia Minor and Greece (Galatians 1:11-24; Acts 9:1-19). Founding a number of churches in these areas, he remained their mentor and guide in the Christian faith through visitation and a series of pastoral letters that are now incorporated into the New Testament. Ultimately arrested for his activities while on a visit to Jerusalem, he was taken to Rome for trial as a Roman citizen. There he continued his ministry while imprisoned and, according to tradition, was martyred for his Christian faith.

Paul's contribution to Christianity lies in his theological formulations, which had the effect of freeing Christianity from an early Jewish Christian perspective that called for gentile converts to Christianity to follow the precepts of the Jewish law. Paul's encounter with Jesus on the road to Damascus was for him the last of Jesus' resurrection appearances. It not only served as Paul's conversion experience but also focused Paul's theological interest on the resurrected Christ and the sacrificial event of Jesus Christ, through whose death God had shown His love to the world. Sinful humanity deserved death but God in Christ overcame the ultimate consequences of that state. The ultimate enemy—death—had been overcome and humanity was offered hope and love through Christ. "Death is swallowed up in victory. O Death, where is thy victory? O Death, where is thy sting?" (I Corinthians 15:54-55). For Paul this message was universal—it offered hope and salvation to all humanity, Jew and Greek alike (Romans 8:21-38).

To experience this joyous salvation, one has only to have faith (trust) in the God revealed in Jesus (Romans 5:1-21). One cannot appropriate it fully by reason and cannot achieve or deserve it by following the Jewish law. Like Jesus' resurrection, it is a gracious gift of God and has the effect of fulfilling the law. If one has faith in God then he or she will do as the law intends, share God's love with all fellow humans. One will live out in daily existence the love God has shared with the believer (Romans 12-15; I Corinthians 5-15).

The effect of Paul's teachings was to make Christianity available to the broad gentile world. As noted in Chapter Three, Paul's challenge to the Jerusalem Christians led to the church's acceptance of gentiles who did not follow the distinctive patterns of the Jewish law (Acts 15). The importance of this decision can hardly be overstressed, since it was among the gentiles that Christianity was to be most successful.

Paul's message was one of several available to Christians of his own time. Matthew's Gospel offered a new "Christian" law in place of the old Jewish law. John's Gospel emphasized the divine or spiritual nature of Jesus. Other gospels offered much of Jesus' own teachings as examples for Christian emulation (Paul draws rarely on the explicit teachings of Jesus). Paul's letters were the first Christian materials to survive in written form and were gathered together early in Christian history, yet it was in the theology of Augustine that Paul's interpretations of Jesus as the "Christ event" came into full flower. Augustine's use of Paul's insights and emphases was to greatly influence Western theology. Luther and Calvin were to return to Paul for their own distinctive interpretations of the Gospel.

BERNARD OF CLAIRVAUX

Reforms instituted in any period usually depend on outstanding leaders, and the monastic reforms of the late eleventh and early twelfth centuries were no exception. The waning of the Cluniac reform was followed by the simplicity of the Cistercian, and chief among its leaders was a French nobleman, Bernard of Fontaines (1090-1153). Disillusioned with the knightly life, Bernard experienced a conversion and determined to enter the religious life. He led thirty of his contempories, including a number of his relatives, to join the Mother House of the Cistercians at Citeaux in 1113. Expanding the strict yet simple rule of the monastery in his own personal devotion, he excelled in austerity and spiritual discipline even to the extent of damaging his own health. Appointed in 1115 along with twelve others to establish a sister house at Clairvaux, he became its abbot, a position he held for the rest of his life, rejecting repeated offers of higher ecclesiastical office.

Concentrating his own devotion on the love of Christ, he formulated a Christocentric style of life imitating the love of Christ. For him this developed into a form of mysticism. Without seriously questioning the medieval formulations of faith and doctrine, Bernard delighted in their mysteries, being convinced that reason could not explain them. This latter attitude made him critical of scholastic learning with its involved theological formulations, particularly those of Peter Abélard (see Chapter Six). His devotion to simplicity and dissatisfaction with the worldliness found within the church made him a sharp and effective critic of much of medieval Christianity. However, his attacks on what he considered the evils of the world, the church, and some of the people who surrounded him were understood by him to be expressions of love. Love in his understanding should be used to eradicate evil.

Although continuing as abbot of Clairvaux, which became a large monastery, Bernard was called on by many for counsel. He travelled extensively, serving as advisor to bishops, Popes, councils, princes, and kings. A persuasive preacher, he was a popular interpreter of the gospel who challenged all to embrace a disciplined life of love. In an election where two popes were chosen by a split College of Cardinals, it was the persuasive ability of Bernard that brought Innocent II to the papacy in 1130. He also wrote a set of ascetic instructions for Pope Eugenius III on his election to the papacy in 1145 *(De Consideratione)*. Convinced of the justice and righteousness of the Christian cause in the Holy Lands, he promoted the ill-fated Second Crusade. In each of these endeavors, it was his own conviction and example patterned after his teaching relative to the imitation of Christ that set the standard for his age—from his example arose a new piety within the period.

Reform led by Bernard was not concerned with theological doctrine or ecclesiastical structure but with the pious and holy lives of Christians in all walks and ranks of life. Reforms occurring in the structure of church or its practice and those in the monastic community were, from his point of view, secondary to the pious application of love in everyday life.

THE COMING OF THE FRIARS

The monastic renewal discussed above was effective in cleansing the spiritual life of the houses that participated and often had, through leaders such as Bernard, a broad effect on the life of the church. Monasticism generally was organized in houses where monks were removed from the general society. Although individuals might be assigned duties requiring contact outside the monastery itself, most members of the order would have little contact with the world.

In the ministries of St. Francis and St. Dominic during the early thirteenth century, a new pattern of monasticism emerged. The son of a wealthy cloth merchant of Assisi, Italy, Francis (1182-1226) as a young man pursued the life of gallantry normal for one of his station. After participating in a war between Assisi and a neighboring state in which he was imprisoned, Francis became disillusioned with this life. He determined to devote himself to prayer and service of the poor. On a pilgrimage to Rome he exchanged his clothes for those of a beggar and was greatly affected by the experience. Returning to Assisi he took the scriptural admonitions relative to poverty and service in Matthew 10 literally by renouncing his own wealth. He began a ministry of rebuilding several churches and giving aid to the lepers of the area. His example was soon followed by others who, under his leadership, formed into a community dedicated to poverty, prayer, preaching, and service. Poverty for members of the order meant owning nothing more than their cowl. In the beginning the order itself could own no property although this was modified so that it might hold houses and churches (this issue caused dissension within the order for centuries). The Franciscans were to live by begging, a major departure from the monastic pattern of self-sufficient communities and the basis of a new name which arose to designate such groups—Mendicant (begging) Friars. Francis travelled widely, even entering Egypt in an attempt to convert the Muslims. His own simplicity, humility and devotion to God and his fellow humans as well as his love of nature made him a saint in his own time. The Friars Minor, as the order became known, soon after Francis' death took major responsibility in areas of education, contributing leaders to the faculties of the rising medieval universities. Their mission work was also widespread, later including America.

Dominic (1170-1221) in 1206, realizing that a mission to the Albigenses (see Chapter Five) had failed partly because it paid little attention to the simplicity and asceticism of the heretics, asked for permission to attempt a mission of his own. Taking the role of poor man and begging for his food, he began his mission. Although the mission was not particularly successful, Dominic retained the pattern of begging when he entered into the task of raising a learned preaching order whose mission would be evangelization of the heretics. Quickly attracting members, the order began a broad mission program sending missionaries along with merchants in a time of expanding trade. Convinced that mission would not be successful without learning, each friar was required to receive at least three years of theological training. The Dominicans or Friars Preachers became renowned teachers (*e.g.*, Albert the Great and Thomas Aquinas), establishing themselves in the universities of the day. Because of their interest in orthodoxy and their sincere piety, they were used by the Popes to implement the Inquisition. They also served the Popes and other leaders of the church as theological and administrative counselors and agents.

Arising from different motivations, the Franciscans and Dominicans effectively created a new monasticism, abandoning the cloisters to minister to the needs of medieval society. Centering their work in the towns where their begging could be supported, their preaching, service, and mission activities did not eliminate contemplation but focused it so that it took on an enabling function for their activities in society. The educational activities of the orders complemented and contributed to a rising interest in knowledge.

WALDO, WYCLIFFE, AND HUS

The need for continual spiritual renewal within the church was symbolized in the Cluniac and Cistercian reforms (see Chapter Three) and the modifications of monasticism brought by the friars. Reform and new patterns of Christian life were not, however, limited to the monastic orders. Peter Waldo (d. 1218)—also spelled Valdes—a wealthy merchant of Lyon, France, took up a life of poverty and preaching. Working largely with memorized portions of the Bible and taking Jesus' Sermon on the Mount as his pattern of life, Waldo questioned, as did Francis, the wealth and worldiness of the church. His preaching threatened the authority of the church by its appeal to Scripture. Although he was orthodox in doctrine, Waldo failed to receive permission from Pope Alexander III to preach except with the agreement of local clergy—an agreement not likely to be obtained in view of his criticisms of the clergy. Waldo's response was to ignore the ruling. He personally escaped the Inquisition, but his followers, taking the name of Waldenses, were grouped by the church with the Cathari and severely persecuted. Consolidated by the persecution they became even more critical of the church. Patterning their activities after their understanding of the Scripture, they went out two by two rejecting oaths, property, and war. They also abandoned the veneration of saints and relics, and the granting of indulgences. They reduced the number of sacraments to two. Response to their teaching was significant even in the face of persecution. Eventually forced into separated communities, the Waldenses survived and still exist as a small group in the Piedmont and Savoy valleys of Italy.

As indicated in Chapter Four, John Wycliffe (1328-1384) in England and John Hus (1373-1445) in Bohemia also found ready response to their respective criticisms of the church. Arriving at many of the same points raised by the Waldenses, particularly the superiority of Scripture over the church and the call for a pious and responsible clergy, Wycliffe and Hus anticipated many of the changes that ultimately surfaced in the Reformation. Wycliffe's teaching that priests and the Pope were stewards responsible to God for their stewardship of His church meant that they could be rejected if they failed to fulfill the duties of their offices responsibly. Authority did not rest on office as much as it did on responsible stewardship of the duties of the office. His rejection of the sacramental doctrine of transubstantiation further questioned the authority and function of the priests. These and other criticisms were broadly publicized by the Lollards, followers of Wycliffe, whom he sent out on preaching missions, in scriptural fashion, two by two. After Wycliffe's death, the Lollards became even more direct in their criticisms of the practices of the church. They rejected exorcisms, priestly pretension, immorality, the simultaneous holding of secular and religious offices, prayers for the dead, pilgrimages, and so on. For their efforts they were severely persecuted and became an underground movement among the poor.

Hus, having arrived at a state of dissatisfaction with the church before he became acquainted with the ideas of Wycliffe, publicized those ideas in Bohemia. His appeal to Christ as the head of the church constituted a direct threat to the power of the papacy. His call for poverty as the Christian ideal for all believers, dependence on New Testament as law for Christian life and the life of the church, and the abolition of clerical abuses of office among other teachings led to his being condemned as a heretic. However, his condemnation strengthened the resolve of his followers and resulted in a revolt against papal leadership.

The connection of both Wycliffe and Hus with universities highlights the role that the universities were to play in renewal and reform. In the next few centuries they were to become centers of questioning and innovation with respect to the religious life of Europe.

BRETHREN OF THE COMMON LIFE

Yet another pattern of renewal arose in the fourteenth century in northern Europe. The call for spiritual renewal heard in many sections of the church met a ready response among persons interested in the mystical traditions which had a long heritage within the church. Emphasis on a mystical approach to Christian faith assuming, as it did, direct personal faith and encounter with God contained a latent criticism or negativism toward the institutionalized sacramental patterns of medieval Christendom. In Holland, Gerhard de Groot (1340-1384), a Carthusian monk influenced by the powerful renewal of mysticism found in the Germans Meister Eckhart (1260-1327) and John Tauler (1300-1361), began to preach a life of inward transformation concentrating on simple spiritual living. The movement that emerged from de Groot's preaching became known as the Brethren of the Common Life. Without permanent vows but living in houses under rules, both lay and clerical participants continued their regular vocations but emphasized service. With a high appreciation and practice of spirituality, they did not necessarily seek mystical union with God. They entered aggressively into the service of the poor and into education, establishing schools in Holland and Germany and gaining a widespread reputation for excellence in education. For supplementary income they also copied manuscripts. Through their schools, the Brethren achieved a wide degree of influence in Europe. Among those trained by them were Erasmus,

Thomas à Kempis, Pope Hadrian VI, and Nicholas of Cusa. Through the teachings of à Kempis incorporated in his work *The Imitation of Christ*, some of their emphases were to have influence on Christians of many traditions from then until the present.

THE SCHOLARLY REFORMERS: ERASMUS, MORE, COLET

As we have seen, reform continually arose in the late medieval period from those seeking simpler spiritual Christianity, and those anxious to serve the poor. Reform from different motivations and with different objectives matured during the intellectual ferment of the Renaissance. With its emphases on renewal of learning and art, accompanied by a rising if rudimentary commercial economic system, the Renaissance placed emphasis on individual humans and their ability to know and transform their world.

The late fourteenth and early fifteenth centuries witnessed the rise of an intellectual movement commonly known as Humanism. Although related to and often promoted by university scholars, humanism found sympathy among intellectuals in all fields. Humanists were intrigued by the study of this world and its cultural affairs buttressed by a deep appreciation of the ancient world and its learning. They emphasized particularly the study of the literature of Greece and Rome. Their object in studying the past was to glean from it the best in philosophy, art, and literature in order to stimulate creative patterns for their own culture. With confidence in humanity's intellectual abilities and potential moral goodness, they looked for the transformation of society.

Many Humanists were clerics and teachers who had patience neither for the intricacies of scholastic learning—the dominant medieval pattern of thought—nor for the bureaucratic orientation of the church. Although generally loyal to the church and seldom willing to join in Reformation splits from it, the Humanists added to the chorus of critics of the church. Their impatience with hair-splitting theology and their love of the ancient world led them to call for simplicity and renewal based on what they understood to be the early church's spiritual pattern. They were critical of indulgences, multiple benefices, absentee priests and bishops, heresy hunting, and the bureaucratic structure and wealth of the church. Their writings and their activities as teachers greatly influenced Protestant Reform leaders as well as reformers who remained within the Catholic Church.

Eminent among a wide movement were Erasmus of Rotterdam (1469-1536), Sir Thomas More (1478-1535), and John Colet (1466-1519). Erasmus, educated among the Brethren of the Common Life, received his education at the University of Paris. Although he was an Augustinian monk, Erasmus ultimately received a papal waiver of his vows in order to pursue his literary activities outside the order. He taught at a number of universities, making several trips to England, where he taught at Oxford. Traveling throughout Europe and for a time serving as a royal counselor to Emperor Charles V, he ultimately devoted his energies to writing and publishing.

He published a Greek text of the New Testament, incorporating corrections of the then known errors of the Vulgate. Later he also published a Latin translation of the Scriptures, which contributed to Biblical scholarship of the day. These two works became the basis of many of the translations of Scripture into the vernacular languages during the Reformation. In addition, he extensively published the early church fathers, including Origen, Cyprian, Jerome, and Augustine. His satirical and witty critiques of medieval culture, including the church, were immensely popular. He entered into bitter controversy with Luther over the question of human free will, with Erasmus defending the common-sense and traditional view affirming freedom of choice in moral and spiritual contexts against Luther's predestinarian understanding that in matters of salvation humanity has no freedom of the will. Erasmus defended the Catholic Church against the schismatic Reformers, yet much of his work was ultimately condemned by the church.

Sir Thomas More, Lord Chancellor of England, held a succession of important political offices. More's home became a center of intellectual life. His most famous writing, *Utopia*, described an ideal community living by natural law and religion. He was critical of the corruption of society and lived a disciplined moral and religious life. Particularly critical of the veneration of relics and the punishment of heretics, More, with other Humanists, contributed to the criticism of the church. More was ultimately beheaded by Henry VIII for refusing to approve of Henry's divorces and for refusing to acquiesce in the Act of Supremacy establishing Henry as the head of the England Church.

John Colet, dean of St. Paul's Cathedral and twice lord mayor of London, was trained at Oxford, Paris, and in Italy. A Greek scholar, he urged Erasmus to study Greek and called for a return to the principles and disciplines of the early church. He was critical of the abuse of power and the worldliness of the clergy. Refounding St. Paul's school, he fostered general, humanistic learning.

Although they clearly were orthodox and worked within the church, Erasmus, More, and Colet along with other Humanists sought genuine renewal of the church from an intellectual basis. This demanded a larger role for human abilities than the mere acceptance of traditional church authority, doctrine, and practice.

PROTESTANT REFORMS: LUTHER AND CALVIN

The major outlines of the Protestant Reformation are discussed in Chapters Four and Five. This most far-reaching reform of Western Christendom, as we have seen, was to some extent the culmination of many renewal movements within the church. Reflecting major theological differences over the nature and source of faith and authority, the actual reforms instituted were often those called for in many other quarters. The centrality and primacy of Scriptures had been asserted by Wycliffe and supported by the work of the Humanists as was the use of the vernacular languages for Scripture and worship. Pilgrimages, veneration of relics, and masses for the dead were questioned. Tributes to Rome, papal anates, and foreign clerical authority were resisted early in England, France, and other countries. The reduction of the number of sacraments had been anticipated among the Brethren of the Common Life and the Waldenses. Interest in simplifying worship and eliminating the intricacies of clerical ceremony was expressed in many previous reform efforts. Critique of the monastic life as a separate and higher life along with questioning of celibacy among clerics was not original with the Reformers. Preaching as a central and essential element had been anticipated among early Franciscans and Dominicans although they did not tie preaching directly to the worship services.

However, the catalyst for the outbreak of the Protestant Reformation lay in the unique circumstances of the sixteenth century, when the questions of many groups and the political climate allowed the foundation of new religious communities separated from the Roman Church. No longer could the church either depend on the state to crush dissidents or its own powers of excommunication to stop dissent effectively.

Nevertheless, while the Reformation clearly served to actualize many of the reforms called for in movements that preceded it, it was not simply a logical or normal outgrowth of such movements. Luther and Calvin, each in their own unique personalities and leadership abilities, sparked the Reformation.

Luther's personality has been the object of extensive research and comment in the modern period.[1] Clearly his passionate, deep-seated emotions contributed to patterns of melancholy and occasional depression, as well as periods of brilliant, creative expression. Pursuing study for a career in law, Luther had already attained Bachelor and Masters degrees from the University of Erfurt when he experienced intense fear of death and became very concerned that he might die before earning salvation. His fears reached a point of culmination when, almost struck by lightning, he vowed to become a monk. In 1505, he entered (over the objections of his father) the Erfurt Augustinian monastery to pursue the holy life in an attempt to guarantee his salvation. An intense disciplinarian, Luther became a model monk, practicing all works of piety, yet finding little comfort in the teachings and practice laid before him in the monastery. He came to feel that there was no way a person could live up to the standard of righteousness demanded by God. Instead of love for God, Luther came to hate him. Fear, anxiety, doubt, and guilt were most often his motivations for the good works which were taught by the church and required by God. This intense struggle in his spiritual life, and his insights into the dark side of life, led Luther away from the Humanists' evaluation of humanity as having innate capabilities for goodness, a popular teaching at that time.

It was in the midst of this struggle that Luther came to his insight that God's

[1] Erik H. Erikson, *Young Man Luther* (New York: W. W. Norton & Company, Inc., 1958).

love is offered to sinful humanity without the necessity that one achieve righteousness as a precondition. Luther's own experience and his insight into human nature (partly derived from St. Augustine) led him to insight on humanity's abject sinfulness and incapacity to do any good outside God's grace. In Luther's view, good flowed from grace rather than being a precondition to it.

This interpretation of humanity, elaborated by Calvin and others, was one of the principal theological positions that would be continually reformulated and occasionally modified in subsequent Protestant theology. Luther's insights into the primacy of the grace of God became the theological basis for instituting the many reforms embraced by the reformers. Luther's adamant resistance of papal authority and his claim of the necessity for direct personal reliance on the grace and mercy of God encouraged others to follow him. The result was reformation that shattered the unity of Western Christian organization and tradition.

Calvin's contributions also reflect a personality that shaped much of subsequent Protestantism. The son of a secretary to the Bishop of Noyon, France, Calvin studied for a legal career at several universities, including Paris. In contact with humanistic scholars, he pursued religious studies and sometime between 1532 and 1534 underwent a conversion experience to reform principles. Working with others who were critics of the church, he was forced to flee Paris and eventually France. Drawn to Geneva by former colleagues in France, he had a major role in shaping that city into a Christian theocracy.

Convinced that Christian love demanded a disciplined life that included Biblical knowledge, a simple life style, and a clear moral code, he was able to build a community of industrious Christians who took their faith seriously in every area of life, including that of work or vocation. The patterns developed reflect Calvin's own example wherein he put precepts into practice. His training as a lawyer and his interest in clarity, order, and discipline allowed him to structure a systematic Protestant theology that issued in a rigidly defined pattern of Christian life applicable to all believers.

Calvin's persistent efforts to mold the Geneva experiment into a clearly regulated Christian state formulated models of church and social organization that allowed Geneva to become for many the ideal Protestant community. As such, it was emulated in France, Holland, Scotland, and Puritan England and, through the colonies of these countries, much of America.

IGNATIUS LOYOLA
AND THE SOCIETY OF JESUS

The widespread movements toward reform and the numerous questions about the state of the church that preceded the Reformation were intensified by its successes. Many Catholics loyal to the church began to look for ways both to reform the church and counter Protestant advances. One of these was a young Spanish nobleman, Ignatius of Loyola (1491-1556). Loyola was wounded in a battle with France and forced into a long convalescence during which he reexamined his life, becoming convinced that the spiritual life leads to true fulfillment, but that such a life must be completed in service. After a pilgrimage to Jerusalem to serve the poor, he returned to seek an education, advancing rapidly through a university at Paris. During this time he formulated the basic patterns of *The Spiritual Exercises* which were designed to carry a person through four intensive stages of spiritual pilgrimage—examination of conscience, meditation, contemplation, and prayer. These were combined to rid one of self-interest and to dedicate one completely to God. *Exercises* was also designed to formulate a program of spiritual retreat that could be followed by any dedicated Christian.

A group of fellow students joined Loyola in forming the Society of Jesus (commonly known as the Jesuits). The purpose of the group was manifold: reform of the church by eliminating the gross abuses of the clergy, dedication to education and mission, particularly to areas where the gospel had not been preached; and service of God through serving the church. To achieve this, Jesuits presented themselves to the Pope as soldiers of God to be used wherever and however the Pope might choose. They intended to act in strict obedience to the command of the Pope—in sharp contrast to the Protestant objectors to Papal authority. Loyola understood that "Man has been created to praise, reverence, and serve God our Lord, and by this means to save his soul."[2] This assumption included belief in free will and the active role of humanity in its own salvation—also a contrast to much of Protestant thought. Confident that persons could be convinced to choose the right path, the Jesuits concentrated on education, rivaling in this area the leadership of the Franciscans and Dominicans. The society was to enjoy great success in missions throughout the world and to influence greatly the shape of Roman Catholicism from then until the present. Loyola's combination of spiritual exercises with their mystical emphasis and complete devotion and service to the church proved a potent impetus to reform and redirection of the church's mission.

MYSTIC RENEWAL: TERESA OF AVILA, JOHN OF THE CROSS, AND FRANCIS DE SALES

In the confusion and corruption of the fifteenth and sixteenth centuries one of the patterns of Christian life which experienced renewal was Christian mysticism. Unrelated to the rise of mystical interest expressed in movements such as the Brethren of the Common Life but responding to similar needs, Spanish mysticism gained renown throughout the church. St. Teresa of Avila (1515-1582) entered a Spanish Carmelite monastery at an early age, but was forty years old when she experienced a conversion to a life of perfection while praying before a statue depicting Christ being scourged. Vowing to seek spiritual perfection, she spent the rest of her life in intense devotion, practicing asceticism and self-mortification. She

---

[2]Ignatius of Loyola, *The Spiritual Exercises,* trans. Anthony Mottola (New York: Doubleday & Company, Inc., 1964), p. 47.

experienced numerous mystical ecstasies culminating in, to use her terms, a "spiritual marriage" with God and a vision of Christ.

Not content with the undisciplined life of her monastery, she sought and gained permission to found a more strict Carmelite house in 1562. Here she insisted that the ancient rules of monasticism be strictly observed and prepared a disciplined program for the mystical life, *The Way of Perfection.* Her autobiography, *The Life of Teresa of Jesus*, and other writings contributed to her wide influence among those interested in mysticism. Unwilling merely to live the life of contemplation, she founded some sixteen houses for women and fourteen for men and effectively reformed the Carmelite order, incorporating mystical interests into its regular program. Eventually these houses were separated into a distinct Carmelite order. Teresa's work was supported and elaborated by St. John of the Cross (1542-1591), a fellow Carmelite whose writings, *Ascent of Mount Carmel* and *Dark Night of the Soul* elaborate the role of discipline and purification of the self in the pursuit of mysticial union. Teresa and John, living as they did during the Reformation period, by seeking both reform and intensification of spiritual life, offered an alternative to the proposals and methods of the Reformers.

Another pattern of mystical devotion is found in Francis de Sales (1567-1622). Bishop of Geneva, although unable to live there because of the Reformation's capture of the city, Francis was devoted to the spiritual life and mystical piety. His *Introduction to the Devout Life* became a popular devotional guide for his own and subsequent generations. His life of contemplation and piety like that of Teresa was joined with a very active pastoral career. He also helped found an order of women devoted to works of charity, The Order of Visitation. Trained by the Jesuits, he aggressively attempted to reclaim Protestants for the faith, actively seeking to convert the Calvinists through a preaching mission.

EVANGELICAL REFORMS: WESLEYAN METHODISM

By the seventeenth century, Protestant movements had matured into Christian churches with modified liturgical patterns, doctrinal confessions, stable church governments and clear moral codes. With such settlement, the fervor and dynamic qualities of the faith that had sparked the reforms in theology and Christian life had cooled. Religion for many often became once again simply a part of the routine of life. The sense of personal contact with God and its exemplification in a disciplined, exemplary life became much less frequent. Religious questions were still actively debated among theologians but often with the hair-splitting tendencies that had characterized earlier scholasticism. Open scepticism was present among many philosophers (see Chapter Six). Religion often consisted of not much more than attendance at services and simple moral teaching.

Several movements arose to counter religious lethargy in the eighteenth century. As noted in Chapter Five, P. J. Spener (1635-1705) and others in Germany encouraged the renewal of a lively faith in the midst of a Lutheranism which had become largely content with dogmatic orthodoxy. Centering in small groups that considered themselves to be little churches within the great church and stressing Bible study and fellowship, this Pietism initiated a renewal of spiritual life.

In England a similar concern surfaced in the rise of societies formed to discuss, study, and implement spiritual renewal in daily life. It was in such a society formed at Oxford University that John and Charles Wesley, George Whitefield, and others dedicated themselves to renew and reform their own lives by Bible reading and intense attention to their spiritual, moral, and intellectual lives (see Chapter Four). Such a society seems also to have been introduced by the Wesleys' mother, Susanna, in the rectory of her husband's parish. Studying works such as Thomas à Kempis' *Imitation of Christ*, the Oxford group sought to find spiritiual substance and to give themselves in dedicated service.

After a disappointing missionary journey to Georgia during which he became acquainted with a group of German Pietists, the Moravians, John Wesley experienced a change in his understanding of the nature of faith and the spiritual life. Previously pursuing holiness in all aspects of life, he was acutely aware of his own inability to achieve it. From his contact with the Moravians he became convinced that one's relationship with God depends not on achieved holiness but on God's grace appropriated by placing one's faith (trust) in God. Holiness was necessary but flowed from faith—a joining of Protestant insistence on faith with the Catholic insistence on holiness. Wesley's theology was a reiteration of tenets found in the theology of the Church of England, which he made alive for his own day.

His greatest contribution to renewal lay, however, in innovations in evangelizing those for whom religion had become irrelevant. These included not only those for whom religion had lost its dynamic qualities, but also the many in English society who had been displaced from traditional religious patterns by the Industrial Revolution. Forming religious societies, he began to use lay preachers to spread the Gospel. Extensive preaching outside the normal confines of the church made the movement popular among the common people and, to a large extent, unpopular among the well to do. Requiring that his helpers itinerate between local societies, he developed local leaders of small classes and bands of persons meeting regularly to examine and renew their spiritual lives. Such a system guaranteed that those entering the new spiritual life would have help and support in their endeavor. The societies were joined together in a "connection" throughout England. This Methodist movement, so called for its methodical patterns originating in the Oxford "Holy Club," gained widespread popularity, ultimately raising the spiritual, moral, and economic level of a substantial segment of the English people. Imported to America by lay immigrants, Methodism became one of the major organized religious groups of the new nation.

Such evangelical patterns were not limited to Wesleyan Methodism. A broad Evangelical Revival incorporating similar movements contributed to a general revitalization of Christian life in the eighteenth century. In America, Puritan divines like Jonathan Edwards, often opposed as a fanatic by his fellow Congregationalists, cooperated with Whitefield and other European evangelicals. Their efforts initiated the Great Awakening that transformed American religious life and practice, introducing the methods of revivalism that flowered in the Second Great Awakening of the early nineteenth century.

NINETEENTH-CENTURY SOCIAL CHRISTIANITY

Change is a constant element in human history yet some periods witness changes that vastly modify life and its setting. Such was the case in the nineteenth century. Europe experienced an industrial revolution that resulted in great wealth, colonial expansion, and military dominance. Accompanying this was an imbalance in the economic system in which a few were very wealthy and most of those who labored were underpaid, lived in congested slums, and were restricted by the most limited opportunities for themselves and their children. In this situation, many Christians turned from interest in reform of doctrinal, theological, and ecclesiastical structures to reforms calling for modification of the repressive societal organization. How could the economic and political system be modified to deal with the root causes of the problems? Were the economic and social systems designed so that true justice and equality were available to all segments of society? Did the structures and institutions of society promote and allow the principles of equality, love, justice, and peace inherent in the Christian message? To deal with these questions, nineteenth-century Christianity fostered reform movements centered not on questions about the nature of the church and its beliefs but about society itself and the applicability of the gospel to it.

In Germany Johann Christoph Blumhardt (1805-1880), an Evangelical pastor from a conservative, Pietist background, developed a ministry at Bad Boll involving prayer and spiritual healing. Most of those who sought his help were the poor who were oppressed by the changing economic situation. Blumhardt's son, Christoph (1842-1919) assisted his father until his father's death. Christoph became interested in the conditions that caused much of the inequity and suffering he found in Germany. He understood the voices of protest in the society—protests against injustice, militarism, war, capitalism—to be the very voice of God arising in the culture. He joined the Social Democratic Party for a period, serving as a member of the Parliament of Württemberg where he was also pastor. Removed from the pastorate because of his criticism of society and the state, he continued to hold up a vision of Christian fellowship that would bring justice and love to all. He understood this to be possible in the coming fulfillment of God's Kingdom—a theology of hope in the midst of squalor and injustice. The Blumhardts emphasized "Christ as Victor," a Christ who could bring help and victory to people caught in the conflicts of modern life.

F. D. Maurice (1805-1872) and Charles Kingsley (1819-1875), worked in the context of the English industrial scene. Convinced that Christianity must respond to the oppression produced by technology, they became leaders of social reform.

They rejected the traditional concept that poverty is the judgment of God. By helping to form cooperatives to improve social conditions and promoting education as a means of social and economic improvement, Maurice and Kingsley became, with J. M. E. Ludlow, instrumental in forming the Christian Socialists—a political movement working for social reform. Maurice's renowned theological work questioned traditional thought, particularly when it tended to make religion so spiritualized as to remove it from life. Kingsley was the popularizer of the movement, writing popular novels that highlighted the degradation and oppression of the common people.

In America similar social concerns arose. The existence of slavery had for some time been questioned, but the abolitionist movement with its objective of eliminating slavery did not become a reality until the 1830s when William Lloyd Garrison (1805-1879), Arthur Tappan (1786-1865), and Theodore Dwight Weld (1803-1895) became its leaders. Through the 1840s and 50s, the movement became a religious issue splitting several of the major denominations (Methodists, Baptists, and Presbyterians). The movement's aim was ultimately achieved only through the devastating Civil War.

The post-Civil War period brought an unprecedented outburst of industrial expansion in America with the concomitant immigration of large numbers of Europeans and others to provide labor. The inequalities and injustices of European industrialization were soon matched in America. Washington Gladden (1836-1918), Josiah Strong (1847-1916), and Walter Rauschenbusch (1861-1918) strongly criticized the social evils of capitalism. While not advocating socialism as such, Gladden did urge public ownership of utilities and increased cooperation between labor and management. He was convinced that churches should not simply concern themselves with the spiritual welfare of individuals, but with the social consequences of industrialization that concentrated wealth in the hands of a few.

Josiah Strong organized a movement that attempted to implement the social Gospel by calling interdenominational congresses on the subject and serving as the general secretary of the Evangelical Alliance. In this position, he had a forum to promote Christian responsibility in all areas of society. Walter Rauschenbusch's experience as a Baptist pastor in an area of New York called Hell's Kitchen made him a compassionate friend of the oppressed and a strong critic of practices that perpetuated suffering. He sought to improve housing, provide recreation, and improve the quality of life rather than simply feed and clothe the poor. His book, *A Theology for the Social Gospel*, detailed the theological base of the movement, which envisioned establishing the Kingdom of God on earth by improving the social conditions and interests of humanity.

These nineteenth-century reformers attempted to shift the focus of Christianity from primary emphasis on the faith of individuals and the internal interests of the churches to an interest in how the Gospel could be applied to the larger institutions of the society. This movement was to be a significant factor in the theology of the twentieth century.

FRANCES WILLARD AND WOMEN'S RIGHTS

Nineteenth-century interest in the social aspects of the Gospel was not confined to the injustices produced by the industrial and economic changes of the day. Many Americans, particularly Protestants with a Pietistic background, began in the 1840s to be concerned about open saloons and the disruptions in social and family life caused by alcohol. Several northern and western states passed laws limiting liquor sales, but a real campaign for the abolition of liquor did not emerge until the 1870s. The Prohibition Party was formed in 1868. But it was with the organization of the Women's Christian Temperance Union in 1874 that the full force of moral indignation against the effects of liquor was organized into a potent social and political force.

Frances Willard (1839-1898), raised in a Methodist home where temperance had been stressed, became interested in the movement and joined the WCTU in its early stages, becoming its president in 1881. She brought to the movement a variety of experiences that contributed to her organizational abilities, including service as president of Evanston College for Ladies and secretary to the Methodist Centenary Fund (a mission campaign). As president of the WCTU, Willard expanded the interests of the union beyond its primary purpose of controlling alcohol sales. Taking an active interest in the plight of the poor and the social consequences of industralization, the union became particularly interested in women's rights—especially labor practices as they related to women, the right of women to the vote, and traffic in young prostitutes (a subject long avoided in public discussion because of the prudishness of the period). A master organizer, Willard created a variety of strategies that resulted in effective political pressure—strategies which in the early twentieth century succeeded in bringing about women's suffrage and the abolition of liquor sales (at least temporarily). Working from a base of Christian principles and stressing the home and the church, she understood her work to be the application of the gospel to life. Within her own denomination, she attempted unsuccessfully to gain the right of women to serve as voting delegates to Methodism's ruling body, the General Conference. The work of the union focused attention for the first time on the American scene on the significance of women's pressure groups seeking women's rights and their potential as a political force.

REBELS, REVISIONISTS, SAINTS:
LEO TOLSTOY AND ALBERT SCHWEITZER

Major change is often dependent on the ability of proponents to found movements or of groups to implement the reforms they seek. The late nineteenth and early twentieth century produced two persons whose witness to the need for renewal was uniquely personal. While neither produced specific or lasting groups, their thought and example influenced many throughout broad areas of the Christian community.

Leo Tolstoy (1828-1910) a member of the Russian landed gentry, studied in Kazan and, influenced by the writings of J.J. Rousseau, became interested in social reform. He published his first novel in 1855, beginning a long and distinguished literary career. Seeking to relieve the plight of serfs, he established schools on his estate, providing much more freedom in education than was normal at that time. Although proclaimed by many as the world's greatest living author, at middle age Tolstoy experienced a sense of the profound meaninglessness of life. Wealthy and with many friends and a flourishing family, for a time he considered suicide. Turning to a study of the world's religions, Tostoy became convinced that an answer to his spiritual quest was to be found in a literal following of the teaching of Jesus in the Sermon on the Mount. Renouncing literary ambitions in 1877 as inconsistent with his new understanding of the Gospel, Tolstoy turned his attention to religious and moral subjects. He became highly critical of the Orthodox Church, particularly its involvement with the state, and of the social system of the day. He sought to live a simple life, renouncing property and family life, practicing manual labor, and working for the relief of social inequity.

Tolstoy's religious beliefs, based on the Sermon on the Mount, led him to embrace principles of nonresistance to evil, unreserved love of all, the wrongfulness of oaths, and the suppression of anger and violence. Such concepts brought him to reject the state, its judicial system, and war. His religious ideas included the rejection of the divinity of Christ but acceptance of radical obedience to his teachings. Excommunicated from the Orthodox Church, Tolstoy's sometimes eccentric endeavor to live a life of ethical integrity made him a lonely but admired figure. In his later novels and short stories, centered around the concepts of radical obedience to love outside institutionalized religion, Tolstoy continued his critique of society and substantially influenced his Russian contemporaries and many in the West.

Albert Schweitzer (1875-1965) provides another example of a unique witness to reform and service. Schweitzer began as a pastor in Strasbourg, where he was later to join the faculty of the university. On the basis of his sudy he began to question the then-current interpretations of Jesus as the outstanding example of moral man. Schweitzer asserted that Jesus' religious teachings, like those of his contemporaries, were based on the eschatological expectation of a Messianic age which would end the world as we know it. Schweitzer went further to suggest that the ethical teachings of Jesus reflecting this expectation were intended for the interim period between his own life and the beginning of the Messianic age. They therefore could not be applied literally in modern life since there was no longer any prospect of an immediate end to life as we know it. The result of Schweitzer's *Quest of the Historical Jesus* was to revolutionize New Testament study putting new emphasis on the eschatological framework of those teachings although few accepted Schweitzer's conclusions completely (see Chapter Two).

Schweitzer also asserted that Jesus' spirit was nevertheless to be taken seriously and could be appropriated in our time. Accordingly, he abandoned a brilliant theological career, earned a medical degree, and spent the rest of his life as a medical missionary in Africa, motivated by a "reverence for life" given in the "spirit" of Jesus. Schweitzer and Tolstoy, by the force of their powerful personalities and personal examples, influenced many to take seriously the radical demands of the teachings of Jesus.

THEOLOGICAL REFORMERS:
KARL BARTH AND REINHOLD NIEBUHR

The work of Schweitzer had a profound effect on the study of the New Testament, particularly its concentration on the human life of Jesus. Liberal theology of the late nineteenth century had built its constructive patterns on humanity's moral ability, enlivened by God's grace, to follow the teachings of Jesus. If, however, Schweitzer was correct in his understanding that Jesus taught from an eschatological context an ethical code meant to apply only to the "end time" then the literal following of Jesus' teachings became a highly questionable activity.

A Swiss Reformed pastor during the difficult days of World War I, Karl Barth (1886-1968), though trained as a liberal theologian, criticized Liberalism's basic tenets, such as the concept that humanity's native moral goodness can build God's ideal kingdom on earth. In his *Epistle to the Romans*, Barth was particularly sharp in his critique of Liberalism's identification with the culture of the time—its "Cultural Protestantism"—as well as its constant attempt to make the Gospel conform, or be relevant, to human history.

Barth became convinced by his study of Paul and other New Testament writings that Christian existence rests on the revelation of God in Jesus—not on human standards of morality or the idealized teachings of Jesus. In fact, Christianity for Barth is not rational in the liberal sense but must be appropriated solely by a leap of faith that affirms the revelation given by God in Jesus. God's Kingdom is not to be built by humanity but will come at God's will and with His power. God is transcendent and cannot be identified with humanity's schemes and history. God makes himself known uniquely in Jesus both as the example who judges humanity's prideful sinfulness *and* as the merciful one who loves and redeems humanity in spite of what it does to Him.

Barth's critique, soon joined by others, was to have a devastating effect on traditional Liberalism. At the same time, it struck a responsive chord among many who had come to distrust humanity's moral abilities and to long for a religion based on the transcendency of God that did not rely on human finitude. The response to Barth's ideas was so great that he was to describe himself as a man who, stumbling in a church tower, had accidently caught hold of the bell rope to steady himself and awakened the whole countryside. Barth understood himself to be recovering the major emphases of Reformation theology. Moving from his pastorate to professorships in theology first in Germany, then when exiled by Hitler, in his native Switzerland, he continued to work at this throughout his long life in a monumental systematic treatment of theology, *Church Dogmatics*, which remained unfinished at his death.

Barth was joined in his criticism of Liberalism by many. But especially relevant for later theology were Emil Brunner, Rudolf Bultmann, and Friedrich Gogarten in Germany, Reinhold and H. Richard Niebuhr in America, and Paul Tillich in Germany, then, when exiled by the Nazis, in America. Reinhold Niebuhr (1892-1971), like Barth, began as a pastor and was especially concerned about the liberal analysis of humanity's moral nature as being essentially good. With a pastorate in industrial Detroit, Niebuhr was conscious of the injustices and inhumanity of much of industrialized society. He saw the foundations of these injustices in human pride and self-interest. His response was to attempt to recapture as a lively theological principle the concept of original sin—understanding it to be an innate universal prideful selfishness in all humans. More impressed than Barth with the inequalities of society, he took up many of the interests of the Social Gospel, but with different theological bases. His works, *Moral Man and Immoral Society* and *The Nature and Destiny of Man*, took seriously the sinfulness of humanity and the possibility of transformation of both humanity and its society by the love expressed in the revelation of Jesus. Niebuhr insisted that such love could only be accepted by an existential, vital, and dynamic faith. Unlike Barth, Niebuhr did not understand himself to be a theologian and did not attempt a grand systematization of his thought, even during the many years he taught Christian ethics at Union Theological Seminary in New York.

He was very active in a variety of liberal political causes and organizations, such as Americans for Democratic Action. He was a strong critic of totalitarian political movements of the left and the right. His dramatic, sometimes prophetic, statement of humanity's condition and the possibilities of God's transforming love were to have a substantial effect on the directions of American theology through the 1950s. His brother, Richard (1894-1962), did much to systematize and formulate a similar pattern of theological realism in America.

BONHOEFFER AND THE STRUGGLE AGAINST TOTALITARIANISM

Dietrich Bonhoeffer (1906-1945), a Lutheran who studied at Tübingen and Berlin, was influenced by the insights of Karl Barth, particularly in his insistence on a confessional faith in Jesus as the central point of Christianity. After studying in America, he became a university lecturer and pastor in Berlin. With the rise of the Nazi movement, he became part of the "Confessing Church." With Barth, he was a signer of the Barmen Declaration in 1934 rejecting Nazi control of the German Church. Later, while working in England, he was called back to Germany to head an underground seminary for the Confessing Church in 1935. Ousted from this post by the Nazis, he was on a lecture tour in America when the Second World War broke out in 1939. Returning to Germany to help continue Christian resistence to Hitler, Bonhoeffer began to take an active role among German dissidents, feeling that a Christian acting from love must struggle against the evil incarnate in the Nazi ideology. As a part of that resistance he served as an agent of communication between the British government and Germans opposed to Hitler. Although not himself actively involved in a plot against Hitler's life, Bonhoeffer was imprisoned and eventually hanged by the Gestapo only a few days before the close of the war.

Bonhoeffer symbolized for many Christians opposition to the Nazis and his *Letters and Papers from Prison* became widely popular after the war. His interest in a Christian gospel that was not bound or molded by the traditional institutions of Christianity—a religionless Christianity—contributed to much postwar ferment in European and American theology. Bonhoeffer's willingness to attempt renewal even by the use of violence in order to avoid the cultural domination of Christianity by non-Christian forces of society has been cited by many third-world theologians as an example of the Gospel being placed first in one's priorities before allegiance to state or ideology.

REFORMERS AND REVOLUTIONARIES IN THE THIRD WORLD: TOYOHIKO KAGAWA AND DOM HELDER CAMARA

Nineteenth-century difficulties with the application of the Christian faith to social and economic patterns of culture were compounded by the mid-twentieth century. Technology, while expanding and enriching the lives of certain nations, also widened the gap between rich and poor in the world. The incessant struggle of differing political and economic ideologies for world dominion has separated the world into an array of parties and camps. In this situation, the social implications of the Gospel become even more acute and require rethinking, as do the theological principles on which they traditionally have been based. The application of the Christian teaching of love as requiring social justice for all has at times had revolutionary results in predominantly non-Christian and Christian countries of the third world.

In 1908, a Japanese seminary student rented a room in a slum section of Kobe called Shinkawa not far from his Presbyterian seminary in order to serve the poor and wretched of the area. Toyohiko Kagawa (1888-1960) thus began a lifetime of service to the poor and socially deprived of Japan. After some years of service in the slums, he studied in America, being particularly interested in the techniques of social modification. Returning to Japan, he began actively to seek change in the social conditions that resulted in the degradation of large portions of Japanese society. He founded the first labor union and the first peasant unions, which effectively sought to change the position of laborers in industry and in farming communities. Active in relief work and continuing to preach in the slums, he founded on the strength of his own pacificism an Anti-war League and was imprisoned for a time during World War II. After the war he worked actively to promote democracy as the form of government for Japan. In all of these concerns Kagawa was basically interested in the welfare of the poor and oppressed. Born himself of a noble class, but disowned when he converted to Christianity, his leadership in movements of social change was revolutionary for his time—yet his reforms were directed toward the improvement of all.

He continued his active Christian mission along with social reforms, forming in 1930 a Kingdom-of-God movement to promote Christian conversions. Kagawa became world renowned for his Christian leadership and service, and was popularly sought for spiritual guidance throughout much of the Western world after the war. His influence on Japanese Christianity was immense and his prolific writings were often translated into English.

In the years following the Second World War, many of the countries of the Far East and Africa gained their independence from colonial European rulers. Joined with the Latin American countries, which had gained independence earlier, into a Third World, they began to seek economic independence and political equality. Actively supporting and often formulating many of these movements have been native Christian leaders trained in Christian schools. Among these, Dom Helder Camara, Archbishop of Olinda and Recife in northwest Brazil, has become a symbol of freedom and love. Camara (1900-), a native of the northeast region of Brazil, served for a number of years as bishop of the *favelas*, the slums of Rio de Janeiro. Here he became interested in the plight of the poor, focusing on an economic system that allowed little upward movement and often produced a basic servitude of the masses to the interests of a relatively few wealthly landowners and merchants. Camara became convinced that the system was not merely one of Brazil's making but the result of an international system that exploited the Third World countries for the benefit of western capitalism. His interest in *real* reforms that would redistribute the wealth of the land led him to work for social and economic reforms. He became an active organizer of a movement called Action, Justice, Peace, seeking reforms in all sections of the society but with particular emphasis on land reform and the improvement of the wages of the poor. Although basically socialist in his concepts, he is interested in new forms that are not patterned after Western or Marxist types of socialism. Convinced that the methods of transformation must be non-violent, he nevertheless is sympathic with the aims of Latin Americans who have chosen violence as the method of reform.

A loyal member of the Roman church actively using his privileges as an archbishop, Camara can also be critical of the church's position in Latin America, which he sees as too often aligned with the ruling classes. Symbolic of his interests is his refusal to live in the Episcopal Palace reserved for him. A bishop of the people, he lives simply as they do, enjoying much direct contact with them. His methods include seeking dialogue with all factions within and without the church to bring about improvement in social and economic conditions and to make the church a servant among the people.

Widely sought as a leader of the Third World, he also has become a symbol for liberation theology, which focuses on reformulating the Christian message in ways that do not necessarily represent Western thought forms—the forms that have been dominant in Christianity for centuries. Liberation theology also has shared Camara's intense concern for justice among all persons. Unlike Kawaga, who sought to spread his message through writings, Camara has preferred to write little but to concentrate on organization and direct action to bring about reform in Brazil.

For both Kawaga and Camara reform has led to daring revolutionary ideas and to much resistance and sometimes persecution. Nevertheless, they have effectively raised the consciousness of the churches and the world toward the social consequences of the Gospel in the modern world.

TWO TERESAS: THE LITTLE FLOWER AND MOTHER TERESA

Two Catholic women of the modern period have taken the name of Teresa, patterning their lives after Teresa of Avila. Their ministries, each successful in its own way, provide witness that lives lived in stark contrast may equally affect and revolutionize the lives of millions.

Saint Thérèse of Lisieux (1873-1897), more commonly known as The Little Flower, was born Marie Francoise-Thérèse Martin in Normandy, France. Raised in a devout family, Thérèse entered the local house of the Carmelite order at the age of fifteen. Two sisters from her own family were already nuns there and another was to join after the death of their father. The Carmelite order, revitalized by St. Teresa of Avila, was a strict order devoted to prayer and contemplation directed toward the life of the spirit in the world. Members of this order took it as their special vocation to pray for missionaries and priests and for the spreading of the Gospel. At Carmel of Lisieux, Thérèse became the ideal nun, giving herself to meditation and prayer, and working obediently in the convent at all of the menial tasks of daily living. Her spirit and expressions of love were such as to become examples for her Sisters of the convent. After some years in the convent she became terminally ill and suffered great physical pain until her death. At the request of her mother superior, she wrote her autobiography, *The Story of a Soul*, in which she recounted her life, especially her spiritual journey.

She considered herself to be especially called to the vocation of a nun and she had early asked God to deprive her of all things attractive on earth that she might be totally devoted to him. In the course of her work, she developed what has, among Catholics, become known as the "little way." Essentially it is the way of a child, the simple trust in whatever is given in life by God and the living of all of the little daily tasks and events of life to the honor and glory of God. Suffering was understood by her to be a gift. Her attention was often on God's compassion even for unbelievers, so her continual prayer was for the message of love to be present and vital in others, particularly unbelievers. In the simplicity of her life and the telling of her story she appealed to common persons and quickly became a saint in their eyes. Miracles and numerous visions were not part of her own spiritual journey, but healing miracles followed her death. The Roman Catholic Church, by canonizing her as a saint in 1925, acted in an unusually short time. She had become the modern saint of unselfish and unassuming love. Devotion to her quickly spread throughout the Roman Church. Her cloistered life of suffering and prayer became an example for vast numbers of the common Christians outside the cloister.

In Mother Teresa of Calcutta (1910-), we meet one equally devoted but whose life has taken a very different course. She has become in her own lifetime a world renowned living saint. Born in Skopje in present day Yugoslavia of Albanian parents, Gonxha Bojaxhiu was raised in a pious, disciplined Catholic household in an area of mixed nationalities and religions. At the age of eighteen, Gonxha joined the Sisters of Loreto to be a missionary. The order, founded on the rules and *Spiritual Exercises* of Ignatius Loyola, was basically a teaching order. Taking the name of Teresa after Teresa of Avila and the Little Flower, Gonxha was assigned to Darjeeling and then Calcutta in India.

Here, for some twenty years, she taught the daughters of India's upper castes. However, her convent was located next to a *baitas* or shantytown where many lived in squalor. In August of 1948, with the permission of her archbishop and mother superior, she left the Loreto convent to live in the streets of Calcutta and minister to the needs of those she found there. Quickly gathering others to help her, she formed an order of nuns, Missionaries of Charity. Living under strict devotional rules, the order is dedicated to service of others based on Jesus' statement that as one feeds, clothes, and cares for others one is caring for Jesus himself. In India, the work is centered in four major areas: Care for the dying in houses for the dying, care for the newborn in homes for children, care for lepers in special colonies, and feeding the hungry. The Missionaries of Charity has now become worldwide with over two hundred houses and more than 2,000 nuns. Joined by a smaller group of Missionary Brothers of Charity and the International Association of Coworkers of Mother Teresa, the work has greatly expanded to be one of the most dynamic of Christian communities of the present time.

As the soul of the movement, Mother Teresa travels the world ministering to the poor and destitute. She has been honored with numerous awards, doctorates, and the Noble Peace Prize in 1979. Taking as her daily prayer the prayer of St. Francis, Mother Teresa has become an internationally known figure who understands the publicity that has come to her work in the past decade as God's means of making the world conscious of the poor and needy—not something she deserves or seeks. In contrast to Dom Helder Camara's politically active role on behalf of the poor, Mother Teresa has been content to minister to their needs although that has taken her into politically sensitive areas such as Beirut at the height of the Israeli-PLO conflict. Her resolution is to speak to humanity's inhumanity to each other—which she calls lack of love—by ministering to the needs of the very body of Chirst as it appears in the hungry, sick, and dying.

DOROTHY DAY AND THE CATHOLIC WORKER

In *The Catholic Worker*, we encounter the unique combination of a newspaper edited by Catholic laypersons on behalf of the workers of American society *and* a social movement that on one hand provides physical help for the hungry and needy, and on the other provides an activist cadre of persons participating in and leading a variety of programs seeking social change within the society. Peter Maurin and Dorothy Day founded the newspaper in the midst of the Depression as a means of speaking out about the plight of the worker and to express Christian concern for the structure of a society that would allow exploitation.

Maurin (1877-1949), a French immigrant, brought to the endeavor an idealistic social concern. After wandering among the poor and outcasts of society for a number of years, he began to write about their plight. A devout Catholic, he had early been a member in France of the De la Salle Brotherhood, a lay organization devoted to service, particularly through education, of the poor. He never lost that interest and brought it into the *Catholic Worker* movement.

Dorothy Day (1897-1980), by the time of the founding of the paper in 1932 had served as a journalist with a number of radical socialist and communist papers and magazines. She had contact with some of the leaders of radical movements, having at one time been arrested for her participation in the suffrage movement seeking voting rights for women. Converted to Catholicism after a life with no religious affiliation, she brought to the *Worker* a wealth of experience and commitment. Her more practical nature and organizational abilities, as well as her abilities as a writer and theorist, ultimately made her the pivotal person in the movement.

The newspaper became the voice of social and cultural criticism within the American Catholic Church and the champion of all sorts of causes. From here, support came for fair wages for cotton pickers in the Depression, the civil-rights movement of Martin Luther King, Jr., the pacifists of World War II, the farm-labor movement of Cesar Chavez, the anti-war protests of Vietnam, and the anti-nuclear activities of recent years—to name only a few. All of this was done within the church to which Day and *The Catholic Worker* were always loyal, even if they were critical. Day's conviction that there could be no mercy without justice led her constantly to question the injustices within the system of the society and the church of which she was a part. Her deep, almost mystical, faith took some of its inspiration from the Little Flower (about whom she wrote a biography). Her interest was in Teresa's concern for the little things of life and the "little people" forgotten and abandoned by society.

The social activism of the *Catholic Worker* movement organized groups throughout the country to carry out lectures, protests, meetings, and retreats seeking new avenues to deal with social probelms. Houses of hospitality provide an opportunity to put belief into action daily by serving meals, and clothing and caring for the needy. St. Joseph's, located in the Bowery in New York, is only one example of a place sponsored by the *Worker* where persons may find help at any time for almost any need.

As the inspiration and binding force of the *Worker,* Dorothy Day offered the unique characteristics of a crusading activist layperson whose saintly life became an example for many within and without the Roman Church. Voluntarily choosing poverty in order to live and work among the workers she sought to serve, Day strove to put the Gospel into concrete action both for the relief of the needy and to change the conditions that create war, poverty, and injustice.

CHRISTIAN NONVIOLENCE AND HUMAN RIGHTS: MARTIN LUTHER KING, JR.

The application of Christian teachings concerning love and equality in American society found another advocate in the movement for civil rights led by Martin Luther King, Jr. (1929-1968). King, having attended seminary at Colgate Rochester, and received a Ph.D. in theology from Boston University, was offered opportunities to pursue his ministry in the North, yet chose to return to the South. While pastor of a black Baptist congregation in Montgomery, Alabama, without a particular plan for reform of the social injustices then a part of the legal structure of the American South, he became involved in the struggle to gain equal treatment for blacks in the public-transportation system of the city. Organizing a boycott of the city buses in 1955, he instigated a successful nonviolent movement protesting the inequalities of segregation. He was instrumental in forming the Southern Christian Leadership Conference, which became a vehicle for political and protest action. Resigning his pastorate in 1960, he turned his full attention and energies to the movement for civil rights of all persons. Arrested in Birmingham as a result of these protests, his "Letter from a Birmingham Jail" became a classic appeal to the Christians of the country to reconsider the injustice of segregation practiced at that time. In it he quotes St. Thomas Aquinas in support of the people's right to disobey unjust laws nonviolently. His other writings were many and influential, including *Stride Toward Freedom* and *Why We Can't Wait*.

King took his inspiration for nonviolent protest from the teachings of Jesus, but patterned his method after that used by Gandhi to achieve India's freedom from Britain in 1947. His insistence that blacks needed to be reconciled with whites

Martin Luther King, Jr. Photo reprinted through courtesy of Religious News Service.

as much as whites needed to be reconciled with the blacks did not interest some blacks, who turned to a more aggressive Black Power movement, including the willingness to use violence.

The efforts of King and others were instrumental in the striking down of traditional segregation laws by the Supreme Court, and Congressional passage of civil-rights legislation to safeguard the equality of all. For his work, King received the Nobel Prize in 1964. Always the preacher, King made his contribution to the civil-rights movement a statement of Christian faith and confidence in the love of God that would ultimately triumph over the pride and egoism of humanity. King was assassinated in 1968.

CHRISTIANS IN COMMUNIST COUNTRIES: HROMÄDKA AND SOLZENITSYN

In the modern pluralistic world where the political, social, and religious options have become myriad, Christians often find themselves in social and political contexts vastly changed from traditional and familiar cultural patterns that through the centuries have molded Christian thought patterns and expressions. Such is the case for Christians living today within Communist countries. The official acceptance of atheistic materialism based on the critique of religion by Karl Marx has been the policy in Communist countries, but Christianity has remained a significant alternative to the official position in many of them. The position of Christianity in Communist countries widely varies from the strongly influential position of the Roman Catholic Church in Poland to suppressed-but-surviving Russian Orthodoxy. Response of the Christians within these countries to their Marxist context has also varied.

In the 1950s Joseph Hromädka, dean of the Comenius Faculty of Theology, Prague, Czechoslovakia, and an active leader in the World Council of Churches, began to publicly question the traditional image and formulation of Christianity. Hromädka, a Presbyterian minister who at one time taught at Princeton Theological Seminary in America, primarily worked in a Communist country still significantly influenced by Roman Catholic and Eastern Orthodox Christianity.

Hromädka's basic concern about modern Christianity was that it has too often been tied to its surrounding cultural and political ideals, principles, and moral patterns. Even in its modern forms, Roman Catholicism has been molded by feudal medieval thinking and practice. Protestantism, on the other hand, arose in the atmosphere of Western democracy and so its concepts of the relation of the individual to society, freedom, and economic principles (which in Hromädka's understanding *do not* provide real equality for all) have been those of liberal democratic capitalism. Hromädka suggested that this cultural formulation of Christianity is neither necessary nor healthy. Christianity as a religion should be Christocentric, concentrating on Jesus and His message expressed in the lives of its adherents without the restraints of political or social ideology. Culture should not define or limit Christianity's forms and patterns. Christianity cannot in its essence be limited to its institutional expressions and can be as viable and vital in communist settings as in others. To do so it must be freed from its Western trappings or, for that matter, from its Eastern Orthodox patterns. In these critiques, Hromädka was in close agreement with much of what has come to be known as liberation theology.

Hromädka also insisted, as many in the Third World have, that Marxism must be taken seriously, particularly in its critique of traditional Christianity. He suggested that Marxism is correct in pointing out that in Western Christianity the ideas of love and justice are espoused but in reality many persons continue to be exploited, hungry, and poorly housed while those in the upper strata of the societies live in "rudely selfish ways." He insisted that religion cannot be understood or practiced as if it only dealt with abstract spiritual values, for it is always tied to the material condition of humanity—Christianity must be concerned with how people are treated and under what physical conditions they live. He further suggested that the "classless society is to be the fulfillment of everything the greatest personalities of history longed for, but never could attain."[3] In these opinions Hromädka came close to accommodating Christianity and communism but his intent as an heir of the Reformation was to call modern Christianity to free itself from attachment to any political and cultural patterns. For him, Christianity could be as viable and valid within communism as outside, but it would not be Western Christianity.

The Russian exiled Nobel Literary Prize laureate, Alexander Solzhenitsyn, presents another view of religion within communism. Solzhenitsyn, born in 1918, was thoroughly indoctrinated in Marxist ideology and served as a front-line Russian officer during World War II. His disillusionment with Stalin found its way into his correspondence during the war and on the basis of this criticism he was imprisoned for eight years and then exiled to the edge of the desert for three more years. Although trained in mathematics and science, and teaching those subjects for much of his life, he understood himself to be a writer. When his writings, which were critical of the Stalin regime, were published they were at first welcomed by Premier Khrushchev but ultimately led to Solzhenitsyn's exile. Although not religious in his early years, he came to embrace the Christian faith during his imprisonment, becoming a staunch defender of Russian Orthodoxy. Critical of its institutional subservience to the state before and after the revolution, he draws much of his moral outrage against communism and the general secularization of the West from traditional teachings of the church. He sees in the traditional Russian Church with its liturgy, worship, and devotion to God the best of Russian culture. Yet it is this that is lost in the Communist society. In his exile, Solzhenitsyn has also been extremely critical of Western Christianity, accusing it of having conformed to the materialism of its culture and having lost real vitality as a dynamic force in the lives of the people. Solzhenitsyn would have Christianity return to its

---

[3]Joseph L. Hromädka, *The Church and Theology in Today's Troubled Times* (Prague, 1956), p. 93.

foundations, "restoring the purity and freshness of primitive Christianity."[4] Both Hromádka and Solzhenitsyn, on the basis of their experiences in Communist societies, would reform the Christian tradition, but in strikingly different ways.

THOMAS MERTON: FROM CHRISTIAN SOLITUDE TO DIALOGUE WITH ASIAN RELIGIONS

Thomas Merton (1915-1968) is widely read by persons within and outside the Roman Catholic Church as one of the most important modern Christian mystics. Merton, born in France and educated in England and America, converted to Christianity in 1938 while he was an English instructor at Columbia University. He had been active in a communist group, worked in a Harlem settlement house and was generally a social activist. His entry into the Abbey of Gethsemani, Kentucky, to be a Trappist (Cistercian) monk meant assuming the life of silence and contemplation, but not a life without communication. A prolific poet and essayist, his writings ranged from works on contemplation and the monastic life to stinging critiques of totalitarianism, racism, materialism, trends toward global war, the Vietnam War, spiritual inertia, and any form of hypocrisy within or without the faith. Active in his order he spent the last three years of his life as a hermit, joining in the monastery only for Mass and a single meal per day.

In his early period as a Christian, Merton was critical of all religions outside of the Roman Catholic tradition. Through the years, however, he came to appreciate the validity and insights of other Christian communities. His mystical study, expressed not only in his lifestyle as a monastic but in his many writings on the life of contemplation, also led him late in life to study Eastern religions. His works on Zen indicate that in the methods and insights of Zen meditation he found a fertile field for active dialogue with other religious traditions. Merton's own religion broadened and deepened through his encounter with other religions and he speaks for many who, conscious of the plurality of the present world, suggest that Christianity must take a serious and sympathic look at truths found in other religions.

QUESTIONS

1. Why is it that the Christian faith has constantly experienced renewal and reform?

2. Which different patterns of reform or renewal can you identify within Christian history and tradition from reading this chapter?

3. Are there patterns of reform that seem continually to recur within Christianity? If so, what does this indicate concerning the nature of the faith?

---

[4] Alexander Solzhenitsyn, "Letter to the Third Council of the Russian Church Abroad," published in Niels C. Nielsen's *Solzhenitsyn's Religion* (New York: Pillar Books, 1976), p. 168.

4. In your opinion, from the reading does it appear that reform and renewal are most often relevant to the forms of institutionalization of Christianity or to its fundamental tenets?

5. It would appear that the call for reform within the faith in the recent past has been most significantly related to the social application of Christianity. What explanation would you give for this phenomenon?

6. Many reformers make their case for reform on the basis of appealing to earlier, simpler patterns of christianity. Why then are they usually considered radical or revolutionary?

7. What, if any, are the reforms that are most needed presently within Christianity as you have experienced it?

FURTHER READING

BAINTON, ROLAND H., *Here I Stand: A Life of Martin Luther*. Nashville, Tenn.: Abingdon Press, 1950.

BONHOEFFER, DIETRICH, *Prisoner for God: Letters and Papers from Prison*. ed. Eberhard Bethge. New York: Macmillan, 1954.

____. *The Cost of Discipleship*, trans. R. H. Fuller. New York: Macmillan, 1959.

DE BROUCKER, JOSÉ, *Dom Helder Camara: The Violence of a Peacemaker*. trans. Herma Briffault. Maryknoll, New York: Orbis Books, 1979.

CALVIN, JOHN, *Institutes of the Christian Religion*, ed. John T. McNeill. Philadelphia, Penn.: The Westminster Press, 1960.

DALY, LOWRIE JOHN. *Benedictine Monasticism*. New York: Sheed and Ward, 1965.

DAY, DOROTHY, *Terese*. Notre Dame, Ind.: Fides Publishers Association, 1960.

____. *The Long Loneliness*. New York: Harper and Row, Publishers, 1981.

ERIKSON, ERIK H., *Young Man Luther*. New York: W. W. Norton & Company, Inc., 1958.

HINNEBUSCH, WILLIAM A., *The Dominicans: A Short History*. New York: Alba House, 1975.

HROMÁDKA, JOSEPH L., *Theology Between Yesterday and Tomorrow*. Philadelphia, Penn.: The Westminister Press, 1956.

IGNATIUS OF LOYOLA, *The Spiritual Exercises*. trans. Anthony Mottola, New York: Doubleday and Company, Inc., 1964.

KAGAWA, TOYOHIKO, *The Religion of Jesus*. Philadelphia, Penn.: The John C. Winston Company, 1931.

KING, MARTIN L., Jr., *Where Do We Go From Here: Chaos or Community*. New York: Harper and Row, Publishers, 1967.

KINGSLEY, CHARLES, *Yeast*. New York: The Co-operative Publication Society, 1899.

KNOWLES, DAVID, *Christian Monasticism*. New York: McGraw-Hill Book Company, 1969.

MERTON, THOMAS. *The Seven Storey Mountain*. New York: Doubleday and Company, Inc., 1970.

McINERNY, DENNIS R., *Thomas Merton: The Man and His Work*, Washington D.C.: Cistercian Publications, 1974.

NIEBUHR, REINHOLD, *The Nature and Destiny of Man*. New York: Charles Scribner's Sons, 1948.

NIEBUHR, H. RICHARD, *Christ and Culture.* New York: Harper and Row, Inc., 1956.

NIELSEN, NIELS C. JR., *Solzhenitsyn's Religion.* New York: Pillar Books, 1976.

OUTLER, ALBERT, *John Wesley.* New York: Oxford University Press, 1964.

PETRY, RAY, *Francis of Assisi: Apostle of Poverty.* Durham, N.C.: Durham University Press, 1941.

RAUSCHENBUSCH, WALTER, *A Theology for the Social Gospel.* Nashville, Tenn.: The Abingdon Press, 1960.

RUPP, GORDON, *Luther and Erasmus: Free Will and Salvation.* Philadelphia, Penn.: The Westminster Press, 1969.

SCHWEITZER, ALBERT, *The Quest of the Historical Jesus.* trans. W. Montgomery. New York: Macmillan Co., 1948.

SERROU, ROBERT, *Teresa of Calcutta.* New York: McGraw-Hill Book Company, 1980.

TERESA OF AVILA, *The Life of Teresa of Jesus,* trans. E. Allison Peers. Garden City, N.J.: Image Books, 1960.

THOMSON, HUGH KERR, *A Compend of Luther's Theology.* Philadelphia, Penn.: The Westminster Press, 1943.

TOLSTOY, LEO, *War and Peace,* trans. Constance Garnett. New York: Random House, 1955.

_____. *The Death of Ivan Ilych.* New York: New American Library, 1960.

VAN DYKE, PAUL, *Ignatius Loyola, the Founder of the Jesuits.* Port Washington, N.Y.: Kennikat Press, 1968.

chapter nine
CHRISTIANITY AND CONTEMPORARY ISSUES

Not too many years ago, one frequently heard predictions of the end of the influence or even existence of religion in the modern world. Some felt that the spread of scientific values and the apparent victory of scientific modes of thinking in the conflicts between science and religion (see Chapter Four) had resulted in the discrediting of religious beliefs and institutions. Others argued that with the increasing ability of humanity to control its destiny through technology—to deal with age-old problems of disease and poverty in practical ways—religious questions about the meaning of life would no longer be of interest to anyone but the emotionally maladjusted. In a novel by Anthony Burgess, for instance, the socially nonconforming poet F. X. Enderby is reconditioned in order to be cured of the compulsion to write poetry. Enderby is retrained for a socially useful role, that of bartender. Unfortunately, or fortunately, the reconditioning fails, and Enderby ends as he had begun—a person who is a frequent source of annoyance and dismay to the plastic or clockwork society.[1]

Predictions of the end of religion or of religious influence in contemporary society have not been borne out, though it does seem that many aspects of major religious institutions are changing. By means of these changes, religion seems to

[1] See Anthony Burgess, *Enderby* (New York: W. W. Norton and Company, Inc., 1963 and 1968). Also Burgess, *The Clockwork Testament or Enderby's End.*

be not only surviving but in some parts of the world gathering strength (though frequently some of the changes are sources of concern to religious leaders and their followers). Both sets of phenomena—the persistence of religion and the changes that are affecting religious traditions and organizational patterns—can be seen most clearly if one considers Christianity in the contemporary world. This is true probably because of its size—Christianity is by far the largest of the world's religions—and because Christianity is found in all types of societies, from the most modern to more traditionally oriented ones.

In the United States, religious affiliation is at an all-time high, and the great majority of those belonging to religious organizations are adherents either of the Roman Catholic or of one of the mainline Protestant denominations. Even among those who have no formal ties to a religious organization, an overwhelming number profess beliefs, such as the belief in God and in an afterlife, drawn from the Judeo-Christian framework. Many express preference for one or another of the major Christian denominations. This is established by numerous opinion surveys. In some ways, in-depth studies reveal a stronger, if more varied, persistence of religious attitudes than the simpler opinion surveys do.

In Europe, the traditional bastion of Christendom for a millennium, sociological research shows a vastly different picture. There is no doubt that during the past two centuries there has been a significant decline in religious participation, even by those who are nominally adherent to Christian denominations. In some traditionally Protestant areas—such as England and Scandinavia—where large numbers of the population are automatically considered members of the established church, perhaps less than ten percent of the nominal members are participants in the actual life of the church to which they belong. In a country like England many of the larger "free" churches, such as Methodism, have experienced dramatic declines in membership and participation. Catholicism has also experienced declining participation and institutional loyalty in most European countries, though much less than that of the extreme Protestant cases. Nevertheless, even in these cases, sociological research suggests that many nominal adherents who never or almost never participate in the religious organizations continue to define themselves and their lives in terms of inherited religious beliefs—sometimes given highly subjective and individualistic redefinition. Such evidence indicates that even the secularized European is more attached to, and probably more susceptible to, the claims of the Christian religion than official participation figures suggest.

Even more surprising has been the persistence of the Christian religion and of Christian institutions in Marxist countries, where for years there have been government-directed attempts to liquidate religious influence. It may be easy to explain the enthusiastic participation of the majority of Poles in Catholic Christianity, given the unpopularity of the Communist regime, the prior commitment of Poles to the Catholic Church, and the identification of Polish Catholicism with Polish nationality.

However, the persistence of Christian participation in Russia itself seems to many both surprising and significant. Since 1917, the Communist government has placed severe restrictions on the practice and propagation of religion. It has tightly controlled the Russian Orthodox Church, limiting the number of churches, clergy, and the amount of theological training that clergy are allowed to receive. During the Second World War, some concessions were made by the government to the church in order to secure support for the defense of Russia against German invaders. By the early 1960s, the Russian government was expressing dismay that after forty-five years of trying to educate the Russian populance away from religious adherence, and after offering incentives and penalties—opportunities for education and advancement in social and economic status having been largely closed to religious adherents—at least half the population of the country continued to have their children baptized. At that time, further severe restrictions on the teaching of religion were placed both on the church and on parents. Nevertheless, participation in the Orthodox Church persists in Russia, and there is a flourishing Baptist movement. Despite the government's persecution, sectarian groups of Pentecostals, Adventists, and Jehovah's Witnesses also have persisted. In China also, where only a small minority of the population has ever professed Christianity, enthusiastic, flourishing groups of Christians have recently emerged from the underground after the relaxation of nearly thirty years of government control and repression.

In Latin America, Christianity at present faces both great challenges and great difficulties. Traditionally Roman Catholic, most Latin American countries have experienced shortages of priests—so that some adherents in interior parts of the country rarely have contact with the official church. The church has also been confronted with the political and economic conflicts these "Third World" countries experience. Traditionally, the church has been perceived as supporting the status quo, the small ruling class that many in the population see as having blocked the needs of the majority for justice and opportunity. In recent years, some Catholic leaders in these countries—bishops, priests, and nuns—have taken strong positions against the status quo. Some have called for nonviolent efforts to bring social change (see Chapter Eight). Some have been willing to collaborate with Marxist revolutionaries, and a few have been killed. Others have been assassinated merely for speaking out, or for working on behalf of social justice. By and large, Latin American countries remain solidly Catholic, though there has been significant Protestant growth, especially among Pentecostal sects, in recent years.

In parts of the world that are predominantly non-Christian, Christianity has made surprising gains. For a decade and a half after the conclusion of the Second World War, it was frequently suggested that much of the non-Christian world of Asia and Africa was likely to be closed to Christianity. Partly, such predictions were based on traditional associations of Christian missionary efforts with European colonialism.[2] After achieving independence, for instance, India imposed severe

---

[2]The disruptive effects of some Christian missionary activity on a traditionally oriented tribal society and its entanglement with European colonialism are excellently portrayed in the novels of the Nigerian writer Chinua Achebe. See especially *Things Fall Apart* (Greenwich, Conn.: Fawcett Publications, Inc., 1959).

restrictions on Christian missionary activity. One of the results of such acts was a greatly accelerated movement toward independence of the native Christian churches, so that they are no longer seen as subservient to Western missionaries, Western control, or Western leadership. In most cases, this has greatly strengthened these groups, both Protestant and Catholic, and has made them largely responsible for evangelistic and missionary efforts in their own and other Third World countries.

Twenty-five years ago, some Western Christian leaders predicted that most of Africa would soon be closed to Christian evangelism, especially because of the large number of conversions from indigenous tribal religions to the Islamic faith. But within the last fifteen years there have been large numbers of conversions to Christianity, sometimes involving entire tribes. Some areas of Africa now represent extremely rapid growth areas for Christian denominations. The greatest growth is occurring where native leadership is strongest.[3]

From all indications, then, the twentieth century is not likely to be a period in which the Christian religion declined in numbers or in influence. However, it may be true that the nature of Christianity's influence and even of its presence in twentieth-century societies has been greatly affected by major changes in modern societies and in the world at large.

RELIGION IN MODERN SOCIETIES

There can be no doubt that underlying economic, technological, social, and political changes in Europe between the thirteenth and sixteenth centuries did much both to cause the breakup of Western Christianity into a number of national churches and separatist sects and to determine the form that these emerging religious organizations took. Such innovations as gunpowder (leading to more powerful weaponry), the magnetic compass, and the printing press stimulated the development of national consciousness and of the national state. It was the emergence of these concepts that made a place for the newer forms of church organization (in contrast to the universal but diverse and flexible Catholicism of the Middle Ages). The nation-state tended to be intolerant and exclusive, power-seeking and concerned about its identity and survival. The national church attempted to express and justify the relative completeness and independence of its nation state. The sect attempted to provide spiritual room or breathing space *outside* the monolithic structure and order of the nation-state for those who felt only marginal ties of loyalty to it but who were nevertheless physically and culturally surrounded by an absolutist society

---

[3]To take just one example: In August, 1982, Bishop Leslie Newbigin, serving in the Church of England after years of leadership in the Church of South India, told a conference on global missions in Ohio, "For the first time the church's mission has a home based in every part of the globe and is growing out of each place." He cited the 3 million-member Kimbanguist Church, based in Zaire, one of the most rapidly growing in the world, as one that has never been dependent on foreign missionary leadership.

and government (Leviathan, as Hobbes called it). Even Roman Catholicism took on a new shape after the Council of Trent. Some regions (like France) functioned almost independently of Rome at times. Overall, though, the Western Catholic Church became, like a vast national church, more monolithic, less diverse, and less flexible.

During the twentieth century, a significant counter-trend has set in. A plethora of new nation-states, formerly subservient to European colonization, has emerged. These states, belonging to the Third World, have some of the same concerns for identity and independence that characterized those of seventeenth-, eighteenth-, and nineteenth-century Europe. Yet they are by and large plagued by poverty, and dependent on the "First and Second" Worlds for technology and economic assistance. The nation states of Europe have, meanwhile, changed from world-controlling empires to participants with other nations in the attempt to secure a future free of the threats to economic, political, and environmental security that the twentieth century has spawned.

The two superpowers, the United States and the U.S.S.R., were never nation-states in the classic European sense. Each, relatively isolated geographically until the rise of twentieth-century modes of transportation, "contains multitudes" and a great diversity of ethnic groups and still untapped potential for growth and further differentiation. Each has in the twentieth century been driven by a preconceived sense of the need not to have the rest of the world closed to it.

In the twentieth century, technology (possibilities of almost instantaneous communication and transportation of messages and destructive weaponry) and economic organizations (such as the multinational corporations that can exert more power than governments) have brought a world into being in which "humankind is the unit of cooperation."[4] This concept was explored and developed by the World Council of Churches during the 1940s and '50s. The related concept of "the responsible society" was intended to provide a norm for all societies in the present world context. According to the World Council's definition, a responsible society is a society.

> where freedom is the freedom of men who acknowledge responsibility to justice and public order, and where those who hold political authority or economic power are responsible for its exercise to God and the people whose welfare is affected by it.[5]

During the 1960s and '70s the same organization came increasingly to see that where "mankind is the unit of cooperation" much of the cooperation (interaction) may take the form of exploitation (of the economically and politically vulnerable Third World countries by their wealthier, more powerful partners). Also, one aspect

---

[4]This concept, originally pharased "mankind is the unit of cooperation," was developed by a meeting of the International Missionary Council held in India in 1938.

[5]Walter G. Muelder, *Foundations of the Responsible Society* (New York and Nashville: Abingdon Press, 1959), p. 19.

of "humankind as the unit of cooperation" has been the threat of the whole world falling victim to a self-produced nuclear holocaust.

During the late 1960s and early 1970s some American political analysts were predicting a trend toward world decentralization, with the great powers retreating into their continental "spheres of influence" and avoiding world entanglements. These predictions were diagnosed by other analysts as having resulted from disillusionment at unsuccessful American attempts to influence events in Southeast Asia and at American dependence on Middle Eastern oil.

The dynamics of twentieth-century economics and technology seem to militate against decentralization. If anything, the difficulties the superpowers have had in exerting influence within their spheres of influence (the United Sates in Latin America; the U.S.S.R. in Eastern Europe and Afghanistan) and the volatile internal social mixtures within each of the superpowers and their spheres would seem to support rather than negate trends toward greater international interaction.

One may be initially at a loss, but should not be surprised, to hear Japanese and Polish country-and-western bands and their vocalists singing about jambalaya and crawfish pie or about a cotton patch down in Louisiana. The process of internationalization of all aspects of life is not likely to stop unless a world catastrophe occurs.

If the twentieth century is seeing the emergence of a truly world society, then one would expect Christian religious groups and organizations to mirror this process. And this is exactly what is happening. The Roman Catholic Church now is a truly international church in a way that it has never been before. Its bishops come from practically all parts of the world. Statements and appearances of its popes, even in non-Catholic and non-Christian countries, are events of first importance. Its leadership is truly international. Priests, theologians, and administrators may shuttle from Dallas or Calcutta to Rome and back just as executives of the multinational corporations do.

Protestant and Eastern Orthodox groups, especially through cooperative efforts like the World Council of Churches, have established international presences and have achieved international consciousness. Even denominations like the Southern Baptists and Churches of Christ in the United States, which do not ordinarily participate in ecumenical organizations, send missionaries to far-flung parts of the world and see their internationally known leaders by way of satellite transmission taking part in world affairs, as in the recent highly publicized mission of Dr. Billy Graham, in the interest of world peace, to Russia.

CHARACTERISTICS OF MODERNIZATION AND RELIGIOUS RESPONSE

Equally important as the internationalization of most of the Christian denominations have been the effects on them internally and in relation to other Christian groups, effects that have emerged in the modernized and modernizing societies of the twentieth century.

Anthropologists explain many of the characteristics of human societies by using a continuum that extends from the simplest to the most complex societies. Such a continuum may begin with hunting and gathering societies and move through non-specialized agricultural, specialized agricultural, non-specialized industrial to the highly specialized industrial societies found in contemporary Europe, the United States, Russia, and Japan. The more complex the society, the more highly specialized are social and vocational roles. In a hunting and gathering society there is almost no specialization in economic or social roles. There is little or no specialized knowledge. By the time an agricultural society emerges, there is a far greater degree of specialization. Usually there will be a priesthood (specialists in religious knowledge), a military caste (specialists in war and in ruling), a class of artisans (specialists in making and building) and the great majority of the population that has no specialized knowledge or skills. Specialization in the economic and social roles of men and women will have begun to develop. Also, the more complex the society, the larger the population tends to become—to the point where increased population becomes socially and economically dysfunctional, and threatens social stability.

The continuation of these trends explains much about life, including religious life, in today's specialized industrial societies. Technological innovations, such as automation, have done much to eliminate the need for a large pool of unskilled laborers. Training for most occupations and professions requires a high degree of specialized training. Paradoxically, however, since many occupations and skills soon become outmoded, a high degree of flexibility is also increasingly built into such training. In a sense, specialized industrial societies require more and more in the way of development of meta-skills and meta-education. Almost mirroring the interchangeability of unskilled workers in nonspecialized industrial societies, the highly skilled workers and professionals of specialized industrial society become more and more interchangeable. With the weakening of the nuclear family, such interchangeability also becomes characteristic of domestic and family roles. In less complex societies, the religious experts possessed almost a monopoly on learning and specialized skills. In modern societies, secular knowledge and skills have eclipsed the religious, leading in some ways to a democratization of religion, since the lay adherents of a religion may be better educated and more literate than its "religious specialists." Thus, skills other than specialized theological or doctrinal knowledge are looked for in religious leaders.

Sociologists have noted a number of characteristics of complex modern societies in contrast to those of simpler, traditionally oriented ones. Characteristics of modern societies may be listed as (1) urbanization, (2) atomization, (3) rationalization, (4) differentiation, (5) privatization, and (6) institutionalization of innovative attitudes.

Urbanization refers to the fact that in modernized societies the great majority of the population will not be engaged in agricultural (primary) economic production but in industrial (secondary) production and in service (tertiary) occupations. The freeing of the majority of the population to engage in production beyond the needs of simple survival has been the key to the economic expansion of industrial societies.

Urbanization has not been without its negative consequences. In industrializing societies, it has disrupted traditional family relations and cultural patterns. Also, the interaction of highly industrialized societies with simpler societies has led to some enormous contemporary problems, (*e.g.*, the growth of population well past the danger point in Third World countries largely caused by new medical technology developed in industrialized societies and applied in the simpler ones). More than a billion of the world's population is now estimated to live in dire poverty, often in starvation or near starvation. The enormous population growth of the twentieth century and the related problem of world hunger are largely results of interaction between the rich nations and the poor.

Atomization refers to the tendency of traditional family, clan, and kinship patterns to break down in modernized societies. Families no longer work as single economic units. Family units tend to become nuclear families—parents (or single parent) and children. Large families are no longer economically functional. In the most modernized societies, the nuclear family, stripped of the traditional support of the extended family, appears to be extremely vulnerable to social pressures and instability. The psychological and social effects of reduction to the nuclear family cannot as yet be gauged. In some ways, with high divorce rates and the tendency of parents to remarry and assume responsibility for multiple sets of children, there may be a trend for a new kind of extended family to develop.

Rationalization refers to the fact that in highly modernized societies the activities, especially economic but also political and cultural, of individuals, groups, and organizations tend to be coordinated by semiautomatic mechanisms (the market, planning by governmental agencies, the communications network, and so on). Information communicated by a government agency in one part of the world concerning the health effects of tobacco use may have a disastrous effect on the economy or a tobacco-producing area. Satellite communication or the world record industry may cause musicians in Japan or Poland to adopt a new musical style. Such effects need not be intended by their originating groups but are highly influential in determining social patterns.

Differentiation refers to the tendency of organizations in complex societies to become more highly specialized. Think of the trends in medicine and in industrial and service occupations in twentieth-century America. The sociologist Talcott Parsons pointed out the drastic effect of differentiation on Western religious organizations and institutions. According to Parsons, much recent talk about secularization in modernized societies stems from the fact that many of the traditional social functions—education, health and welfare, charity, even entertainment—formerly performed by Christian churches have been taken over by government at various levels. This fact possibly as much as any other has led to a *perception* (whether justified or not) of a declining role or influence of religion in society.

Privatization refers to a tendency in modern societies for the areas of subjective involvement of individuals to be rather sharply separated from those of public (political and occupational) activity. A person may be an engineer, a lawyer, or a mechanic, but the area of life in which he or she finds subjective satisfaction may be the activity of an amateur actor, yachtsman, or football fan. The sociologist Thomas Luckmann has argued that, increasingly in modernized societies, religion for many individuals has come to belong to the private, subjective sphere of life rather than to the public realm. To the extent that this may be true, it goes against much of the recent effort of Christian denominations, Catholic and Protestant, to be socially relevant and to apply the Christian message to the needs of society. (See Chapters Five, Seven, and Eight for discussion of the Social gospel ideal of twentieth-century Protestantism and the social involvement of twentieth-century Catholics expressed in papal encyclicals and liberation theology.)

Luckmann's position has been described as follows:

> In relatively simple societies the sacred ... cosmos permeates social institutions such as labor and kinship. The religious representations serve to legitimate action in all areas of life and are mediated through all institutions in the society. But more complex societies tend to develop specialized institutions to maintain and transmit the sacred cosmos.[6]

As noted above, Luckmann believes that the phenomenon of privatization (a consequence of rationalization and differentiation) is leading to a new role for religion, or a new form of religion, in modern industrialized societies. In earlier stages of society, religious ideas and feelings gave an overall meaning to life. Religious organizations gave their blessing to the state, work, education, and family life. In modern societies, each of these areas of life—even marriage and the family—has tended to be separated from its earlier religious ties. Each has become rational in relation to the functional requirements of the particular institution or area of life.[7]

The Protestant Reformers interpreted one's work as the major way by which the individual responded to God's call to serve neighbors. In modern societies, work may be seen either as a boring economic necessity or as the way one climbs the social ladder. The same applies to education. It formerly was seen as a way of fitting oneself to serve God. Now it is generally presented to young children as a necessity if they are to do well economically and socially. Work and education are presented as requirements that society imposes on the individual with little concern for his or her interests and choices.

In this situation, according to Luckmann, the unique or subjective characteristics of the individual are of no imporance to the organization or social institution,

---

[6] Emily C. Hewitt, Lawrence H. Mamiya, and Michael C. Mason, *Models of Secularization in Contemporary Sociological Theory* (New York: Studies in Education, 1972), Publication #1, p. 23.

[7] See Thomas Luckmann, *The Invisible Religion* (New York: Macmillan, 1967), pp. 195-196.

and the individual, though perhaps occupied for many hours a day and dependent for a livelihood on participation in the organization (*e.g.,* the company for which the individual works) invests little or no subjective interest in it. This lack of personal investment of meaning may apply not only to the political sphere, to one's occupation, but to one's family life and roles as well. This may mean that the individual, though conforming to the political, economic, and social demands of society, will find the meaning of life elsewhere. The result, according to Luckmann, may be that

> the large primary institutions of modern society—notably, government, business, and industry—operate according to their own "functional" and "rational" norms and are not guided by religious sanctions. Such institutions are meaningless to the people who work within them.[8]

They are, that is, subjectively meaningless, though objectively they require large amounts of the individual's time and energy. Thus the man may do his duty as breadwinner and father, but find his real satisfaction in watching the Denver Broncos, Washington Redskins, or Dallas Cowboys on Sunday-afternoon television. Or a young woman may be a straight-A student in college, but find vacation trips to the coast or the mountains the really important events in her life.

In modern societies, then, according to Luckmann, *religion* becomes privatized, a largely personal, subjective affair. Individuals are not subject, unless they choose to be, to institutional religious control or guidance. For some, religion itself, as traditionally defined, becomes meaningless. Others will be affected by deep anxiety at the apparent loss of the controls that traditional values and norms have exercised on society and seek through participation in sectarian or cultic movements to find something in their personal lives to take the place of the lost center of meaning. Still others will seek through political and communications activities to restore the directing role of religious values to the society. Some will seek to make the religious organization more relevant to the society, to meet the needs of individuals adrift in the secular sea or to forge a new way of interaction between religious values and secular institutions. For still others, religion may be a very important, indeed the most important, dimension of life, but confined to the private sphere—a subjective task, a lifelong quest for inner meaning, for self-discovery.

Institutionalization of innovative attitudes designates the deliberate, formalized, and institutionalized expectation and promotion of change—a pro-change orientation—throughout contemporary societies. This promotes in every social institution an openness to diversity. However, it may also encourage the planned obsolescence not only of products and fashions but of beliefs, attitudes, ideas, organizations, communities, and persons.

---

[8] Hewitt, et. al., p. 14.

RELIGOUS ORGANIZATIONAL STRUCTURE IN MODERN SOCIETIES

Given the preceding discussion, it seems reasonable to suggest that the different Christian organizations—churches, denominations, sects, and cults—will offer a full range of options for individual adherents. However, it also seems reasonable to believe that the great majority of Christian churches and groups in modern societies will tend to approximate the *denominational* type.

The *church* type of religious organization is one which for all practical purposes includes the whole society. One is born into it. It usually makes a clear distinction between clergy and laity, between the realms of the sacred and the secular. It *is* the custodian of the religious institutions of the society. There will be two set standards of behavior for the society—one for the full-time religious and another for the secular. But control will be exerted over all. The secular government is the church's ally in enforcing religious and moral conformity.

In contrast, the *sect* type of religious organizaion is one in which membership is voluntary. In important ways, it calls on its members to withdraw from significant parts of the society, seeking to separate the holy people from the corrupt and worldly. In theory, all adult members are sanctified, saintly, or perhaps priests or clergy. Though membership is voluntary, strict control is exerted over individual members or they are expelled.[9] The tendency of the sect is to become an isolated, separated community (like the Amish in the American Midwest); or to attempt to become a church through the conversion of the whole society (early Christianity in the Roman Empire); or to move toward denominational status (Methodists and Baptists in the United States).

The *denomination* is an organization characteristic of modernized or modernizing pluralistic societies. In some ways it is church-like, stressing nurture and education rather than adult conversion. Membership in it is voluntary, but may be a result of family tradition, personal convenience or habit. It exerts much less control over the behavior and consciences of its members than either the church or the sect. In fact, it is sometimes characterized as a focus of secondary rather than primary loyalty. To the extent that this is true, it does not necessarily follow that the members of the denomination do not make a primary religious commitment. It may simply be the case that they have become relatively autonomous religiously—with their subjective religious attitudes having primary significance in their lives but their denomination producing an important objective vehicle for their expression, fulfillment, or personal growth.

Thus if it is true that the so-called mainline religious organizations, including even the Roman Catholic Church, in contemporary advanced societies tend to approximate the denominational pattern, this does not mean that the importance of their role in individual and social life is diminished, only that it has changed. We

---

[9]The term cult is usually used to refer to a small group dominated by the personality and teachings of a powerful individual. After a generation or two the cult usually dies out or develops into a sect or denomination.

may expect to see in modern pluralistic societies a continued subjective intensity and individualism in which participation of individuals in religion is enabled and balanced by religious organizations serving as carriers, interpreters, and modifiers of objective religious tradition. It is entirely possible that for both individuals and organizations the interchangeability of individuals and the sharp separation between the private and public spheres of meaning will prove untenable. Individual and group life may ultimately become too precarious in privatized societies to be tolerated by individuals seeking wholeness in individual life and as persons-in-community.

CONTEMPORARY ISSUES AND CHRISTIAN RESPONSE

Christianity and the Values of Society

In the context of the preceding discussion, one of the major issues faced by Christian churches is how to relate to the societies in which they find themselves located. Two contrasting dangers for religious organizations in contemporary societies present themselves. One was noted by Dietrich Bonhoeffer (see Chapter Seven) while in prison for his anti-Nazi stance. Bonhoeffer noted that when humanity's major struggle was against *nature*, the Church had a large field of activity, since the church could step in with its answer—God—everywhere human ability to control life broke down. In modern times, however, humanity has become increasingly able through social and political organization and science and technology to deal with the problems that earlier were left to religion. So the church has been pushed to the margins of society, dealing only with the leftover ultimate questions (*e.g.*, death, guilt, and so on).[10] Bonhoeffer felt that the church should seek its place at the center of society. It should become involved in the secular, since it is the secular that largely shapes and affects the lives of people now, and Christ above all was and is "the man for others." Note the ambiguous possibility here: The Church might seek to remake the secular in accordance with some set of religious values or it might attempt to interpret the meaning of secular involvement for its adherents and society—to witness and serve rather than direct and shape. The second possibility is the way advocated by Bonhoeffer.

If Bonhoeffer saw the danger of an increasingly marginal role in society for Christian organizations, Martin Luther King, Jr. frequently expressed the fear that the churches too often are only vehicles for perpetuating and reinforcing the accepted values of the society—they are thermometers instead of thermostats. In fact, Bonhoeffer's and King's diagnoses probably accurately describe the fundamental temptation of the characteristic types of religious organizations of their own societies—the established church in Bonhoeffer's Germany and the denomination in

---

[10]Dietrich Bonhoeffer, *Letters and Papers from Prison,* The Enlarged Edition (New York: The Macmillan Company, 1972).

King's America. As King saw, the American church is likely to become simply another civic organization or service group under constant necessity to demonstrate its social usefulness and progressive spirit.

Christianity and Social Evil:
The Holocaust

Modern Christians also find themselves faced with social evils that are the direct consequence of their own historical prejudices and biases, which do not conform to traditional teachings of Christian love. The conflict of Jew and Christian in the Middle Ages was typified by the Inquisiton and the official stance of Western Christianity that Jews (who were frequently blamed for the death of Jesus) were "deicides"—killers of God. Jews had little hope of escaping latent and active anti-Semitism. Nevertheless, reflecting the attitudes the Enlightenment fostered, Jews, particularly in Western Europe, became convinced that if they lived actively as citizens contributing to their societies, acceptance would be inevitable and anti-Semitic prejudice would die. In much of Europe this was not the case. The late nineteenth century brought renewed anti-Semitic outbursts in France and Germany.

Also in the nineteenth century, Russian Judaism was accused by the Russian Orthodox Church of undermining the church and the established order of the tsar since church and state were one. Although not responsible for the initiation of charges of the "blood-libel", a superstitious belief held by some Christians that Jews practiced ritual murder, Russia proved fertile ground for such accusations.

At the beginning of the twentieth century, Jews throughout Europe were subject to racial prejudice and in Eastern Europe to persecution. Enjoying relative economic independence and freedom in the West, they found that the old anti-Semitic prejudices had been aggravated by the new social mobility and visibility of Jews prominent in the arts and professions. In the aftermath of the First World War, Germany's economy and its traditional political life were devastated. The rise of National Socialism under Hitler was a response to the disappointed hopes and fears of many in the new, disturbing situation. In his program for German recovery, Hitler incorporated racist myths according to which Jews were a threat to the pure Aryan Germans. Given latent and frequently overt anti-Semitism, it was not difficult for Hitler to make the Jews scapegoats for all of Germany's problems. Restrictions on the Jews began with the promulgation of laws that limited Jewish participation in society in 1935. These were followed by destruction of synagogues in 1938, concentration camps in 1939, and finally a program of systematic extermination. These policies were applied to all captured countries so that much of the Jewish population of Europe was destroyed; some 6 million Jews lost their lives by the end of the war.

The effect of the Holocaust on Jews and on Jewish-Christian relations has been more far-reaching than many Christians realize. Recognition of worldwide interdependence of Jews has resulted in significant emphasis on unity and the defining of Jewish identity. It has also brought a resurgence of interest in and study of ancient religious and cultural identity. The creation of a Jewish state was certainly augmented by the Holocaust. In recent years, literary treatment of the Holocaust in novels, plays, and films have been numerous. The works of Elie Wiesel and other Jewish writers have raised questions about why the holocaust happened and how its having happened can be appropriated by Jews—and Christians—in terms of their attitudes toward each other and their beliefs about God. Questions about the meaning of evil and its relation to God—and whether in the light of the Holocaust Jews and Christians can continue to believe in a God who is good, powerful, and loving—have been explored by Jewish theologians, including Richard Rubenstein.

Christian thinkers have also sought to understand the Holocaust. They have been particularly concerned about what the Holocaust says about the meaning of human life and the relation of human beings and groups to one another. They have been concerned about the involvement of Christians in the horror, as well as the lack of protest by Christians who knew of the events, or should have known, while they were taking place.

Ecumenical Relations

One pressing issue for contemporary Christian organizations concerns their relations with each other. There has probably never been as much cooperation and good feeling between the different Christian denominations as there is now. Very large steps have been taken between the Roman Catholic Church and the Church of England and between the Roman Catholic and European Lutheran churches toward doctrinal and practical agreement. There have been mergers between many of the Protestant denominations—in Canada and in India, for instance. In the United States, major progress toward union or unification of more than ten mainline Protestant denominations in a Consultation on Church Union was made during the 1960s before negotiations came to an at least temporary deadlock.

In spite of this ecumenical interest, it seems likely that the future of the majority of Christians, for the present, will be denominational. In contrast to sects or churches, denominations do not define themselves as antagonistic to each other. Their tendency is to approximate each other, to become similar, and yet to provide enough diversity to attract a maximum number of adherents. This does not mean that cultic and sectarian groups will not have significant influence in contemporary society. Sectarian gorups (perhaps in unorthodox forms) may indeed exert a large influence on the denominations. Yet it is clear that the majority of persons in contemporary society will not be attracted to cults (like the Unification Church) or to sects. Historically, sectarian movements have frequently brought renewal to the Christian movement as a whole. The various monastic renewal movements within Roman Catholicism functioned as sectarian groups that stayed within the church (see Chapters Three and Eight) thus providing new options of participation. Even within a single denomination, congregations of various types (*e.g.*, from high church to low) will attract a larger and more diverse membership than will uniform or interchangeable units.

Another important issue concerns the relation of Christian to non-Christian religions, especially in those parts of the world where non-Christian religions predominate. Perhaps its claim to exclusiveness—to exclusive access to God—has been one of Christianity's traditional strengths. Yet many contemporary Christians (*e.g.*, Thomas Merton) have seen great strength, truth, and beauty in the religious traditions of Buddhism, Taoism, and Hinduism without necessarily sacrificing claims to the uniqueness of Christianity. Will contemporary Christianity be strengthened or weakened by an attitude of openness toward and cooperation with the other world religions?

Judaism and Christianity:
Their Continuing Uneasy Kinship

Throughout Christian history, relationships of Christians to Jews have been marked by tension. Animosity often has run deep, for they were grounded in differences of faith, in variant understandings and treatments of common scriptures, and in differing interpretations of the will of a commonly acknowledged God. Obvious contrasts in life style and patterns of worship compounded tensions between the two religious communities. From an early time, Judaism was the minority group.

Christian ambivalence toward Jews and their religion arose early, as indicated by the Apostle Paul's comments in the Letter to the Romans, Chapter 11. There, the Jews are seen as disobedient to God's commandments. This disobedience is not seen by Paul as having had totally negative results. According to him, it resulted in the possibility of non-Jews being included in God's plan for the Jews. Paul sees the Jews as incorrect in their beliefs and attitudes, yet he insists that they are God's chosen people and will be brought back to their privileged position in and through Christ. Such a position laid the groundwork for Christian endeavors through the centuries to convince the Jews of the falsity of their beliefs and their need to accept Christ. Such endeavors, no matter how well meant Christians may have believed them to be, frequently intensified antagonism and increased Judaism's sense of being a persecuted minority.

Misunderstanding and mistrust between Jews and Christians from this source has been especially significant in America. Much of American Protestant Christianity, stressing personal religious experience, came to accept a conversionist attitude toward religion. Such an understanding has placed great emphasis on the initiation into the Christian life as an experience requiring conversion or "new birth." This understanding assumes that prior to conversion, one's religious convictions and experience are inadequate and incorrect. It also assumes that it is the duty of converted Christians to seek to lead others, including adherents of non-Christian religions, to such a conversion experience, and that non-Christians should welcome such evangelistic efforts to unite them to Christ. Jews are likely to reject these assumptions, feeling that their religion is quite adequate and seeing no need to change. In fact, their religious perception is very different from that of conversionist Christianity. For Jews, religion is a part of the givenness of life. Typically, Jews do not expect or want non-Jews ot convert to Judaism. They expect persons to live faithfully within their inherited religious milieu. Failure of religious life means failure to live with moral and spiritual sincerity, observing precepts and laws that may require renewed commitment but not conversion. Jews do not share the Christian belief that Christianity is the completion or fulfillment of their religion. Many zealous Christians have found this fact hard to understand and appropriate.

The twentieth century brought efforts by many Christians and Jews to eliminate prejudice and anti-Semitic practices. In the United States, the National Conference of Christians and Jews was founded in 1928 to promote mutual understanding and cooperation. While there was no concentrated Christian effort to protest Germany's progressively more and more virulent anti-Jewish policies between the world wars, some Christians spoke out against them. Groups such as the Quakers attempted to intervene, to exert direct moral influence on the German government on behalf of Jews. The Quakers and others facilitated escape from Germany and resettlement in other countries for Jewish refugees. In the aftermath of the Holocaust, the world Council of Churches denounced anti-Semitism. The Second Vatican Council of the Roman Catholic Church (1965) promulgated a far-reaching schema on the Jews and other non-Christian religions. In it, the view of the Jews as perpetrators of deicide (killers of God) was rejected. Jewish organizations such as B'nai B'rith have worked since the nineteenth century to spread information among Christians about Judaism and to defend Jews from prejudice and falsehood.

Since World War II, the study of Judaism by Christian scholars has greatly expanded, leading to numerous attempts to promote understanding and rapprochement. American colleges and universities, some sponsored by Christian denominations, have included the study of Judaism and have employed Jewish scholars in their departments of religious studies. Such inclusion has been possible because Judaism is seen not only as one of the major world religions but as an American religious tradition with the same status as other religious alternatives. Christianity and Judaism seem as inextricably joined to each other now as they were in the past, in ways that perhaps go far beyond what most Christians who live in Christian-majorities realize. Openness and joint interest, particularly in the face of the threat to both religious traditions by attitudes of increasing secularism, have not totally eased the tensions in Christian and Jewish relations. Karl Barth, perhaps the greatest Protestant theologian of the twentieth century, denounced anti-Semitism as a terrible crime and saw the the continued existence of the Jews as a sign of God's faithfulness to His promises. Nevertheless, Barth seemed to think that a major task for Christian self-understanding is the continued theological re-thinking by Christians of the relation of Christianity to Judiasm.

Ethnic, Cultural,
and Racial Differences

Not only are attitudes toward other religions and cultures a crucial issue for contemporary Christianity, attitudes toward ethnic, cultural, and racial differences *within* the Christian world are still of decisive significance. Most of the mainline Christian groups now admit that in much of the past there was too ready an identification of European or American cultural values with the values of Christianity. Now it is largely agreed that the gospel can find its setting in a large variety of cultural contexts (how one covers one's torso, or whether one has tea at four P.M. is of little significance for the gospel). It is still a major agenda item for Christian religious groups in the twentieth century to see what this will mean for doctrinal expression, organizational structures, liturgical practices, and codes of morals and etiquette.

As for the question of *race*, in theory this may have been solved by Paul when he wrote in his Letter to the Galatians:

> There is neither Jew nor Greek, there is neither male nor female, for you are all one in Jesus Christ.

(GALATIANS 3:28)

In practice it has not been solved. The American denominations contributed significantly to the struggle for civil rights by black Americans during the 1960s. Yet American churches still are largely segregated, and many black Americans believe that the civil-rights struggle died prematurely during the 1970s. A theology of racial differences was elaborated largely in the modern period to justify first slavery, then unequal treatment of blacks. Such a theology is still used to justify the racist society of South Africa in spite of heroic protests by black and white Christians.[11]

The Meaning of Being Human

Perhaps the major complex of religious and moral isues in contemporary societies is centerd on the question of what it means to be human. As Bonhoeffer noted, humans are no longer constrained by nature in many ways that obtained in the past. Technology has opened vast possibilities for changing or redefining the meaning and limits of human existence.

Ecology. One important task undertaken by Christian theologians has been a rethinking of the very concept of nature. This has included new attention to a Christian understanding of the natural environment that humans share with each other and with nonhuman forms of life. Since the rise of modern science and technology, humans in industrializing societies have tended to take an exploitative view of the environment and the nonhuman world, often justifying this view by elements

[11] See Alan Paton, *Too Late the Phalarope* (New York: Scribner's, 1953).

of the bilblical tradition (Genesis 1-3, for example) that set humans above the rest of the created world.

With new perceptions of the dangers both for human life and for the other species that unrestrained technological exploitation of the environment has brought, many Christians are beginning to look at other elements within the Christian traditions: The view that humans have a duty to protect and care for the created world and the sense of kinship of humans, exemplified in such Christians as St. Francis of Assisi, with nonhuman forms of life. The Protestant theologian James Gustafson has recently engaged in a major effort of theological re-thinking embracing these issues.

In recent years, there has been a small but growing movement among some Christians toward vegetarianism. Sometimes this is an expression of kinship with nonhuman forms of life. More frequently, perhaps, it is a response to the problem of world hunger, expressing the belief that it is wrong to spend the world's resources in the rather uneconomical production of meat while millions of fellow humans are starving.

Work.   The meaning of work—occupation or vocation—is changing rapidly and radically in contemporary society. In the past, work was variously characterized by Christians as a penalty imposed on humanity for Adam's sin or as an opportunity to serve God and neighbor through practical action. More recent secular prophets—Marz and Freud—have looked at work as fulfilling innate human needs for creative expression either when it is freed of the fetishistic demands of capitalist economics (Marx), which place the functioning of the impersonal system above the needs of living human beings; or when it is freed of neurotic fantasy elements (Freud), which distort the realities of the present in terms of unconscious conflicts carried over from the past. One of the problems that contemporary religious thought must engage is that of the meaning of human work as an aspect of human activity generally. The idea of status-seeking through climbing the socially prescribed occupational or career ladders would seem to be as vulnerable to Christian as to Marxist or Freudian critiques.

Medicine, Technology, and Bioethics.   A host of issues cluster around new medical technology that allows new ways of terminating, prolonging, and even creating human life. During the past few years, the issue of abortion has become one of the most explosive and divisive on the contemporary American scene. Traditionally oriented Catholics and Protestants have argued that abortion is equivalent to murder, since the fetus from the moment of conception is a unique human being endowed by the Creator with full human dignity and significance. Other Christians have argued in the name of autonomy and of the communal shaping of personality that women have a nearly absolute right to the control of their own bodies. Also, the fetus does not become distinctively human except through the process of socialization, they argue. Perhaps the majority of American Protestants and some Catholics have tended to take an intermediate position, being opposed to abortion in most cases but willing to grant it in others—in cases of pregnancy resulting from rape, danger to the life of the mother, or serious malformation of the fetus. Since the 1973 Supreme Court ruling that struck down existing state laws forbidding abortion, abortion has become a major method of birth control in the United States. A vigorous, often religiously motivated single-cause anti-abortion movement has exerted political power in an attempt to reverse this trend. There have been many attempts to use philosophical and theological analysis to clarify the issue, but positions seem simply to have hardened.

Sexuality, Marriage, the Family. The issue of abortion raises profoundly the question of the nature and significance of human life. So do the related technologically created possibilities of pregnancy by artificial insemination and *in vitro* fertilization. It is clear that technology has produced the need for a radical re-thinking in religious circles of the meaning of human sexuality, marriage, parenting, and the family. To mention the first of these, note that traditionally the Christian churches have regarded marriage as a sacrament or quasi-sacrament and have opposed divorce. The Catholic Church has held firmly to this position, though it recently has shown increased willingness to grant annulments of marriages. Many Protestant groups have greatly relaxed their positions in this respect, by and large accepting, without always recognizing divorce, and granting remarriage at will. Traditional Christian attitudes toward human sexuality have been mixed, seeing sex as a part of the natural goodness of the created order but also at times associating it with the fall and original sin. For centuries, the highest forms of Christian life were understood by many Christians to be the celibate life. Many traditional Christian attitudes toward sex and sexuality, including attitudes toward homosexuality, are being reexamined in the light both of scholarly interpretations of Biblical texts and of data from the behavioral sciences.

The Position of Women. Questions concerning human sexuality, marriage, and the family lead ultimately to questions concerning the position and rights of women. It frequently has been claimed that the position of women—in contrast to their position in the Roman Republic and Empire—was significantly elevated in Christian teaching and practice. One text cited is Paul's saying that in Christ "there is neither male nor female."

Paul also held an elevated view of male responsibility in the marriage relationship and in religious roles (I Corinthians 14:33-35). He is often given a major share of responsibility for the traditional Christian attitude supporting male dominance in family, church, and society. However, in what seems to be a crucial, if difficult, passage, Paul admits a mutuality between the two sexes, according to which neither is dominant, God is (I Corinthians 11:2-16). It cannot be denied that attitudes supporting male dominance developed early in Christian thought and practice:

> With the rise of asceticism as a major factor in the life of the church, the conservative view of the role and status of women became more pronounced. From the standpoint of the ascetic, who had withdrawn to the desert to flee the wickedness of the world, women became sources of temptation; after all, Eve

had been the one responsible for Adam's fall, for the entry of evil into the world. Women were blamed by such writers as John Chrysostom and Ambrose for being immature and ignorant, conditions which, where they existed, are easily explained by the educational neglect of and social discrimination against women characteristic of the period. Clement of Alexandria, however, argued that by nature there was (and ought to be) complete equality between the sexes. (He did believe that there should be some differences in vocation.) It would be fair to say that the social position of women in the Roman Empire remained largely unaffected by the spread of Christianity. This is seen in the minimal role allowed to women in the institutional life of the church. In the Eastern part of the Empire (and perhaps also in the West) there *was* a regular *ordination* of deaconesses. Deaconesses were allowed, however, to minister *only* to women, and they were not allowed to perform ecclesiastical functions thought to be proper to the male, such as teaching or praying aloud in worship services or approaching the altar. This is in stark contrast to the practice of many of the heretical sects of the period, such as Montanism, in which women were allowed more active roles. With the onset of feudalism, women lost many of the rights they had had in the urban setting of the Roman empire.[12]

In recent years, the Roman Catholic Church has done much to recognize and augment the role of women in the church, such as designating outstanding women saints of the past (Teresa of Avila and Catherine of Siena) as doctors of the Church. However, recent popes have continued to affirm that there can be no reconsideration of the traditional denial of the status of priesthood to women. Some Protestant groups, such as the United Methodist Church, have recently allowed full rights of the ordination to ministry to women. In some United Methodist seminaries, as many as 40 percent of preministerial students are women. Other groups, like the Episcopal Church, have been largely negative toward allowing women in ministry, though there are increasing numbers of women who have been ordained by willing bishops. Certain theologically conservative Protestant groups, especially Pentecostals, have always allowed full rights of ordination to women. Others, like the Southern Baptists, though ultimately congregationally controlled (*i.e.*, each congregation is free to adopt its own policy), have been largely negative toward ordination of women.

In addition to the question of the role of women in religious organizations, the churches increasingly will have to confront the larger question of the significance of the largely economically motivated emancipation of women in modern societies. Although many Christians have supported women's liberation on the basis of their understanding of the Gospel, they have perhaps not yet fully examined to what extent the economic basis of the movement masks new forms of the exploitation of women, thus giving some justification to conservative critics of the feminist movement, who have argued that women possess more rights and better protection where there are unequal roles and treatment. To take just one example: Many who have seen athletics in the United States, from public schools to universities to

[12] Robert C. Monk, et. al., *Exploring Religious Meaning*, 2nd Ed. (Englewood Cliffs, N.J.: Prentice-Hall, Inc., 1980), pp. 254-255.

professional sports, as frequently being based on exploitation of the athletes and institutions involved have felt little enthusiasm for the recent drive to incorporate full-scale programs of women's athletics into the existing systems.

World Order, Justice, and Peace

Political and Economic Justice. Another cluster of problems centers around issues of justice, order, and peace in the contemporary international system. Leaders in the World Council of Churches (Protestant and Eastern Orthodox) and many Roman Catholic thinkers became sensitized during the past two decades to the growing disparity between standards of living in the advanced industrial societies and those in the Third World. They were inclined to sympathize with Third World voices, even Marxist ones, who blamed the industrialized societies for their exploitation and neglect of the Third World. This has led to some negative reaction against the World Council in the Western countries, especially the United States, and against Catholic and Protestant leaders by ruling groups in certain countries, especially in Latin America. Critics have charged those sympathetic to Third World liberation movements with being gullible tools of cynical Marxist revolutionaries. Other, more sympathetic voices, have charged that the Western capitalist countires misperceive the world when they see it as dominated by capitalist-Marxist conflict, since the real issue is that of the exploitation and neglect of the poor by the rich. These voices argue that to interpret revolutionary struggles in such places as Nicaragua and El Salvador as primarily conflicts between international Marxism and the free world is naive, misleading, and potentially disastrous. The diverse movement called liberation theology—emphasizing the need of oppressed majorities and minorities for liberation from political and economic exploitation—has been the most vital theological movement of the past decade and a half.

Nuclear War. The other major problem concerning international order is the threat of nuclear war. Roland Bainton has pointed out that traditionally there have been three Christian positions about war. One has been the pacifist position of such groups as the Society of Friends, the Church of the Brethren, the Mennonites, and of such individuals as Leo Tolstoy, Muriel Lester, and Martin Luther King, Jr.

The second position has been that of adherence to the criteria of justified war, criteria that must be met before a war can be begun or waged.[13] According to such theorists as Augustine and Aquinas, these criteria are universally recognized among civilized nations and are known by natural reason. They include protecting civilian populations from direct attack, being certain that the damage inflicted by waging the war is less than the harm of not waging it, aiming at a better condition for all affected as a result of the war, and having a reasonable expectation that the aims of the war will be achieved.

[13] For a brief discussion of just war theory see Monk, *et al.,* pp. 248-251.

A third position, that of the crusade, was introduced to account for *some* wars (especially those of the Old Testament Israelites against the heathen Canaanites) waged at the direct command of God. In the present international context, some Christians have argued that a militant crusade against godless communism, even if it resulted in the destruction of all life on earth, would be justified. More have asked whether, given the threat of total annihilation that nuclear war poses, the criteria of justified war could ever be satisfied in international conflicts involving even the threat, much less the use, of nuclear weapons. As this book goes to press, the leaders of many Christian organizations, including the bishops of the American Roman Catholic church and leaders of many American Protestant groups, are attempting to re-think the entire question of nuclear war in order to give guidance to their constituencies in a period in which the threat of nuclear war seems to have increased dangerously.

Theological Questioning

Contemporary societies provide a large arena for theological re-thinking.

Understanding Jesus and the Christ Event.   In earlier chapters, it has been noted that the present century has been one of major theological re-thinking among Protestants and Catholics. The process continues. In Chapter Seven the concept of the incarnation held by conservatives was described as saying that God took on human nature in Jesus Christ. For liberal Christians, this doctrine might be described by saying that Jesus expressed God fully. In Chapter Five, the modal orthodox view was described as holding that in the man Jesus (not to be thought of as existing prior to or independent of the incarnation) God expressed or revealed Himself fully. A recent, worldwide debate has raised questions about whether the traditional language of incarnation, and of the Trinity, of three persons within one nature, or of two natures within one person, is at all adequate anymore.[14] Essentially this debate stems from the larger question of whether traditional orthodox theology, by adopting categories of Greek philosophy to interpret what happened in Jesus Christ, does not falsify the essential event of the gospel proclamation. The idea that the use of Greek philosophical concepts (substance, nature, and so on) in some ways distorted the Christian message has frequently been expressed—by such persons as Rudolf Bultmann, Reinhold Niebuhr, Leslie Dewart, and others. *Their* position has frequently been contested.

Also, the idea that the Christian message was originally proclaimed in a language heavily dependent on myth and mythological concepts and that such myth-impregnated thought forms make the gospel unintelligible to people in scientifically dominated societies has been advocated by Bultmann and others. *This*

---

[14] See John Hick (ed.), *The Myth of God Incarnate* (Philadelphia: The Westminster Press, 1977). Also Michael Green (ed.), *The Truth of God Incarnate* (London: Hodder & Stoughton, 1977) and Michael Goulder (ed.), *Incarnation and Myth: The Debate Continued* (Grand Rapids: William B. Eerdman's Publishing Company, 1979).

issue also has been variously discussed, with some theological conservatives denying that the Christian language uses myth and thinkers like Tillich, Reinhold Niebuhr, and Jaspers who argue that myth is indispensible for the communication of religious truth. Such debates have called into question traditional Trinitarian and incarnational concepts. Many have rushed to defend these concepts, impressed with the resilience and durability of the language and concepts of orthodoxy.

The debates are not yet finished. They have encompassed a broad range of topics. Catholic and Protestant theologians are currently reexamining the nature of the church. One issue that has received much attention is the contrast between the church as an institutional structure and as a community (people of God). Catholic theologians, especially, have reexamined the significance of tradition, the nature of authority as related to ecclesiastical offices, and the relation of Christianity to non-Christian religions.

Theology as practiced within the Christian churches and academic communities at present is a sign of the continuing vitality of Christian belief and commitment. It is also at times a source of intense controversy. The fact that religious studies and sometimes theology have a setting in contemporary secular academic contexts is itself a source of diversity and at times of controversy. There continues to be pressure on theologians to conform in their theological conclusions both to the expectations for commitment of traditional religious communities and authorities as well as to the objective critical standards of the secular academy.

Liberation Theology. As noted previously, the attempt by Christian denominational leaders and theologians to think through the political and economic implications of the Gospel, particularly as related to the Third World experience of oppressor and injustice, has given rise to liberation theology. Particularly strong in Latin America and arising from both Catholic and Protestant sources, this movement has been varied and influential. Within economically powerful Northern, industrial societies, it is usually studied in theological seminaries. It has been welcomed by some as restoring a genuine, frequently lost dimension of Christianity's proclamation of God's will for all of life. Others have charged it with substituting popular political slogans for the gospel and of being uncritical in support of left-wing, including Marxist, movements.

Black Theology. A response by black Christians to continuing racist patterns of oppression and injustice in church and society, and to religious justification of such patterns, has been the attempt to reflect on and draw strength from the black experience of oppression, endurance, hope, and struggle. This has resulted in black theology, one of the many variant forms of contemporary liberation thought. Most black theologians encourage members of other oppressed ethnic, cultural, racial, or sexual groups to join the attempt to find new relevance in the gospel by reflecting on their experience in similar ways.

Feminist Theology. Much has been written in earlier sections on perceptions of the need to examine and recast many traditional patterns based on male-dominated or patriarchal patterns imposed on earlier expressions of Christianity. Feminist theology, which can be considered a form of liberation thought, attempts to do this. It is an activity carried on by women who believe that such re-thinking is necessary before any in society can become truly free. It shows great variety, taking more moderate to more radical forms.

The New Evangelical Theology. As mentioned in Chapter Five, post-fundamentalist conservative or evangelical theology, especially in America, has shown increasing vitality. A broad-ranging debate concerning the Bible has recently emerged among American evangelical thinkers. Theologians like Jack B. Rogers and Donald McKim have raised questions concerning the traditional conservative concept of Biblical inerrancy while wanting to maintain a distinctive Evangelical attitude toward scripture. Another characteristic note among present neoevangelicals is increased willingness to make political judgments and to become involved in political protest or activism. These can extend from individuals or groups supporting the Moral Majority and right-wing causes to others like Jim Wallis and his coworkers, publishers of *Sojourners* magazine, who, from a radically evangelical Biblical perspective, support nuclear pacifism and identification with the poor of the Third World.

Contemporary Forms of Witness, Life, and Expression

If the sociological theory developed in earlier pages of this chapter is accurate, we may anticipate a wide variety of forms of Christian witness and life style in contemporary societies. Many of these are illustrated in Chapter Eight. Two not discussed there that perhaps show contrasting extremes of Christian expression, life style, and witness will be briefly examined here.

Simone Weil was a Frenchwoman who came to maturity between the two world wars. She was of Jewish background, a brilliant student of mathematics, literature, and philosophy. She was a fellow student of Simone de Beauvoir and Jean-Paul Sartre, developers of the philosophy of atheistic existentalism. She became convinced of the truth of the Christian gospel, though she was attracted to such nonorthodox expressions of it as the Albigensian radical separation of spirit and body. Her closest advisor was a Catholic priest. Nevertheless, she refused baptism, believing that God had called her to be a Christian outside the established church. She was concerned about the lot of French working people and worked in a factory, refusing the advantages and comforts that her middle-class background could have given her. When Germany defeated France during the Second World War she went to England to work with the free French reistance. Refusing to eat more than she believed the population of occupied France received, she died, partly as a result of malnutrition, during the war. Highly individualistic and deeply Christian, though unbound either by traditional orthodoxy or church structures, her deeply mystical writings have influenced many. She was impressed with the uprooting of people in the contemporary world and believed that people could find roots only by turning to God. For her, the religious life was one of suffering and inner purification, involving sharing the lot of the world's poor.

Billy Graham, an American, was born just a few years after Simone Weil. He came to maturity in roughly the same time period, but in a vastly different social and cultural setting. An American Southerner and a Baptist ministerial student, according to his biographers he made a deliberate decision to turn his back on the historical critical approach to the Bible. He accepted, in American fundamentalist fashion, the "literal inerrancy" of the Scriptures. In the late 1940s he came to national, then world, prominence. He had adopted the methods of his great nineteenth-and twentieth-century predecessors—Protestant evangelists who held revivals in major metropolitan centers of America and Europe using tents or municipal auditoriums. Billy Graham used the devices of revivalism in America and Europe, especially England, holding campaigns that lasted in some cases for several weeks. To the traditional revivalist methods he added modern technology, radio and television, becoming one of the pioneers of the electronic church. He differed from many evangelists of the electronic church in that he insisted on cooperation of (mainly) evangelical Protestant denominations in sponsoring his appearances. He urged converts to affiliate with a local church and denomination of the individual's choice. He promoted ecumenical cooperation among the various evangelical denominations.

His message was apocalyptic and simple. He stressed the imminent literal Second Coming of Christ and the sinfulness of the contemporary world. He proclaimed that humanity was living in the last days, using the threat of nuclear war, the breakup of the family, and rising crime rates as evidence of this. Graham was criticized for the simplicity and lack of social relevance of his message by such a spokesman of twentieth-century Christianity as Reinhold Niebuhr. Nevertheless, during the course of his ministry, Billy Graham began to speak out in support of civil rights for American ethnic groups. This stand was almost unheard of at the time among prominent white Southern Protestant fundamentalists. More recently, he has taken a strong and controversial stand in support of nuclear disarmament, alienating some of his traditional followers. Up to date in terms of programming and organization, striking those who hear him as eminently sincere and committed, Dr. Graham is perhaps the best known figure of contemporary world Protestantism, although be beongs to a denomination, the Southern Baptists, some of whose representatives refuse the designation Protestant.

Both individuals, Simone Weil and Billy Graham, one apparently free of tradition, the other seemingly tradition-bound, incorporated elements of Christian religious tradition, while rejecting others, in their approach to Christian life and witness. Each, however, was willing to incorporate new insights, in some ways to develop and others to transform earlier positions in the attempt to express what it means to be Christians in unique cultural settings.

What of the individual Christian in the contemporary world? We can expect that the majority of individual Christians will be tolerant of Christians in other denominations, and even within their own denominations, who hold significantly different religious positions from their own, though on some issues, more frequently moral and political than doctrinal or liturgical, there will be tension and conflict. Individual Christians will be interested in their own ethnic and denominational roots, to the extent of wanting to internalize them—wanting to become true Catholics, Presbyterians, Baptists, Disciples, or Nazarenes. But they will be relatively autonomous or individualistic in doing this—wanting to become Catholics, Presbyterians, Baptists, Disciples, or Nazarenes of their own kind. Perhaps the major task of Christian groups in modern societies will be to assist them in doing this rather than to indoctrinate or mobilize them to fulfill organizationally defined goals.

QUESTIONS

1. How has the concept of Christian missions changed since the Second World War?

2. How do the differences between simple and complex societies and the characteristics of modernized societies affect religion and religious organizations in the modern world?

3. Explain the differences between church, sect, and denomination as types of religious organizations.

4. How are changing attitudes about the role of women in society affecting religious organizations and attitudes?

5. How are the two aspects of international relations discussed in this chapter interrelated?

6. What questions about major traditional Christian theological beliefs and practices have been raised by the Holocaust, and by Christian-Jewish relations generally?

7. What are the major sources and emphases of liberation theology, black theology, and feminist theology?

8. Why and how have traditional Christian theological concepts, including those of the Trinity and incarnation, been questioned in recent theological discussions?

FURTHER READINGS

ABRECHT, PAUL (ed.), *Faith, Science and the Future.* Geneva: World Council of Churches, 1978, Philadelphia, Penn.: Fortress Press, 1979.

BAINTON, ROLAND C., *Christian Attitudes Toward War and Peace.* New York & Nashville, Tenn.: Abingdon Press, 1960.

BERRY, WENDELL, *The Gift of Good Land.* San Francisco, Calif.: North Point Press, 1981.

BOSWELL, JOHN, *Christianity, Social Tolerance, and Homosexuality.* New York-Oxford: Oxford University Press, 1980.

BOULDING, KENNETH E., *The Meaning of the 20th Century.* New York: Harper & Row Publishers, Inc., 1964.

CLARK, ELIZABETH and HERBERT RICHARDSON, *Women and Religion: A Feminist Sourcebook of Christian Thought.* New York: Harper & Row, Publishers, Inc., 1977.

DEWART, LESLIE, *The Future of Belief: Theism in a World Come of Age.* New York: Herder and Herder, 1966.

FRADY, MARSHALL, *Billy Graham.* Boston/Toronto: Little, Brown and Company, 1979.

GRAHAM, DOM AELRED, *Conversations: Christian and Buddhist.* New York: Harcourt Brace Jovanovich, Inc., 1968.

GREELEY, ANDREW M., *Unsecular Man: The Persistence of Religion.* New York: Schocken Books, Inc., 1972.

GUSTAFSON, JAMES M., *Ethics From a Theocentric Perspective: Theology & Ethics,* Vol. I. Chicago, Ill.: University of Chicago Press, 1981.

KATOPPO, MARIANNE, *Compassionate and Free: An Asian Woman's Theology.* Geneva: World Council of Churches, 1979. Maryknoll, N.Y.: Orbis Books, Inc., 1980.

KÜNG, HANS, *Does God Exist?* Garden City, N.Y.: Doubleday & Company, Inc., 1980.

——. *On Being a Christian.* Garden City, N.Y.: Doubleday & Company, Inc., 1976.

LONG, EUGENE THOMAS, *Jaspers and Bultmann: A dialogue between philosophy and theology in the existentialist tradition.* Durham, N. C.: Duke University Press, 1968.

MOLLENKOTT, VIRGINIA RAMEY, *Women, Men & the Bible.* Nashville, Tenn.: Abingdon, 1977.

MOLTMANN, JÜRGEN, *Experiences of God.* Philadelphia, Penn.: Fortress Press, 1980.

MONK, ROBERT C., et. al., *Exploring Religious Meaning.* Second Edition. Englewood Cliffs, N. J.: Prentice-Hall, Inc., 1980.

NIEBUHR, H. RICHARD, *Christ and Culture,* New York: Harper & Row Publishers, Inc., 1951.

OGDEN, SCHUBERT M., *The Point of Christology.* New York: Harper & Row, Publishers, 1982.

OTWELL, JOHN H., *And Sarah Laughed: The Status of Women in the Old Testament.* Philadelphia, Penn.: The Westminster Press, 1977.

PARSONS, TALCOTT, *Sociological Theory and Modern Society.* New York: The Free Press, a Division of the Macmillan Company, 1967.

PÉTREMENT, SIMONE, *Simone Weil.* New York: Random House, Inc., 1976.

RICHARDSON, HERBERT, *Nun, Witch, Playmate.* New York: Harper & Row, Publishers, 1971.

ROGERS, JACK B. and McKIM, DONALD, K., *The Authority and Interpretation of the Bible.* San Francisco, Calif.: Harper & Row Publishers, 1979.

SCHALLER, LYLE E., *Understanding Tomorrow.* Nashville, Tenn.: Abingdon, 1976.

SCHELL, JONATHAN, *The Fate of the Earth.* New York: Knopf, 1982.

SCHILLEBEECKX, EDWARD, *Jesus: An Experiment in Christology.* London: William Collins Sons & Co. Ltd., and the Crosslands Publishing Company, 1979.

SHANNON, THOMAS A., (ed.), *War or Peace?* Maryknoll, N. Y.: Orbis Books, 1980.

STROBER, GERALD S., *Graham: A Day in Billy's Life.* Garden City, New York: Doubleday & Company, Inc., 1976.

WARD, HILEY H., *Religion 2101 A.D.* Garden City, N. Y.: Doubleday & Company, Inc., 1975.

WEIL, SIMONE, *Waiting for God.* New York: G. P. Putnam's Sons, 1951.

APPENDIX ONE:
JEWISH AND CHRISTIAN CATEGORIZATION
OF JEWISH SCRIPTURES

Note: In most instances the Christian arrangement follows that of the Septuagint (the Jewish translation of the Hebrew Scriptures into Greek made ca. 300-100 B.C.).

The Hebrew Bible (Masoretic Text)	The Christian Old Testament (which follows the Septuagint with some differences in *names* of books)

I. **The Torah**	I. **The Pentateuch**

The Five Books of Moses

Genesis
Exodus
Leviticus
Numbers
Deuteronomy

II. **The Prophets**	II. **Historical Books**
Former Prophets	*Joshua*
Joshua	*Judges*
Judges	*Ruth*
I-II Samuel	*I-II Samuel*
I-II Kings	*I-II Kings*
	I-II Chronicles
Later Prophets	*Ezra* (or *I Esdras*)
Isaiah	*Nehemiah* (or *II Esdras*)
Jeremiah	**Tobit* (in Protestant
Ezekiel	**Judith* Apocrypha)
The Twelve	*Esther* (with * additions)
	*I-II Maccabees (in
Hosea, Joel, Amos	Protestant Apocrypha)
Obadiah, Jonah, Micah	*III-IV Maccabees* (never
Nahum, Habakkuk, Zephaniah	recognized as Canonical
Haggai, Zechariah, Malachi	by Christians)

III. **Writings**	III. **Poetry and Wisdom**
Psalms (Songs of Praise)	*Job*
Job	*Psalms*
Proverbs	
	Proverbs
The Festal Scrolls	*Ecclesiastes*
	Song of Solomon (Song of
Ruth	Songs)
Song of Songs	

Ecclesiastes
Lamentations
Ester
Daniel
Ezra-Nehemiah
I-II Chronicles

*The Wisdom of Solomon
*Ecclesiasticus (the Wisdom
    of Jesus ben Sirach)

IV. The Prophets

Isaiah
Jeremiah
Lamentations
*Baruch
*Epistle of Jeremiah
Ezekiel
Daniel (with * additions)
Hosea, Joel, Amos, Obadiah,
Jonah, Micah, Nanum,
Habakkuk, Zephaniah, Haggai,
Zechariah, Malachi

*These books, included in the Catholic scriptures as indicated, are included in the Protestant intertestamental apocrypha and are not recognized by Protestants as Canonical (see Chapter Four). Also included in the Protestant apocrypha, and since the sixteenth century printed in the Catholic Vulgate as appendices to the New Testament, are works entitled I and II *Esdras* (by Protestants) and (by Catholics) *III* and *IV Esdras*. Some other works, not listed here, are included in the Protestant Apocrypha. There is great variation in spelling of the names of many of the Biblical and apocryphal books as listed in Roman Catholic and Protestant versions.

APPENDIX TWO:
WHAT IS THE NEW TESTAMENT?

The New Testament is a collection of writings that originated in the early Christian Church. None of these writing is lengthy. Most, perhaps all, of them originated during the first eighty years of the Christian movement. They were circulated among the various Christian congregations of the ancient world and ultimately became part of the New Testament canon because of their nearly universal use and recognition as scripture or inspired writings among Christians.

Gospels

Collections of stories about Jesus and his teachings with interpretations of them by the early Christian community (including the author of each gospel). Although the gospels form a unique literary genre, they differ among themselves by resembling different literary genres current in the ancient world. Each gives a connected account of the ministry, crucifixion, and resurrection of Jesus.

Matthew) the
Mark) Synoptic
Luke) Gospels

John

History

An account in two parts, by the same author, of the significance of the ministry of Jesus and beginning and expansion of the Christian movement against the background of world history. Though "Luke" is placed with the gospels, it is the first part of a work to some extent modeled on ancient (Greek and Roman) historical writings.

(Luke)-Acts

Letters

Communications from Christian leaders to Chrstian congregations or (more rarely) to an individual Christian dealing with specific problems involving belief or conduct. Usually—Paul's Letter to the Romans is an exception—these are genuine letters dealing with one or more specific, practical problems. Romans, which also deals with a number of specific issues, gives a systematic, connected account of Paul's teaching about God's redemptive act in human history.

Letters by Paul	Letters attributed to Paul but thought by many scholars to have originated from a later "Pauline" circle	Letters not originating from Paul or his circle
I Thessalonians	*Ephesians*	*I Peter*
II Thessalonians	*I Timothy*	*II Peter*
		Jude

I Corinthians *	*II Timothy*	*II John*
*II Corinthians**	*Titus*	*III John*

Galatians +
Philippians+
Philemon +

Romans
Colossians

Theological and Homiletical Treatises

These are writings, inspirational and homiletical—
sermonic—in nature. Though each is called a
letter, and to some extent is, formally, they are
more like devotional essay or meditations
(*I John* and *James*) or even treatises (*Hebrews*)
than like the other New Testament letters.

Hebrews
James
I John

Apocalyptic Writings

There is one fully developed Christian
Apocalypse in the New Testament.
(*I Thessalonians, II Peter, Jude,* and the Synoptic
Gospels contain apocalyptic elements). This is
the Book of Revelation or the Revelation to John.
Most scholars believe that it was written during
a period of intense persecution of Christians by
the Roman Government, perhaps the first (under
the emperor Nero) or second (under Domitian)
persecution, which provided a severe shock to the
fledgling Christian movement. Using all the
symbols of popular apocalyptic writing,
Revelation seeks to urge Christians to remain
loyal to their faith, promising that God will
soon vindicate them by overthrowing the
demonic powers that control the Roman Empire.
Although affirming its spiritual validity for
present-day Christians, most scholars believe that
interpretations which tie *Revelation* to specific
present (*e.g.*, twentieth century) and future
events and dates fundamentally misinterpret it.

Revelation

---

*I and II Corinthians viewed as a unit seems to contain more than two related letters not
necessarily now in the sequence of their original composition.
+These contain important autobiographical materials.

INDEX